NEW DIMENSIONS IN HEALTH

Simple Secrets to Creating Optimal Health

MICHAEL BROOK

BALBOA.
PRESS

A DIVISION OF HAY HOUSE

Balboa Press books may be ordered through booksellers or by contacting:

Balboa Press
A Division of Hay House
1663 Liberty Drive
Bloomington, IN 47403
www.balboapress.com
1 (877) 407-4847

Because of the dynamic nature of the Internet, any web addresses or links contained in this book may have changed since publication and may no longer be valid. The views expressed in this work are solely those of the author and do not necessarily reflect the views of the publisher, and the publisher hereby disclaims any responsibility for them.

The author of this book does not dispense medical advice or prescribe the use of any technique as a form of treatment for physical, emotional, or medical problems without the advice of a physician, either directly or indirectly. The intent of the author is only to offer information of a general nature to help you in your quest for emotional and spiritual well-being. In the event you use any of the information in this book for yourself, which is your constitutional right, the author and the publisher assume no responsibility for your actions.

Any people depicted in stock imagery provided by Thinkstock are models, and such images are being used for illustrative purposes only.
Certain stock imagery © Thinkstock.

Printed in the United States of America.

ISBN: 9781-4525-1495-6 (sc)
ISBN: 978-1-4525-1496-3 (e)

Library of Congress Control Number: 2014908813

Balboa Press rev. date: 06/26/2014

Dedication

To People everywhere who are committed to the pursuit of Truth, Healing and Wholeness, the manifestation of spiritual values in their daily life and a world that works for everyone.

A deep heart-felt thanks to JMH, GMJ, Dianna, Charles, Terry, Kerry, Lauren, Kevin, Tansy, Susan and my parents Tom and Willa Brook for sharing their insights, goodness and their unique contribution of BEING to my life.

A special thanks to Dr. C. Samuel West who articulated a vision that I always sensed but never put into words. It continues to be the vision to which I aspire. "To raise up a people, regardless of race, creed, color or religion; who conquer disease, live in peace with no poor among them."

Illustrations by Kathy Hawke.

www.newdimensionsinhealth.com

CONTENTS

PREFACE

I had just finished a year of touring on the professional freestyle skiing circuit and it was one of those dream experiences. I had won the majority of contests in the aerial acrobatic event and was considered to be one of the best aerialists in the world. This dream year included winning a car and thousands of dollars in prize money, making a movie, an appearance on CBS Sports Spectacular, a very nice write up in Skiing Magazine and a number of other publications.

Running on a parallel track, I had been on a very intense spiritual quest for several years. I felt like I was being driven by something deep within, a powerful yearning of "I have to know," not merely believe, but know. I had explored a number of different spiritual belief systems, religions and philosophies. Although they all had some value none of them fulfilled the inner desire for a direct experience of God. This inner drive "to know spiritually" had been as intense as my athletic pursuits and this spiritual experience was realized around the same time as my freestyle experience.

My experience in the mind / body connection came from my training in trampoline, diving and acrobatic skiing. I don't know if I intuitively learned how to visualize or was driven into mental training. Some of my junior high school classes were so painfully boring that I had to find an escape and I remember practicing trampoline skills in my mind for hours. Over the years I learned first-hand how thought and emotion translated into physical performance. It wasn't until the second year on the freestyle circuit that I experienced the role one's soul or higher-self played in guiding one's life through effects on the physical body.

I trained hard the summer between seasons and when the snow started to fly I was ready. For some unknown reason on the second day after the ski area opened my knee started to hurt as I was training. I didn't fall, twist it or do anything else I was aware of, but the more I skied the more it hurt. I layed off a day or two, massage and iced it but it was getting worse. I went to the doctor to have it checked out and after the examination he looked at me and said "there is nothing wrong with your knee." You can imagine my frustration. I had a contest coming up and obligations to my sponsors. It was getting to the point where walking was becoming difficult. I tried to train, more ice, more massage and anything I could think of but all to no avail. I decided to try another doctor and after he checked me out his conclusion was the same as the first one. "There is nothing wrong with your knee."

For the rest of the season I took it easy so my knee could heal but there was no improvement. I went to six different doctorsthat ski season and they all came to the same conclusion. "There is nothing wrong with your knee." Needless to say, I was angry, frustrated and at a total loss as to what to do. I had gone from being one of the best in the world to nonexistent, letting my sponsors down with a helpless feeling of not being able to do a thing about it. At the end of ski season, I was sharing my disappointment and frustration with a friend. He told me, "There is an exceptional orthopedic surgeon in town, and if anyone can find the problem, he can."

I made an appointment and went in to see the doc. He examined my knee thoroughly, twisting, tweaking, pulling, pushing and listening. It was the most thorough exam I'd ever had and whenhe was done he looked at me and said, "There is nothing physically wrong with your knee." I couldn't believe it. After such high hopes of recovery I was stunned. While I was sitting there feeling frustrated and totally lost this surgeon placed his hand on my knee and closed his eyes. We sat there for about a minute or so in silence, and I'm thinking, "What now?" He opened his eyes, looked at me and asked, "Do you meditate?" My immediate thought was, "What a weird question for a surgeon who is treating a knee to ask." Fortunately for me this doctor wasn't just a surgeon treating a knee. He truly was a healer working with the whole person. "Yes, I do," I responded. "Well, you need to do a lot more," was his reply. "There is absolutely nothing physically wrong with your knee; however, there is definitely something wrong in your life, and it is showing up in your knee." WOW!

We talked for another ten of fifteen minutes about life, one's purpose, their spiritual path and what their unique gift to life was. (I'm so glad he wasn't a managed care doctor) I had achieved and exceeded all of my goals as a professional skier, and now it was time to redirect that energy by giving back. I walked out of his office reassessing where I'd been and where I was going. Life now had my attention.

This was my introduction to the mind/body/spirit connection and the understanding that one's soul or higher-self will use physical challenges to redirect us and move us forward on our path. I've come to understand that one's spiritual path is intertwined with the process of health, healing and wholeness and it is the interrelationship of these that we will explore as we move into a New Dimension of Health.

CHAPTER 1

EXPLORING THE PATH TO HEALTH AND WHOLENESS

Optimal health is not only an experience or condition it is a process of becoming. It is the result of understanding and living in accordance with the natural laws that govern the physical, emotional, mental, spiritual, social and economic arenas of our lives. Whether you are struggling with difficult health challenges, or striving to raise your levels of performance and enhance the quality of your life, there are techniques, information and resources that will support and dramatically accelerate your process. This path toward optimal health is also a process of personal and spiritual growth. Growth takes place when we stretch outside of our comfort zone of what is familiar, and explore new possibilities and challenges. In many cases this is necessary if we are to experience true health and healing. The process of healing and building high levels of health is very much a spiritual endeavor, although it may not be presented in religious terms.

It's been said that we not only walk on the path of personal and spiritual growth but that the path itself is constructed as a result of our own experiences. The more we understand this the more effective we will be in growing from the experiences that life sends us. As we started out in life, each of us had a desire to experience the goodness of life in a greater way. We pursued the things we thought would make us happy. Some of those things when accomplished did bring us a measure of happiness and some did not. Many people started out enthusiastic, confident and optimistic about life. However, ill informed, poor choices and wrong turns may have led them to a state of unhappiness, poor health and an overall feeling of dis-ease with the experience of life. Others may have started on their path with difficulty, health issues, family challenges and financial obstacles, but by persistence and right choices overcame the liabilities by turning them into assets that created happiness, health and success in all areas of life.

Let's begin by examining the roots and the meaning of the words, *health* and *wholeness*. The word *health* traces its roots back through the old English and German to the prehistoric German word *khailaz*. The word *whole* originally meant *undamaged*, and traces its origin back to the same root word. Other derivatives of *khailaz* are *heal*, *hallow* and *holy*.[1] The process of creating health and healing is the process of becoming "whole" in all areas of your life. As you truly become whole - physically, emotionally, mentally and spiritually - you do indeed become holy in the true sense of the word.

The process of personal and spiritual growth is the process of developing wholeness and optimal health. The more we understand this process the more effective we will be in charting our course. Much has been written about the experience of walking the spiritual path. However, as we touched on earlier, a key part of the process is learning to construct the path as we move forward on it. In a sense, the path already exists. At the same time, it must be discovered and created within us. Some schools of thought teach that we tread the path by becoming the path. Although personal and spiritual growth is an individual experience, in many ways, the journey is the same for everyone.

As we progress, we begin to understand the laws and principles that govern growth. If we understand these forces, we are able to work with them and progress smoothly. If we are ignorant of these principles and forces, or if we unknowingly work against them, our progress will be thwarted and our experience will be fraught with unnecessary difficulties.

There are natural laws and universal principles governing all areas of health: physical, emotional, mental, spiritual, social and economic. As we live our lives in accordance with these natural laws and principles, we grow in our experience and expression of health and wholeness. When we violate these laws or principles, knowingly or unknowingly, we experience a loss of health and inner fragmentation moving us away from a state of wholeness. Consciously choosing to develop physical, emotional and mental health is an essential part of the process of personal growth. The growth process and adherence to developmental principles lay the foundation for soul awareness and greater spiritual development.

When we become conscious of the principles required to create health and wholeness, we have a choice to work with those laws or not. When we choose to work with the laws, they bring forces greater than ourselves to assist our progress. When we violate a principle, knowingly or not, we inevitably reap the consequences. If we act out of ignorance, and reap unwanted results, we may feel like a victim of forces that are beyond our control. We may not always see the cause and effect relationship between our thoughts and actions, and the experience that life brings us. However, as our level of awareness grows, we develop a greater ability to work with the natural process of life, health and wholeness.

Yes, there are forces greater than ourselves that are beyond our control. However, understanding these principles gives us greater, more intelligent choices as to how we respond. We have control of our lives and health to the degree that we understand and work with the laws of health.

As we explore and apply the physical, emotional and mental principles of health that lead to a strong, healthy, well-balanced, fulfilling life, we increase the rapidity with which we move along the path. We also discover some of the forces that are greater than we are, and explore different ways to work with them to our advantage.

This personal growth and health creation process is like the experience of climbing a mountain. Each step takes effort and a commitment to keep moving upward. The higher we ascend the better the view and the more amazing the experience. Often, the higher we ascend the greater the obstacles, challenges and pitfalls. However, as we grow wiser from the experiences gained along the way, we obtain the resources necessary to deal with them. Our skill and capacity increase by choosing to face these challenges. Once on top, the view, the feeling of growth and self-fulfillment are magnificent. As we reflect on the challenging ascent, in spite of the pain and difficulty, the reward is well worth it.

So it is with our experience of life as we proceed upon the path to optimal health. To grow in all areas of life takes effort and commitment. There are people in the roles of friends, mentors, teachers, and business associates who have walked the path before us, who can offer wise insight and support, and point the way. Great spiritual leaders, scientists and others who have climbed much higher and revealed great truths can support and help in our development.

Each of us can recognize those people who, through their experience and knowledge, have reached out in some way and helped us climb higher. Through their support, we have grown into a greater experience of this gift of life. In the same way they reached out and helped us, so do we have an obligation to reach to those who haven't yet reached the point where we are and help them in their growth process. Although someone may be higher in their ascent and have more experience, that certainly doesn't mean they are better than others. It does mean that they have a greater responsibility to reach out to others, to serve and uplift. If we have knowledge that can benefit others we have a moral obligation to share it.

Working with the laws of health is very much a part of creating and moving forward on our spiritual paths. One of the goals of the process is to become what is known as an "integrated personality." This means that the physical, emotional and mental arenas of life are coordinated and working in harmony with each other. The emotional arena can be particularly challenging, as few of us are taught how to effectively work in that arena.

The result of this integration process is a greater experience and expression of life. The words *optimal health* and *wellness* are used to denote the highest level of physical, mental, emotional and spiritual expression that we are capable of experiencing at any given point. As we move forward, that experience and expression grows.

We will examine the principles of health in each individual arena, keeping in mind that each is a necessary part of the greater whole. As strength is built in each arena, and our lives move into alignment with the principles that create health, we will see a higher quality of life expressed on all levels. Naturally, as we grow, this will continue to evolve to higher and higher levels of expression. Since our quest is a continual aspiration to embody greater levels of consciousness and healthy living, we will use the Wellness or Living Continuum in figure 1 to illustrate the process.

High-level wellness is where we experience vibrant and radiant physical, mental, emotional and spiritual health. At this level, there is a high quality of life experienced in all arenas. Ideally, this is what we aspire to become. This is where we all want to experience life. Unfortunately, most of us aspire only to be "not sick" and we think that we are healthy, as long as there is nothing apparently wrong and there are no visible problems.

When we fall into the area of illness and disease on the continuum, we experience the pain and discomfort associated with those states. The purpose of pain is to get our attention. Often, this is the only thing that will motivate us to change. When we are sick we focus all of our attention on treating the pain and getting rid of the discomfort or "dis-ease." When the pain goes away, we move back up the continuum to health, or not sick.

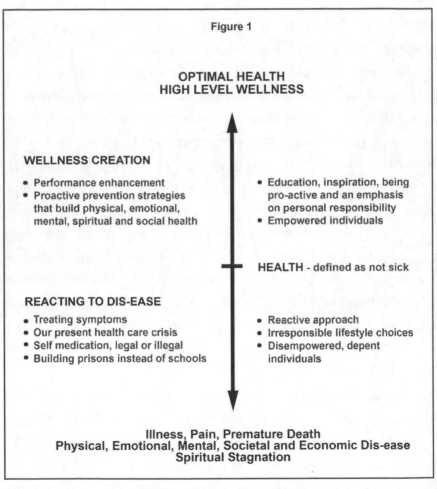

Figure 1

OPTIMAL HEALTH
HIGH LEVEL WELLNESS

WELLNESS CREATION

- Performance enhancement
- Proactive prevention strategies that build physical, emotional, mental, spiritual and social health

- Education, inspiration, being pro-active and an emphasis on personal responsibility
- Empowered individuals

HEALTH - defined as not sick

REACTING TO DIS-EASE

- Treating symptoms
- Our present health care crisis
- Self medication, legal or illegal
- Building prisons instead of schools

- Reactive approach
- Irresponsible lifestyle choices
- Disempowered, depent individuals

Illness, Pain, Premature Death
Physical, Emotional, Mental, Societal and Economic Dis-ease
Spiritual Stagnation

Wellness/Living Continuum

Unnecessary disease and poor health are appallingly prevalent in our society. Each day in the United States, over four thousand people die from heart disease, cancer or stroke. That equates to 120,000 people a month from these diseases alone. To put this into perspective, during the Viet Nam War 58,000 soldiers died. Yet within our borders, every month 120,000 men, women and children die from these diseases. These numbers are bad enough in and of themselves, but what makes this truly tragic is that many of these problems are preventable. According to *The New England Journal of Medicine,* 70 percent of the diseases we experience are preventable. [2]

Disease, whether physical, emotional or psychological, affects not only the individual, but the entire family and the larger organizations and communities of which we are a part. The economic burden on a family or business can be devastating, creating unnecessary and crippling hardships for years.

Please take a moment to reflect on this. In your own life how has this affected you? Have you, or anyone you know, suffered from these or any other form of degenerative disease? Have you lost a loved one to one of these conditions? Are you or someone you know in chronic pain? How has this affected you and your family emotionally, financially and in the over-all quality of your life? Let's drop that New England Journal of Medicine percentage down from 70 to 50 percent. Now consider there is a 50 percent chance that this pain and suffering, as well as the emotional and financial consequences associated with it, could be prevented.

Now ask yourself this question. If I could do something about this in my own life and for those around me, would I make the commitment and effort to do it? As you go through this book you will learn some of the key causes of these problems. However, only committed application on your part will produce any positive results.

As you read this I hope you will continue to make that commitment, to invest in the health and well being of yourself and your loved ones.

If you are among those searching for ways to restore health and create high level wellness, consider taking a different approach to dealing with dis-ease, rather than the traditional, reactive "fix it" model. There is a difference between healing and curing. True healing addresses the underlying causes of illness and moves a person towards a state of greater health and wholeness. This approach is quite different from treating symptoms to make them go away. The cause of a headache is not an aspirin deficiency, however if the medicine makes the pain go away we would say we were cured.

The healing versus curing orientation is beautifully summed up by the adage: *"The foolish physician treats the disease. The wise physician fulfills the conditions of health and the disease will leave of its own accord."* As a guiding principle in our lives this seed of thought provides a foundation for understanding the difference between fighting disease and building true health.

A Different Approach

We can say there are two ways to deal with dis-ease regardless of the form it takes, physical, emotional, economic, environmental, social or conflict between countries. We can fight the disease, i.e. declare war on cancer, declare war on drugs, declare war on poverty, declare war on terrorism, etc. Or, we can choose to support the processes that create health and lead to wholeness in all arenas of life.

The fight-and-attack method does have its place in emergency situations. However, if we really take a look at the results this approach has produced, we will often see there is more damage created by "the war on symptoms" than on the actual cause or condition itself. One of the brilliant descriptions of this process came out of the Viet Nam conflict when one of its generals said, "We had to destroy the village in order to save it." Another version of this thinking is that we have to poison the body (toxic chemicals, radiation, chemo therapy) in order to save it from the cancer. Depending on which statistics we use, the deaths that result from side effects of prescription drugs is between the fifth to the third leading cause of death in the United States. According to the *Journal of the American Medical Association,* more than 300,000 deaths every year are the result of medical mistakes and side effects from prescription drugs.[3] Since only ten percent of drug reactions are reported to the Center for Disease Control, the real number is much greater. This means that following your doctors' or the pharmaceutical companies' directions for taking medication could kill you. In 2003 three medical doctors, one of them also a naturopath and two PhD's published a report called Death by Medicine. They concluded that the number one cause of death in America is the health care system. In spite of the miracles of our amazing medical technology, our present system kills tens of thousands of people every year.

In defense of the medical and pharmaceutical industries, it's only fair to point out that in most cases it is the violation of the laws of health that puts people in a condition where medication may be necessary. Caring for the body you were given is ultimately your responsibility, not the doctor's, not the insurance companies, not the drug companies and not the government's. Those industries have their place but if you chose to depend on them for your health and well-being you will be greatly disappointed and probably end up as one of the statistics. Medication certainly has its place, and many people have benefited from it. There are times when fighting disease with medications may be necessary. However, there is another way.

By identifying the underlying causes of the problem, whether it is cancer, heart disease, poverty, drug abuse or war, and by using the natural principles that create health and wholeness, we are able to bring about true healing. In short, fulfill the conditions of health and the disease will leave of its own accord. As you discover these principles of health, take time to note them and write down how you will apply them in your own life.

As we aspire to live higher levels of health, we experience a growing understanding that health is the natural state of the body. There is an innate intelligence or wisdom that operates this wonderful body we are living in. When the blocks are removed, and the conditions of health are fulfilled, the innate wisdom of the physical body does its own healing. As we progress, we will see how amazing that inner intelligence really is.

Dr. Jonas Salk expressed this simple truth a little differently when he said, "Unless we place emphasis upon the need to understand equilibrium in all aspects of the human organism, individually and collectively… we will always be predominately preoccupied with the pathological, with reducing the negative rather than enhancing the positive. Until we see the sources of pathology as partly attributable to ignorance of what is required for maintaining health, we will continue to search for causes which can be eliminated or prevented, when, in fact, some of the pathology we seek to suppress is the result of our failure to do certain things that actively evoke and maintain a state of balance."

Cellular Systems

This state of equilibrium or balance of which Dr. Salk spoke needs to be achieved on all levels, internally and externally, from the microcosm to the macrocosm. On a microcosmic level, consider that our body is made up of 50 to 70 trillion individual cells. Each cell is a living organism and is made up of thousands of smaller components. Cells need food and oxygen to support them and they must eliminate waste. They respond to stimuli and can adapt to their environment. They have organs that generate energy and repair damaged parts. They have the intelligence to build complex structures. The 60 trillion cells in the human body have the ability to send and receive information, and are affected by this process just as we are. Each has a specific job description, depending on the organ of which it is a part. Each cell is an entity unto itself and is affected by its external environment as well as having an impact on its surroundings.

If the conditions of health for these individual cells are met, if they receive the proper nutrients and the waste is removed, if the stimuli or information they receive is positive and wholesome, then the result is a state of health. In this state, they are able to perform the jobs needed by the particular organ of which they are a part. As a result, the organ is healthy. When the organ is performing well, the system of which it is a part is effective in accomplishing its needed tasks. When all the organs and systems of the body are functioning at optimal levels, the result is vibrant health in the greater organism.

The reverse is also true. If the cells are unable to get the nutrients they need, if they are unable to clear away the waste, if stimulus they receive is stressful and the information communicated is negative or incorrect, the result is a state of dis-ease. The individual cells struggle to survive and can't do their needed work. The organ of which they are a part breaks down and is unable to fulfill its role and make its needed contributions. The result is a state of dis-ease affecting the whole body.

Taking this analogy to a higher level, we can view individual people as the cells that make up the greater organizations of which they are a part, and organizations as living organisms are made up of individual members. As individuals, we are the cells that make up families, clubs, businesses, churches and other organizations of which we are a part. These organizations (organs) make up the community, state or nation of which we are a part.

If, as individuals, we are healthy, physically, emotionally, mentally and spiritually then that health is more likely to be reflected in the life of the family, business, church, community, nation and world. If our conditions of health are not met on all levels and we are out of balance then dis-ease will be reflected in the organizations of which we are a part.

The state of the body affects the health of the cells, and the health of the cells affect the health of the body. The state of the family, business or nation will affect the health of the individual. And the physical, emotional, mental and spiritual health of the individual will affect the health of the family, business or nation of which they are a part.

To create a healthy, happy, successful life resulting in high-level wellness, we must fulfill the conditions of health on all levels, internally and externally, individually and collectively.

As you move through this book and ponder its contents consider it to be an invitation to actively pursue high-level wellness. Naturally, we will start where we are and learn how to effectively move up the living continuum, creating a greater experience of health and higher quality of life. Or, if you prefer the mountain metaphor, we will to learn to identify our point on the path and turn the challenges and obstacles into the steps that will assist us in the climbing process. Throughout this book, we are going to explore the conditions of health from the cell to the society and from the person to the planet.

Albert Einstein once said that a problem cannot be solved by the same level of thinking that created it. Applying the knowledge in this book will most assuredly support you in your ascension process as you move up the mountain. It will provide valuable information and it will move your thinking and the way you view health, yourself and the world to a new level. It will provide a means to understand and grow from the inevitable challenges that come, as you move forward, on that beautiful unfolding process which is life.

CHAPTER 2

SIMPLE SECRETS OF PHYSICAL HEALTH

The Lympathic System

Physical health begins at the cellular level. If all your cells are healthy, your body is healthy. To be healthy each cell needs nutrition coming in and the waste removed, just as your body does. The circulatory system brings nutrition to the body and the lymphatic system carries the waste away. Most people, including many doctors, know very little about the lymphatic system.

The International Society of Lymphologists is the premier organization of research scientists and doctors presently studying the lymphatic system. This society was formed in 1966 by Dr. H.S. Mayerson, a pioneer in the field of lymphology. The Society meets every other year in different places around the world to discuss its findings and exchange information.

A number of years ago, Dr. Casley Smith, President of the International Society of Lymphologists, issued what he called the Lymphatic Manifesto. In this Manifesto, Dr. Smith stated, "While the Lymphatic System is one of the 12 to 14 systems of the body, it receives almost no attention from the medical profession. In textbooks of medicine, surgery, pathology, physiology or anatomy, it rarely occupies more than one-half to one percent of the space. And, while this may improve over time with the efforts of people such as us, the fact remains that many people will suffer because of this widespread ignorance. Many will lose their lives, some will lose their limbs, many will suffer needless pain and incapacity, and many researchers will get incorrect results. All this, because of simple ignorance of the importance of lymphatics." In the context of our present health care crisis how does this affect you, your family, your finances and nation as a whole?

The lymphatic system has been called the garbage disposal of the body, the vacuum cleaner of the body, and the white blood stream. All of these names are descriptive of the many different functions performed by the lymphatic system. This system permeates every part of our body. In a sense, the lymphatic system runs parallel to the venous part of our blood circulatory system.

Figure 2 is a simple explanation of how the lymphatic system interfaces with the blood circulatory system to deliver nutrients to the cells and remove waste. Blood is pumped by the heart first to the lungs where it is oxygenated and then sent to the rest of the body. It travels away from the heart through the arteries into the blood capillaries. As the blood moves through these tiny capillaries it delivers oxygen, minerals and nutrients to the cells. After the blood passes through the capillaries, it returns to the heart via the venous system.

The walls of the capillaries are porous. Some of the blood plasma diffuses through the capillary walls in order to carry oxygen and nutrients to the cells. When the blood plasma leaves the capillary and moves into the spaces around the cells it is called interstitial fluid.

The fluid works its way through the cells, irrigating them as it goes. It delivers needed nutrients or "the groceries" and picks up "the garbage," wastes given off by the cells resulting from the metabolic processes. The interstitial fluid moves around the cells and then is drawn into lymphatic terminals. Next, the lymphatic terminals siphon off the fluid and move it into the lymphatic capillaries. These tiny capillaries converge into larger vessels as they move upward with other lymphatic tributaries, contributing their fluid as the system works its way upward. These vessels eventually join into the thoracic duct, the largest lymphatic duct, which is located in the chest. It then deposits the lymph fluid into the left subclavian vein located at the base of the neck.

As the fluid moves through the lymphatic system, it is cleansed each time it passes through the lymph nodes. There are between 400 and 700 of these lymph nodes positioned throughout the body to act as a filtration system. Lymph nodes also store lymphocytes, white blood cells that have the ability to neutralize, dissolve, and destroy bacteria, viruses, cancer cells and cellular debris. The lymph fluid picks up garbage from the cells, waste products, toxins and other metabolic debris, and carries it away as it moves through the system. This poison-laden fluid is cleansed and purified in the lymph nodes and then returned to the circulatory system at the subclavian veins.

BLOOD CIRCULATORY

Figure 2

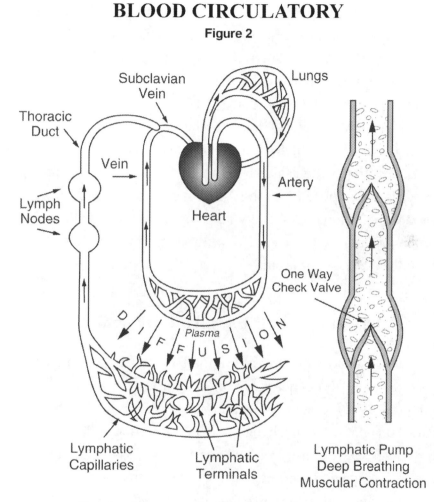

Plasma diffuses through the blood capillary walls.
It works its way through the insterstitial spaces between
the cells and is siphoned off by the lymphatic terminals
which draws it into the Lymphatic Capillaries.

Blood Circulatory

Our bodies are about 70 percent water. Of all the fluid in your body, about 60 percent is fluid within and around your cells, about 10 percent is blood plasma and about 30 percent is lymph fluid. You have approximately three times more lymph fluid than blood. If you've ever had a water-blister, the clear fluid inside is lymph. In addition, there are four times more lymphatic vessels throughout your body than there are blood vessels. So you have a very intricate and extensive lymphatic network.[4]

Let's review this again. Blood and blood plasma leave the heart, travel down through the capillaries, diffuse through the capillary walls, and irrigate the cells. Then the fluid picks up the waste from the cells and is pulled into the lymphatic terminals and drawn up through the lymph nodes. Everything harmful is filtered out, and the lymph fluid returns to the circulatory system at the subclavian veins. Then the cycle begins again.

Circulatory System and Lymphatic Dynamics

The circulatory system is pumped by the heart and moves approximately three quarts of blood through 60,000 miles of capillaries every minute. The lymphatic system, however, does not have a pump. Instead, the lymph fluid moves through a series of one-way check valves. There are millions of these little one-way check valves throughout the body. For the system to move there must be more pressure behind the valve than in front of it. This forces the fluid forward. The way the check valves are constructed prevents fluid from flowing back. When it is moving well, the lymphatic system circulates 20 milliliters or one and one-third tablespoons per minute. It's a very slow-moving system.

Our hearts pump approximately three quarts of blood through 60,000 miles of capillaries every minute, carrying oxygen and nutrients to the cells. How does this delivery process take place?

Figure 3 was adapted from the book *Introduction to the Science of Lymphology* based on information taken from the *Textbook of Medical Physiology*, by Dr. Arthur C. Guyton. This textbook is used in many medical schools around the country.

Consider that the pressure inside the capillary is high, and the pressure outside is low. The walls of the capillary are porous, which allows blood plasma to leave the bloodstream by diffusing through the capillary walls. It is this pressure differentiation of high pressure inside, and low pressure outside that causes the blood plasma to seep through the pores of the capillary walls, thus allowing the fluid to carry nutrients to the cells.

One example demonstrating this diffusion process would be a hose with holes punched in it. When connected to a pressurized source of water, the pressure in the hose forces the water out through the holes. This same principle applies to a blood capillary. As a result of this process, the fluid delivers oxygen and nutrients to the cells.

Once the blood plasma moves outside the capillary, it becomes interstitial fluid, or lymph. The fluid flows around the cells and delivers the food that the cells need. At the same time, the interstitial fluid picks up the cellular garbage and carries it off to the lymphatic terminals. From the lymphatic terminals, it is pulled off into the lymphatic system, and then the cleansing process begins.

HEALTH & DISEASE STATES

Figure 3

3 qts a minute x's 80 = 240 qts or 60 gal a minute

Conditions of Health

Dry State
Electrical Generators On

Conditions of Disease

Excess Fluid, Excess Sodium
Toxic Swamp State
Electrical Generators Off

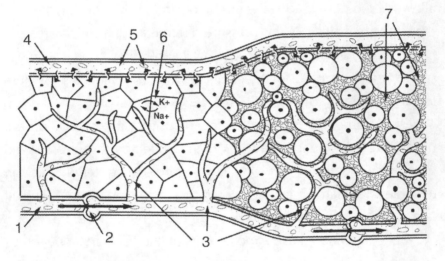

1 Lymphatic Capillary
2 One Way Check Valve
3 Lymphatic Terminals
4 Blood Capillary — Pressure high inside, porous walls allow plasma, carrying nutrients and oxygen to irrigate the cells
5 Blood Proteins — albumins, globulins and fibrinogens
6 Sodium Potassium Pump
7 Trapped Blood Proteins

Health and Disease States

Fig 3, from *Introduction to the Science of Lymphology*. Used with permission.

20

Within the bloodstream, there are the blood proteins of albumen, globulin and fibrinogens. These proteins perform different functions but one of the jobs they have in common is to hold the water inside the capillaries. This is a key point to remember. You might find it helpful to think of these blood proteins as little magnets that attract and hold water.

Blood plasma is 93 percent water. The other seven percent of the bloodstream consists of dissolved solids. Why do we need blood proteins within the bloodstream to attract and hold water? Because the pressure inside the capillary is high, and the capillary walls are porous, the plasma is constantly being forced out through the capillary walls. The pressure is forcing the plasma out, and the blood proteins are holding the plasma in. If all the plasma were forced out due to the inner pressure, the capillary would collapse.

For a long time it was believed that because the pores in the capillary walls are small and the blood proteins are large, that blood proteins are too big to fit through the pores and exit the capillary. In the 1930's, Cecil Drinker of Harvard Medical School challenged this assumption. His experiments led him to believe that the blood capillaries continuously leak plasma proteins; however, he lacked the technology to prove it conclusively.

It wasn't until the late 1950's that Dr. Mayerson discovered that these blood proteins do, in fact, continually seep out of the capillary. In his experiments, Dr. Mayerson tagged the blood proteins with radioactive iodine. He found that as many as 50 percent would leave the capillaries within a 24-hour period.[5]

As an example, imagine trying to push a water-filled balloon three inches in diameter through a hole only two inches in diameter. The pressure exerted by your hands would be able to rearrange the shape of the balloon, allowing it to work its way through the hole. In a similar way, the high pressure inside the capillary forces the blood proteins through the porous openings in the capillary wall.

The pressure inside the capillary is high, while the pressure outside is low. Once these blood proteins leave the capillary, there is no way for them to get back in. There is nothing that is going to force them back through the openings in the capillary wall. The only way for them to get back into the circulatory system where they belong is to work their way through the spaces between the cells, and then into the lymphatic terminals. They then travel through the lymphatic system and are eventually returned to the circulatory system at the subclavian veins. That is the only way for the blood proteins to get back into the bloodstream. Then the process starts all over again.

How important is this removal of blood proteins by the lymphatic system? In the *Textbook of Medical Physiology,* Dr. Guyton made this statement, "The lymphatic system represents an accessory route, by which fluids can flow from the interstitial spaces around the cells, back into the blood. And, most important of all, the lymphatics can carry (blood) proteins and large particulate matter, such as dead cells and other toxic materials, away from the tissue spaces, neither of which can be removed by absorption directly into the blood capillary.

Dr. Guyton continues his explanation of the importance of this process by saying, "We shall see that the removal of the blood proteins by the lymphatic system is an absolutely essential function, without which we would die within 24 hours. This is one of the most important but least understood functions of the lymphatic system."[6]

If your lymphatic system fails to work properly and does not remove these blood proteins, you will die within 24 hours. Perhaps this is one of the reasons why Dr. Casley Smith, when he issued the Lymphatic Manifesto, was so emphatic in stating that "many people will lose their lives, some will lose their limbs, many will suffer needless pain and incapacity, and many researchers will get incorrect results, all because of a simple ignorance of the importance of the lymphatics."

How can these blood proteins cause disease if they are not removed by the lymphatic system? As mentioned before, these blood proteins are very large and one thing that begins to happen is that they start to get clogged or trapped in the interstitial space around the cells. Remember, the purpose of the blood proteins is to attract and hold the fluid within the capillary. It does not matter where they are within the body, they attract and hold fluid. What happens once they get outside the capillary wall into the interstitial space between the cells? They attract and hold fluid. When the blood proteins come out faster than the lymphatic system can pull them off, they start to clog around the cells and retain excess fluid. The result of this is that it becomes more and more difficult for the nutrients and oxygen to get to the cells and it becomes more and more difficult for the cellular garbage to be removed.

In a sense, we have a repeat of the New York garbage strike that happened a number of years ago. People kept putting garbage outside their house and no one took it away. After a while, there was so much garbage piled up in front of their house that they couldn't even get out to go to the store to buy food. The same thing happens on a cellular level within us. If the toxins, garbage and cellular debris are not removed, then the cells end up living in their own waste. How healthy do you think those cells will be as time progresses? How healthy do you think you would be, living in an environment surrounded by your own waste? As disgusting as this thought may be, it is exactly the same kind of environment that trapped blood proteins will produce within us.

The optimal condition of health takes place when cells are in what is known as "the dry state." This is the state that exists when there is only enough fluid surrounding the cells to fill the crevices between the cells. Earlier we talked about the pressure inside the capillary being high and the pressure outside the capillary being low. The pressure needed to create this dry state is known as "sub-atmospheric pressure." An example of sub-atmospheric pressure is best described by using a balloon. If you blow it up, the pressure inside the balloon is greater than the pressure outside. If you let the air out the pressure is neutral. There is the same amount of pressure inside as there is outside. If you were to suck all the air out of the balloon, it would be considered to be sub-atmospheric pressure. The pressure inside would be less than outside. This dry state is the necessary condition for optimal health. Remember, our goal is to fulfill the conditions of health and the diseases will leave of their own accord. This is the internal state we want to create. It is this sub-atmospheric pressure that produces the dry state around the cells in healthy tissue.

What happens when we have blood proteins constantly seeping out? What happens when they are not being pulled off by the lymphatic system? What happens when they start to clog up around the cells? What happens when they attract and hold excess fluid and sodium? As this process continues, it becomes more and more difficult for the oxygen, minerals and nutrients to get to the cells and more and more difficult for the cells to get rid of the waste. At this point, we start moving away from the dry state necessary for health into a state of excess fluid and excess sodium and this creates a state of disease.

At the top of figure 3 we have a formula that says three quarts a minute times 80 equals 240 quarts or 60 gallons a minute. What this means is that our heart pumps three quarts of blood through 60,000 miles of capillaries every minute. As the three quarts of blood moves through the capillaries they diffuse through the capillary wall 80 times per minute. Remember, the purpose of the blood proteins inside the capillary is to hold the fluid there. At the same time, because of the high pressure inside the capillary, the blood plasma is being forced out through the pores in the capillary walls. Fluid is pushed out under pressure, delivers the groceries to the cells, is pulled back in by the attractive effect of the blood proteins, and then picks up more groceries to deliver to the cells. Under pressure, a measured amount is forced out. Then some is pulled back in. Pressure forces it out and attraction pulls it back in.

This diffusion process happens 80 times a minute. Take a moment to think about this and let it soak in. This process takes three quarts of blood, and by diffusing it back and forth 80 times, your body has the use of 240 quarts, or 60 gallons of blood a minute to irrigate the cells.

One of the reasons the dry state is so important is that in order for these cells to be irrigated and fed by the plasma diffusion process, they must be packed very close to the capillary wall. When that diffusion process happens at a rate faster than once a second, you can see that the further away the cells are from the capillary walls, the more difficult it is to make the nutrient exchange.

Activating the Lympathic System

Lymphologists debated for a long time as to what really caused the lymphatic system to circulate. One group argued that "muscular contraction," or exercise, caused the circulation. The other group insisted that deep breathing stimulated circulation.

In 1979, lymphologist Jack Shields photographed for the first time the flow of lymph fluid inside the body. During the test, he had a patient do some mild exercise, and the flow of lymph did, in fact, slightly increase. Then he had the patient take a deep breath. As soon as he did, the lymphatic system started to squirt like a hose. This settled the debate once and for all. Deep breathing is the key to accelerating the flow of the lymph system. How does breathing deeply accomplish this? Dr. Shields says, "Deep diaphragmatic breathing stimulates the cleansing of the lymph system by creating a vacuum effect which pulls the lymph through the bloodstream. This increases the rate of toxic elimination by as much as 15 times the normal rate."[7]

Deep breathing takes the pressure off the top of the check valves, creating a suction effect. This effect takes the pressure off the top of the valves, causing them to open, thereby increasing the movement of lymph fluid. To increase the flow of your lymphatic system and increase its effectiveness, become conscious of breathing deeply.

Because the lymphatic system is a very slow moving system, the build up of trapped blood proteins and excess fluid can outpace the ability of the lymphatic system to draw them off. If we don't do something to circulate lymphatics, we move away from a dry, healthy cellular state into a state of fluid retention and a state of disease. This is good incentive for all of us to find some kind of exercise we enjoy and to start becoming conscious of breathing deeply.

Healthy Cell State

We have explored the environment necessary to fulfill the conditions of health in order to maintain healthy cells. Now, let's take a look at Figure 4 showing the conditions within the cell necessary for optimal performance.

For the cell to remain healthy the potassium level within the cell must remain high and the sodium level must remain low. The walls of the cell are permeable. This allows certain substances to seep in and others to seep out. If there is a high concentration of a substance within the cell and a low concentration outside the cell, then each side will automatically seek balance.

CELLULAR HEALTH STATE
Figure 4

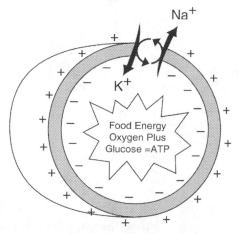

Condition For Healthy Cells
High Potassium (K^+) within the cell
Low Sodium (Na^+) within the cell

ATP is the Fuel that runs the
Sodium-Potassuim Pump

Cellular Health State

As an example, imagine an aquarium filled with water and a permeable partition separating each side. If you were to add a high concentration of sodium to one side, what would eventually happen? The sodium would eventually seep through the partition and balance itself out. Any substance will automatically move from a high level of concentration to a lower level in an attempt to seek balance. This same principle applies to the cell.

The conditions of health within the cell require a high level of potassium and a low level of sodium. Since the wall of the cell is permeable, the potassium is constantly leaking out and must be pumped back in. The sodium is constantly seeping into the cell, and must be pumped out. It is this constant rotation of positive sodium and potassium ions, into and out of the cell that has come to be known as the sodium-potassium pump.

In addition to keeping the potassium level high within the cell and the sodium level low, this rotation of positive sodium and potassium ions generates electricity. Every cell in your body generates electricity and works as an electrical generator. The muscles work by an electrical impulse from the brain. The nervous system is electrical. There are photographic techniques that take pictures of the electrical field that surrounds the body. Researchers have learned that an imbalance, or disease, will show up in the electrical field first, before it shows up in the physical body. Interestingly, science is finding that thoughts and emotions are electrical and energetic in nature. We are, in fact, energy beings, electrical in nature. There are a growing number of studies showing the role that electricity and magnetism play in health and healing. The sodium-potassium pump is the mechanism whereby electricity is generated on the physical level.

Let's explore this energetic/electrical connection a little further. If we break down physical matter into its basic building blocks we have atoms. Atoms are comprised of protons, neutrons, electrons and other subatomic particles that are electrical in nature. It is interesting to note that an electron can sometimes act as a particle, and sometimes act as a wave. This indicates that an electron is both matter and energy at the same time. If the atomic particles that are the building blocks of creation are electrical and energetic in nature, then it stands to reason that the molecules made up of the atoms are electrical and energetic in nature. The cells that are made up of the molecules are electrical. Therefore, your entire body is electrical and energetic in nature. We will investigate this in greater detail a little later.

How is that electrical energy generated within the body? An article entitled "Electricity in Plants" published in *Scientific American,* beautifully described this process. The opening sentence in the article states, "The processes of life have been found to generate electrical fields in every organism that has been examined. It is the delicately balanced distribution of inorganic salts, in and around a living cell, whether plant or animal, that accounts for its electrical properties."[8]

What happens to this "delicate balance" if we have blood proteins clogging the spaces between the cells, attracting and holding excess fluid and excess sodium? What happens to the cellular environment if this interstitial traffic jam is preventing the oxygen and other life-process fuels from getting into the cells and the metabolic waste from being removed? First, we start moving away from the dry state, the state necessary for health, into a state of excess fluid retention which creates the state of disease. As we move into a state of excess fluid and excess sodium, in a sense, the cells start to drown. Perhaps the best description of this state is the "swamp state."

A second result of this disease state is that as the trapped blood proteins clog around the cells they start to shut down the sodium-potassium pump. As the sodium-potassium pump shuts down, the electrical fields shut down, our health shuts down, and the healing process shuts down. At this point, the cells start to degenerate and die. As the cells reproduce, they do so in a degenerated or mutated form. This is the beginning of a degenerative disease. It really doesn't matter what part of the body or in which organ this process takes place. This process is a key underlying cause of all degenerative disease. It is also descriptive of the aging process.

In his wonderful book, *Food is Your Best Medicine,* Henry Bieler, MD, shares some insights of another doctor, "After many years of practicing medicine and often working with patients who were beyond his ability to help them, Dr. John Mackenzie concluded that disease is the end result of a long process whereby the body is saturated with toxins. This degenerative process is caused by poor dietary habits, wrong thinking, and lifestyle. Dr. MacKenzie and many others believe that depending on where the toxin is localized will determine the type and nature of the disease. If it's in the joints, it will manifest as arthritis, in the pancreas, it will be diabetes, the liver, hepatitis, and so on."[9]

Consider this fact: your body creates several hundred billion new cells every day to replace the several hundred billion that die. If each succeeding generation of cells is slightly weaker than the preceding one, a gradual degenerating process takes place. This is the process of aging. However, what would happen if each generation were as healthy and strong as the one being replaced? What would happen if each succeeding generation of cells were healthier and stronger than the one before? Understanding this process gives us a tremendous amount of control over our health and how we age over time. As we shall see, it is not natural for the body to degenerate and break down. It was designed and engineered to run effectively much longer then we are actually experiencing.

In order for the sodium-potassium pump to run, it needs fuel. The fuel that's required by the cell to fire this pump is called adenosine triphosphate (ATP). ATP is the pure energy needed by the cell to run the sodium-potassium pump. This is somewhat of an oversimplification, but oxygen, glucose and phosphates combine to produce ATP. These are produced from the air we breathe and from the food and water we ingest. ATP is the energy that fuels the cell and runs the sodium-potassium pump, which in turn produces electricity. It is this electrical energy produced by the life process of the cell that creates health and stimulates healing. This is a key point to remember. When the electrical generators are on, your level of health is high and the innate intelligence within has the ability to heal the body because the life process generates electrical energy. One way to define health would be to say that health is the generation and balance of electrical energy.

Oxygen is the most important ingredient of ATP. It must constantly be supplied from the bloodstream to be combined with the glucose and phosphates in the cells to create the ATP. These sodium-potassium pumps generate the electrical energy that is essential for the normal, healthy functioning of all organs and other physical characteristics of our bodies. What will happen if we are not able to get oxygen into the cells? When the delivery of oxygen to the cell is blocked, the glucose within the cell ferments. In its attempt to survive, the cell will live off of the fermentation of glucose. This abnormal diet of fermentation causes a mutation of the cell that we know as Cancer in all of its forms. Cancer cells thrive in this polluted environment.

A medical doctor and Nobel Prize winner, Otto Warburg, who worked at the Max Plank Institute for Nutrition and Health in Germany, performed the following experiment. Dr. Warburg took perfectly healthy cells, withdrew the oxygen from those cells and found that they turn cancerous every time. When there is no oxygen, the glucose ferments, and cancer cells live off of the fermentation of glucose. Dr. Warburg said, "There is no disease more well-known than cancer."[10] In one of his lectures he stated, "Cancer, above all other diseases, has countless secondary causes. But, even for cancer, there is only one prime cause. Summarized in a few words, *the primary cause of cancer* is the replacement of the respiration of oxygen in normal body cells by a fermentation of sugar." It has been known for a long time that lack of oxygen produces cancer. As Dr. Warburg taught, trapped blood proteins in the interstitial spaces around the cells are the primary cause of cellular oxygen starvation.

As we have seen, cells are like tiny batteries that produce electricity necessary for health and vitality. Dr. Warburg points out that through the activity of the sodium-potassium pump, healthy cells generate between 70 and 90 millivolts. This is the level of electricity necessary for a healthy cell. If the voltage of the cells is reduced due to toxicity and stress, it is less able to produce the needed energy. If the cellular voltage drops to 50 millivolts, the person experiences a loss of energy, chronic fatigue, and is more susceptible to illness. If the voltage drops to 15 millivolts the cell becomes cancerous.

Through his research and experience, Robert Olney MD, demonstrated that blocked oxygenation is the primary cause of all viral, malignant, bacterial and allergenic diseases. When we think of a swamp, we automatically think about a smelly, foul environment that provides a breeding ground for creepy, crawly things. The internal swamp created by trapped blood proteins and fluid retention works exactly the same way. Dr. Olney found that in the absence of oxygen, even microorganisms that are normally beneficial to our health and well-being, become parasitic. His work proved that lack of oxygen in micro-organisms causes them to be pathogenic and parasitic, and that when this condition is corrected these organisms become non-pathogenic, non-parasitic, and non-virulent.

Instead of playing their necessary part in the process of health creation, these microorganisms start sucking energy and health from the host. His observation has been that with this knowledge, and what is already known, it should be possible to virtually wipe out cancer and infectious disease.

A respected molecular biologist and a geneticist, Stephen Levine, and Dr. Paris M. Kidd, Ph.D., in their book, *Antioxidant Adaptation*, point out "Oxygen plays a pivotal role in the proper functioning of the immune system. We can look at oxygen deficiency as the single greatest cause of all diseases."

Again, think of this state of fluid retention and excess sodium, resulting in stagnation, and lack of essential nutrients and oxygen, as a swamp. What lives in a swamp? All sorts of creepy, crawly, slimy, little things. When the cells and tissues of our bodies are in a polluted, toxic, stagnant state they become the breeding ground for countless viruses, bacteria, parasites and other unpleasant creatures to live and propagate. This polluted environment also inhibits the process necessary to fight disease.

Part of the disease-fighting process is for the white blood cells to attack and destroy any foreign substance that is not part of the body. These foreign substances, or antigens as they are called, are marked for destruction by cells in the immune system using substances called antibodies. When the internal environment is in the dry state, then the white blood cells can work, even in the absence of antibodies. They search and destroy anything that is foreign to the body. If the cells are in the dry state, infections and allergies cannot exist.

However, where there are trapped blood proteins causing fluid retention, creating an internal swamp and a lack of oxygen, the white blood cells cannot work. Research published in *Scientific American* by W. Barry Wood Jr. revealed that if there is fluid retention in the spaces around the cells, the white blood cells cannot ingest bacteria.[11] It is the fluid retention caused by trapped blood proteins that makes our bodies subject to infectious disease.

The pH Balance of Acid and Alkaline

The term pH stands for "potential of hydrogen" and is a measurement of electrical energy. As we have seen the body is energetic and electric in nature and maintaining an optimal state where cells can generate electricity is a key to our health. In the Textbook of Medical Physiology Dr. Guyton states, "The first step in maintaining health is to alkalize the body. The second step is to increase the number of negative hydrogen ions." As the number of negative hydrogen ions increase there are more electrons available. The pH is described using the terms of acidity or alkalinity of a liquid. These words indicate the electrical potential available. An acid state will steal electrons resulting in lower energy while an alkaline state will donate electrons raising energy hence the terms acid and alkaline can be thought of as electron stealers and electron donors.

When electrons are stolen from an atom it creates an imbalance called a free radical. That atom will look for another place it can take an electron to reestablish balance. As this condition progresses over time it destabilizes the cells that make up the tissue of organs and eventually leads to a dis-eased state. As the number of negative hydrogen ions increase there are more electrons available to donate. As extra electrons become available the surplus helps to reestablish balance in atoms that had previously lost electrons. This stabilization helps to neutralize the damage caused by free radicals and provide the body with the electrical energy necessary to create high levels of health. Having the body in an electron giving alkaline state is essential for health.

Disease will thrive in an acid state however it cannot live in an alkaline state. As we have seen, healthy cells are between minus 70 and 90 millivolts. As the voltage drops to minus 50 millivolts cells become fatigued and if the voltage drops to minus 15 millivolts the result is cancer. By raising the pH above 90 millivolts we are providing the body with electrical energy it needs to heal.

A Potential for Hydrogen chart goes from 0 to 14 with 7 being a state of balance. The pH, the electrical balance for a healthy person is between 7.1 and 7.5. If one is dealing with a disease, the body is in an electron stealing acidic state. If health is to be regained the body must be restored to an electron giving, energy producing alkaline state. The most important measurement of the levels of your health is the level of alkalinity and the amount of oxygen in your blood.

Remember, fulfill the conditions of health, and disease will leave of its own accord. Keep your body in an alkaline state and disease can't exist. Create the dry state and the cells generating energy and there is no room for disease. If our bodies are in the dry state, and the life processes of the cell are switched on, then you can't be sick. Conversely, anything that will cause the blood proteins to come out faster than the lymphatic system can pull them off will move us into a state of disease.

Anatomy of Pain

We have seen the role that oxygen plays in creating and maintaining cellular health. Let's examine its role in the prevention and reduction of pain. The presence of oxygen prevents and relieves pain. Unoxygenated blood cannot relieve pain. As an example, you no doubt have had the experience of sitting on a hard surface such as a wooden chair at a desk, a church pew or on the ground for an extended period of time. What happens? After awhile your seat starts getting sore and you start shifting around. That discomfort is caused by the pressure on your rear end, which is preventing the blood from getting to the tissues. What do we do? Stand up, move around, and give ourselves a little massage to get the blood flowing again, right? However, it is not the increased circulation of blood that relieves the pain. It is the oxygen being carried by the blood to the tissue that assuages the pain.

Here is an example of how one can move from a state of health, the dry state, to a state of dis-ease, fluid retention and pain in a matter of minutes. Have you ever had the experience of swinging a hammer, missing the nail and smashing your finger instead? Agghhhh! You yell, scream, grab your finger and hold it tight. In a few minutes you let go to take a look at the damage. Within an hour your finger has swollen up and is so tender that you can't even touch it without excruciating pain. Often, the injury hurts more an hour later, after it swells up, than it did when the initial trauma occurred.

The hammer blow to the finger traumatized the cells. When cells are damaged they give off two substances, called histamine and bradykinin. These two substances have the effect of attacking the pores of the capillary walls and causing them to open up or dilate. Because the pressure inside the capillary is high and outside is low, the result of these pores opening up is that the blood proteins rush out, taking the fluid with them. Once they are outside the capillary, they continue to attract and hold fluid. Your finger goes from a healthy state to a diseased state in a matter of minutes. As the fluid surrounds the cells, the oxygen is unable to reach them and the result is pain. Sometimes it takes two or three days for the slow-moving lymphatic system to pull off the excess fluid so the healing process can even begin. During that time, even if you barely touch the finger, the pain is tremendous.

Other than not traumatizing the cells in the first place, is there anything that can be done to prevent this diseased state of pain from occurring? The next time you smash your finger, grab it and hold on tight. Continue holding it for 20 to 30 minutes, and it won't even swell up. Here is why. When you grab the finger and hold it, you neutralize the pressure. There is the same amount of pressure inside the capillary as there is outside the capillary. Even though the pores are dilated, the blood proteins won't rush out because the pressure inside the capillary is the same as it is outside. If the exit of blood proteins does not occur, then they won't draw the excess fluid around the cells. Your finger won't swell up.

In about 20 minutes, the histamine and bradykinin stop attacking the capillary walls and dilating the pores. Even though there is damage caused by the hammer blow, you have prevented further damage from occurring, by stopping the movement of the damaged tissue from the dry state, to the diseased or swamp state. You don't have to wait for the slow-moving lymphatic system to remove the excess fluid. The oxygen can reach the cells, the generators are on, and the healing process can begin immediately. Without interference from additional swelling to the damaged area, the healing process speeds up tremendously, sometimes within hours rather than days or weeks.

I had an opportunity a number of years ago that gave me a firsthand experience of this process. I was visiting a friend who lived in the mountains and we were doing a little rock climbing. As I attempted one tricky move I slipped and fell about six feet. Although I landed on my feet, when I hit I felt a little twinge of pain on the front of my ankle. It was hardly noticeable so I continued my activity. We climbed for another 15 minutes, ran a mile or so back to his house, and visited for another 10 minutes, before I started home. By the time I arrived home an hour and a half later, my ankle and foot had swollen so much I had to hop into the house on one foot and had a considerable amount of painful difficulty taking off my boot.

What had happened? Although the initial trauma was relatively slight, it was enough to damage the cells in that area. The histamine and bradykinin attacked the capillary walls causing the pores to dilate. Under pressure, the blood proteins rushed out taking the fluid with them. The damage was very slight in the beginning and I was able to continue climbing, running and working the injured area. Two hours later, the escaped blood proteins had attracted so much fluid that my ankle looked like a balloon. All I could do was lie there and ice it. It hurt too much to stand, even without putting pressure on it. It took a couple of days for the swelling to go down, and almost a week before I could walk normally.

Since that time, I have had similar injuries at that same site. However, I immediately stopped what I was doing, even though it didn't hurt that much, and grabbed my ankle with both hands. I held it tightly for about 20 minutes. The pain left, and it never swelled up. In most cases, I was able to continue the physical activity. Needless to say, a serious injury will require more extensive care. However, where possible, if you remember to hold or wrap the injury firmly in order to neutralize the pressure and prevent fluid build-up (swelling), you will minimize the additional damage as a result of oxygen starvation, help to prevent further injury, and speed up the healing process. For injuries where fluid retention from trauma cannot be avoided, there are techniques that can be used to facilitate and stimulate lymphatic activity that will also help speed the healing process by removing excess fluids, blood proteins and toxins from the traumatized area. These other techniques will be discussed and illustrated later.

Physical stress or shock, have the same effect on the body that the localized trauma had on the finger as a result of the hammer blow. How does this process work? Again, Dr. Guyton gives us the answer in *The Textbook of Medical Physiology*. He says, "Almost all tissues of the body respond to tissue damage, whether the damage results from simple trauma or from cellular disease by the process called inflammation. The first stage in the process of inflammation is a leakage of large quantities of plasma-like fluid out of the capillaries into the damaged area followed by a clotting of the fluids." Physical stress is simple trauma, which causes tissue damage.[12] This tissue damage is a milder version of the smashed finger scenario. It has the same effect of dilating the capillary pores, moving one from the dry state to the diseased state.

If tissue is damaged as the result of poor posture, a repetitious overworking of a certain area of the body, too much or too intense of a sports activity, then the conditions that lead to pain and disease are being created. As this process continues over time, it results in a state of chronic pain, which means it hurts all the time. When the generators are shut off, healing can't take place. And, when oxygen can't get to the cells, the result is pain. If we understand this process, we can learn how to prevent blood proteins from becoming trapped, and learn how to move the trapped blood proteins out of the interstitial spaces. By doing so, we will be able to prevent the conditions from occurring that lead to degeneration and chronic pain and promote physical health.

CHAPTER 3

SIMPLIFIED NUTRITION AND CLEANSING

Let's take a brief look at the role nutrition plays in the creation of health or disease. In the early 1900's, a dentist named Dr. Weston Price wanted to find out what the relationship was between diet and the incidence of dental caries and decay. He traveled all over the world to study different cultures: the people, their diets, and what happened when they were introduced to the modern diet of processed, refined foods. At this time, it was still possible to find groups of people who had been isolated from the outside world and had lived on a natural, traditional diet for centuries.

One of the areas he studied was a remote valley in Switzerland. The community there consisted of about two thousand people whose diet had been based primarily on home-grown rye. Their milk and cheese came from their own goats and cows. When Dr. Price examined the mineral content of the soil, he found that it was far above average. The community had no doctors or dentists because there was no need for them. Interestingly enough, there was no need for policemen or jails, either. When he examined the children, ages seven to sixteen for dental caries, he found only 0.3 per person. This means that it was necessary to examine three children to find one cavity. Two out of three children had perfect teeth.

When Dr. Price visited a neighboring community having almost identical characteristics, his observations found dramatically different results. When he examined the children for dental caries, the incidence was 20.2 cavities per 100 teeth. Every child had an average of six to seven cavities. The only difference between the two communities was that a number of years before, a road had been built allowing the valley inhabitants to be introduced to the modern diet of sugar and other refined foods.

In addition to an increase in dental caries, Dr. Price observed other forms of degenerating health resulting from societies adopting a "modern diet." He noted that malformed facial bones and dental arches produced a crowding of the teeth. These malformations correlated with a lower IQ and an increase in personality disorders.[13]

There has been a dramatic increase in problems such as ADD and ADHD in our country over the past few years. Should we not consider these statistics in connection with the trend showing a marked decline in the percentage of the children in the United States who receive adequate levels of nutrition? Perhaps fulfilling the conditions of health nutritionally would be a more effective way to address these problems, rather than just drugging children.

The relationship between diet and behavior takes us into a whole new area that is well worth investigating, but beyond the scope of this book. For those who are interested in the nutrition/behavior connection, three excellent books to read are *Diet, Crime and Delinquency* by Alexander Schauss, *Smart Moves: Why Learning is Not All in Your Head* by Dr. Carla Hannaford and *Diet for A New America* by John Robbins.

Dr. Price also noted that the incidence of birth defects greatly increased in the second community. The difference between healthy children born before their parents adopted the use of refined foods, and those children born to them after was often dramatic. In some cultures, where degenerative diseases such as cancer and heart disease had been virtually non-existent, their appearance followed soon after the introduction of the modern, refined diet. When we view pictures of people who lived on their traditional diet in perfect health compared to those who became victims of the modern diet, the contrast is startling. We can't help but acknowledge the unsettling feeling of what we have done to ourselves and what we are doing to our children.

What happened? How could a society that had lived in a relative state of health for centuries move into a state of disease so quickly? Think of it this way. Imagine that you are instructed to go to a building site and build a house. We will assume that you already have the knowledge, instructions and blueprints. You arrive at the site ready to start your project only to find that there are no building materials to use. There are no bricks, mortar, lumber or nails. You call the person who gave you the assignment and say, "There's nothing here. I can't build a house without building materials." To your chagrin, the person at the other end answers, "I don't want any excuses, I want results. Now get busy." Don't laugh. Some of us have worked for people like that. What could you do about building the house? Obviously you must have building materials.

As absurd as this little scenario may sound, this is exactly the situation in our body. It needs fuel to burn and building materials with which to construct tissue. When those materials are not available, the body adjusts the best it can. However, there will come a time when it has exhausted all of its reserves in its nutritional savings account, and the body is bankrupt. The inner wisdom is doing everything it can to supply the body with the needed nutrients to maintain health, and there is nothing there it can use.

Additionally, the process of digestion is one of the most energy-consuming processes of the body. It takes energy to break down food, extract the nutrients, convert it to energy and eliminate the waste. Think of this in terms of living expenses. If your income is five thousand dollars a month and your expenses are six thousand dollars a month, you have a problem. If you can't increase your cash flow to meet expenses the extra money has to come from somewhere. In most cases people borrow money or sell off assets to make up the difference. In either case, there will come a time when a person can't borrow anymore or doesn't have any other assets to sell. If earning and spending haven't balanced there will be a crisis.

The energy-in, energy-out exchange in the body works very much the same way. If the body has all the nutrients it needs for fuel and building materials, there will be a high level of health. If the body is expending more energy than it is taking in, it must compensate in some way. It will start extracting nutrients from other parts of the body to maintain the most important vital functions. As the nutrients are depleted, parts of the body start to break down because they don't have the building material needed to build and repair.

As an example, B complex and calcium are required to break down and metabolize sugar. If there is not enough calcium in the diet, the body will go into the bones and extract it to break down the sugar. What do you think that does to the skeletal system? As we continue to ingest non-foods, we are not replenishing our nutritional bank account and our body must make up the difference somehow. When it reaches a point where the inner wisdom cannot "borrow" any more from other parts of the body there will be a crisis.

A major problem facing us today is that our modern diets are missing many of the nutrients needed by the body to maintain a state of health. The degenerative condition that Dr. Price observed in many formerly healthy societies, and much of our present health crisis, is the result of a nutritionally bankrupt diet.

In addition to modern refined foods, modern farming techniques have also contributed to nutritional deficiency. In the past, the ground had been allowed to lie fallow for a period of time so that the minerals in the soil could be replenished. The minerals in our food come from the earth. The plants we eat are the medium through which we receive the minerals; however, the earth is the source. If the minerals aren't present in the soil, how can they get into the plants to become our food? And how valuable is that food to our bodies? Without healthy, mineral-rich food, the cells will not have the building materials they need to produce health.

Today, for the most part, the mineral content of depleted soil is supplemented with petrochemical fertilizers. This is the basis of modern farming. This often produces a fruit that looks wonderful but is tasteless. Have you ever had the experience of biting into one of those big, juicy, luscious strawberries, anticipating the gush of sweetness, only to find that it tastes like wet cardboard? Welcome to the petrochemical strawberry. Yum!

As we consider the Standard American Diet (appropriately abbreviated as SAD) and the growing health care crisis in relationship to the findings of Dr. Price, it becomes clear that part of the solution lies in each of us being more conscious of the food choices we make for our family and ourselves.

Although the subject of nutrition can be complicated, it is also very simple. If you ever want to be totally confused, just get a group of experts in nutrition together and try to figure out what is right. There are some basic guidelines to follow that apply to everyone. The best approach I've heard comes from Dr. Charlie Cropley whose course, "Food is Your Best Medicine," is based on Dr. Henry Bieler's book with the same title.

Dr. Cropley keeps it very simple: Eat only food. The substances we see as we visit the grocery store, and that most of us put in our bodies, have been altered, processed and refined in some way and simply cannot be classified as food. The further a food has been processed away from its original state, the more difficult it is for the body to use. A simple rule to remember is, "The closer you can eat food to the way God created it, the more life is in it and the better off you'll be."

People experience remarkable benefits from this three-week class. Those who were over-weight, lost weight and those who were underweight gained it. People who were experiencing high or low blood sugar problems and the resulting mood swings experienced stabilization. Those with arthritis noticed a lessening of pain and stiffness. For some, their depression left. Many who came into the class on medication no longer needed it. In short, the conditions of health were fulfilled. Toxins were removed and the body began receiving the nutrients it really needed. And, true to natural law, the diseases left of their own accord.

There are five basic principles that Dr. Cropley has successfully used for years on thousands of patients. The first principle is that food should be natural. This means that it doesn't come in a can, a box or a wrapper. When you look at the way a banana is packaged it doesn't need any expiration date. You'll know when it has reached that point.

Second, food should be alive. The vitality you experience in life is in direct proportion to the vitality in your food. When you pick an apple off the tree, it is full of living energy. It is alive, and when you eat it, the life force in the apple becomes a part of you. Life begets life. Every cell in your body is intelligent and it knows how to relate to life. It can't relate to or use something that is dead.

The third principle is to keep it simple. When one eats many different foods together, it makes digestion extremely difficult. As an example, when you eat protein, it is broken down and digested with hydrochloric acid, which is very acidic. When you eat starch, the enzyme that breaks it down is amylase, which is alkaline. When you mix acid and alkaline together, they neutralize each other making digestion ineffective. The food putrefies in the stomach and your body has to work overtime to accomplish the job. This increases the amount of energy consumed in the digestive process. Below is a basic diagram about food combining that will help you optimize the food you eat.

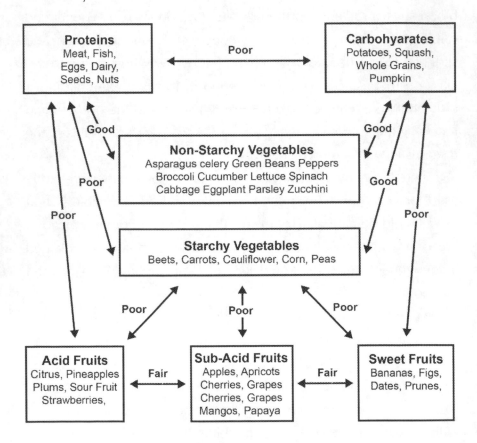

The fourth principle is clean. This is more than washing your food. This means that we don't use healthy, live food as a means of transporting dead food into your body. As an example, don't use salad as a means of carrying blue cheese dressing into your body. Eating clean means that we minimize the use of sweeteners. Most of us are aware that refined sugar is poison; however, high usage of honey and maple syrup can cause damage as well because they are 90% sugar. When dealing with these sweeteners, less is better. A good choice for sweeteners is stevia. A little goes a long way and research has shown that it actually aids in healing the pancreas and liver.

The fifth principle is whole. The concept to keep in mind is that the whole is greater than the sum of its parts. If you had a radio and you took it apart, you'd have all the parts. Would that pile of parts accomplish what the assembled radio would? Obviously not. Whole foods are complete foods. There are numerous vitamins, minerals and enzymes that act in a synergistic way, producing a greater effect than each individual nutrient would have, even if they were all mixed together. Just as there is a difference between a complete radio and a pile of parts, so is there a difference between a whole live food and a bunch of synthetic nutrients manufactured to make a supplement. We are not going to improve on the wisdom of nature and it could be argued that when you extract and isolate a substance from a whole food such as a vitamin you no longer have a food. You have a drug.

When you use these five principles as guidelines, your eating and health will automatically improve. Remember the simple rule of thumb: the closer you can eat food to the way God made it the better off you'll be.

It's helpful to keep in mind that individuals have different body types, and this means that we have different requirements. It is true that one man's food is another man's poison; however, the basic nutritional laws hold true. Take the time to learn your body's needs. You may be surprised to find that foods you thought were healthy are actually toxic to your system.

Cleansing and Detoxification

Remember, creating and maintaining health and high-performance living is a life-long process. Make haste slowly. Start the transition by eliminating the dead, denatured, processed foods one by one, and replacing them with whole, live, natural foods. One of the things you will find as you progress with this transition diet is that the non-food substances that taste so good will gradually lose their appeal as your taste changes. As your body cleanses itself, you will find it's easy to give up foods you no longer want. There are also cleansing diets and fasts that can be very beneficial; however, start slowly.

One of the reasons that fasting can be so beneficial in the healing process is that it helps your body burn the garbage. After the third day of receiving no food, the body needs fuel to burn in order to continue performing its functions. Since there is no food available, it begins to consume itself. It does not do this indiscriminately, however. It first begins by consuming the weak, deteriorating, unhealthy cells. It consumes the toxic garbage, which had been accumulating in the swamp state, and helps the body detoxify faster.

I have a friend who was diagnosed with advanced colon cancer and given six months to live. In addition, he was dealing with adult-onset diabetes and candidiasis. Having been trained in allopathic medicine, he was well aware of the more traditional and common treatments of attacking the disease with radiation and chemo. Instead he chose another route, attending a clinic where the emphasis was on cleansing, purifying and detoxification by fasting and other natural means. This approach included strong nutritional support, correct food combining and other holistic practices that would enhance the healing process.

The results were dramatic. In three months the cancer was completely gone as were the diabetes and candidiasis. He runs regularly and is experiencing an energy level higher than he has experienced since his 20's (he is now in his mid-fifties). How does one go from a condition of deadly disease to such high levels of energy? There are a number of things that contributed to this remarkable turn-around, and many are covered in this book. Applying the basics of good nutrition and internal cleansing are essential to putting the cells in a condition where they can thrive and perform optimally. Cleansing will support you in the pursuit of higher levels of health and energy.

Since cleansing and purification are a part of healing and creating wellness, let's take a brief look at the elimination and cleansing process. As digested food leaves the stomach, it travels through the intestines. The small intestine is about 25 feet long. The intestines are lined with millions of tiny finger-shaped extensions called "villi." The villi help push the food through the intestine where the nutrients are absorbed through the intestinal wall into the bloodstream. The villi also dramatically increase the surface area of intestine to increase the ability to absorb the nutrients. The surface area inside a 25-foot tube is relatively small; however, the millions of villi increase the absorption surface area to the size of a tennis court! If the assimilation of nutrients is to effectively take place, it is imperative that the intestines are kept clean and the villi healthy and functioning well. Unfortunately, the "Standard American Diet" of refined and processed foods leads to insufficient digestion, poor absorption and can actually damage the villi.

Unless the diet consists mainly of whole foods that cleanse as they go, toxic garbage accumulates inside the intestines. This inhibits the villi's ability to absorb the needed nutrients and move the waste through. If this condition persists over time, your blood absorbs poisons from the waste in the intestines rather than needed nutrients. Then your blood carries these toxins all over your body. No wonder so many people feel tired all the time. In many cases you may be so used to your sub-standard energy level that you think of it as normal, never realizing the greater energy and the higher quality of life you could have.

Compounding this problem further is a condition called leaky gut syndrome. When in good health the walls of the intestines and colon are slightly permeable allowing only small molecules of nutrients to pass through whole keeping harmful toxins such as bacteria, fungus, parasites and heavy metals in the colon where they can be neutralized and excreted. When the structure of the colon wall is compromised due to poor diet, over use of antibiotics, chronic stress and environmental contaminants it becomes hyper-permeable and larger spaces develop in the colon wall. This allows large protein molecules, toxic substances and parasites to pass through into the blood. They are then transported all over the rest of the body and deposited in the tissues contributing to the disease process we have already seen.

Obviously, the first step is to start cleaning up your diet. Stop poisoning yourself. The second step is to clear the pipes. Many good intestinal and colon cleansers are available in your health food store or through network marketing companies that distribute vitamins, herbs and other health-enhancing products. One of the best detoxification programs is called Arise and Shine. Fasting, enemas and colonics can also be valuable in aiding this cleansing process.

As nutrients are absorbed through the wall of the intestine into the blood they are transported to the liver. The liver filters the blood, removes the impurities and forms a secretion called bile. The bile is excreted into the duodenum, a part of the small intestine, and passed out with other waste. Bile, in a healthy system, is a bright yellow similar to urine. If the blood is too toxic and there is a lack of alkalinity in the liver to neutralize it, the bile will be acidic and dark green or black. If the bile is too acidic, the corrosive effect can damage the liver and gall bladder and cause bile burns inside the small intestine as it passes through. As this mixture passes through the intestines, much of this waste is reabsorbed into the blood.

If the food is pure and the digestive tract clean, the stress on the liver will be minimal. As a result, the blood will be clean and better able to carry oxygen and nutrients to the rest of the body. The body's energy will be used in creating vitality rather than clearing toxins. Dr. Henry Bieler in his book, *Food is Your Best Medicine*, says, "If the liver could keep the blood stream clean by filtering out damaging poisons, man could live indefinitely, barring physical accidents."[14] Basically, the aging process is a result of slow poisoning causing cellular degeneration over time. Dr. Bieler refers to the digestive system as the first line of defense against disease, and the liver as the second.

A Word on Water

The traditional approach to measuring the amount of water needed for optimal health has been the 8 glasses a day as rule of thumb or one half ounce of water for every pound of body weight. While liquids like milk and juice carry nutrients, pure water is essential in cleansing the body. It is safe to say that most of us do not drink enough water and over time this can lead to dehydration and insufficient cleansing. These conditions will contribute to a number of physical problems. Keep in mind that if one's diet is primarily fresh fruit and vegetables, which are mostly water, you will require less water. However, a good rule of thumb is ½ ounce for every pound you weigh.

Naturally, the quality of the water is important and there are three characteristics you will want to be aware of to assure you are receiving the maximum health benefit possible. The first thing to be sure of is that the water you drink is alkaline. Surprisingly, most bottled and reverse osmosis water is acidic. As we have seen, keeping the body in an alkaline state is one of the most important things you can do for your health.

Ideally your water should be micro clustered. The number of atoms in a normal water molecule is between 15 to 18. The number of atoms in a micro clustered water molecules are around 5 to 7. This allows the water to be transported into the cells quickly and efficiently. Micro clustering means the surface tension is lower and the water is absorbed into the tissues much easier and is more effective at eliminating waste.

Third, the water you drink should ideally be high in anti-oxidants because they help to neutralize free radicals and support the body's ability to restore electrical balance. This quality in your water has a powerful healing effect by giving your body a surplus of electrical energy needed to restore and maintain healthy cellular function.

Nutritional Supplements

The question of food supplements often comes up. For most people, a high-quality, natural, whole, live food supplement can make a tremendous difference in preventing disease and restoring high levels of health. I always suggest that people take a look where they are on the wellness continuum. If their health is vital and robust and they normally avoid dead food and eat nutritionally potent, organically grown, live foods with the bulk of their diet consisting of fresh fruit, vegetables and whole grains, supplementation is probably not necessary. If you're in the lower half of the continuum, or hovering around the not-sick area, then taking a good food supplement could make a big difference. However, make sure the supplements are used in addition to a quality diet and not to support you nutritionally while you continue to eat lifeless, dead or toxic foods.

With the pace of life today and the amount of stress with which we all deal, nutritional support is quite beneficial. Only about one percent of the children in the wealthiest country on the planet receive adequate nutrition. Considering the reality of present day health statistics, a good food supplement plan is a wise investment. You are likely to be preventing health problems from occurring later on in life. If you use supplements make sure they come from a whole food base.

Let's put this in perspective. Think of how much you or your employer spends on health insurance each month. For most people and families it can range between $600 and $1200 a month or more. Here is a thought to consider:Do you really want to use your health insurance and get your money's worth out of it? Chances are you would probably rather stay healthy and not have to use the insurance. So, let's think about this. You spend several hundred dollars a month paying for something you don't want to use. How much do you spend on yourself and your family to make sure they stay healthy? Is it wiser to spend money on something you never want to use, something that is designed to treat disease after you have it, or is it wiser to invest in your health and prevent the illness or disease in the first place?

I'm not suggesting you cancel your insurance policy. Good insurance coverage is a wise safety net to have. However, most people make their insurance payments religiously but don't spend a fraction of that in the process of building health. Quality food supplements, educational seminars and workshops, other health-enhancing products plus exercise are the best health insurance policy you could have. Health enhancing products don't cost, they pay.

In addition to being nutritionally dead and therefore useless as far as supplying fuel or building material to the body, certain foods have an effect on the body similar to that which occurs when the cells are traumatized. This trauma causes capillary pores to open up and blood proteins to rush out. Salt, sugar, caffeine and alcohol, to name a few, have the effect of dilating the capillary pores and increasing the exit of blood proteins. Once outside the capillary wall, they attract and hold excess sodium and excess fluid, moving one into the "swamp state."

The body has been designed to balance itself. The natural, built-in intelligence within our physical make-up works very hard to maintain a state of health. When it becomes overloaded with toxins, it does its best to cleanse itself. In some cases, what appears to be an illness is really our body's attempt to eliminate the toxic garbage that has accumulated. Poisons are coughed up from the lungs, excreted from the bowels in the form of diarrhea, vomited up, oozed out from the eyes, and drained from the nose. Sometimes, our bodies become so toxic that poisons are excreted through the skin. These processes are the body's attempts to cleanse itself and move back into a state of health.

When we find ourselves experiencing any of these symptoms, how do we respond? The normal, well-educated American who has been "schooled" and trained by television commercials, may take a drug to dry up the nose, a cough syrup to suppress a cough, or use an ointment on the skin to stop a rash. Our bodies try to purify and heal themselves after we pollute them. But do we really want to stop the cleansing process?

When you watch television, listen to what the commercials are really saying: Cough *suppressant*, for relief of *symptoms*, etc. If all you want to do is treat symptoms, then, by all means, buy those products. They may temporarily move you out of the diseased state back to being healthy, if you define healthy as not sick. However, if you truly want to heal the illness and start building high-level wellness, then you must address the underlying causes.

To build health, we need to minimize the input of poisons and help our body cleanse itself. We already know that deep breathing and exercise will help stimulate the lymphatic system. And by just eating a clean diet of fresh fruit, vegetables, and whole grains, you will help your body begin to cleanse. Although individuals and body types differ in their requirements, as a general rule, these foods should be the mainstay of your diet. If you eat meat and dairy, consume them in moderation.

Often, people become inspired and decide to really clean up their act and "get healthy." They stop eating dead food, start eating only raw food, and perhaps go on a cleanse, or a fast. What happens? Their body starts to dump poisons into their lymphatic system and bloodstream so fast that it can't get rid of them, and they become "sick." If they don't understand that their body is actually cleansing itself so it can heal, their response is, "I'm trying to clean up my act and eat better. And what happens? I get sick. Forget this health stuff. I'm going back to burgers, soda and greasy fries.

Remember the transition diet of gradually eliminating the dead food and replacing it with live food will move you forward consistently a little at a time. If you do this now, and participate in a cleansing process from time to time you may well be preventing yourself from having to deal with a serious condition in the future. These are two things that will dramatically move you up the living continuum and enhance your quality of life.

As we conclude this section on nutrition and cleansing I'd like to share some thoughts that may help you redefine what health is and a vision of what is possible. One of the most famous experiments of the past century was performed by Nobel Prize winner, Dr. Alexis Carrell while working at the Rockefeller Institute of Medical Research. Dr. Carrell wanted to see how long a cell culture would remain alive outside the body. He took a tissue culture from the heart of a chicken embryo and placed it in a nourishing solution. On the 66th day it began to beat rhythmically. That little group of cells was kept alive for 29 years and the only reason the experiment was terminated is because the researchers concluded it would continue forever. Dr. Carrell stated, "The cell is immortal. It is merely the fluid in which it floats which degenerates. Renew this fluid at intervals, give the cell something upon which to feed and, so far as we know, the pulsation of life may go on forever."

In his book *The Golden Seven Plus One*, Dr. C. Samuel West included a letter he received from a cancer researcher who had worked at Boston University Medical School, Tufts Medical School and Southwestern Medical School conducting research in cell biology and biochemistry. She says, "any researcher who has worked with tissue cultures knows that cells can be kept alive indefinitely, but you must keep the proper chemical balance in and around the cell and eliminate the waste products of their metabolism.[15]

These two examples provide us with a whole new vision as to the possibilities for living a vitality and energy-filled, disease-free, high-quality life.

CHAPTER 4

EXERCISE AND LYMPH FLOW

Next, let's take a look at the role physical exercise plays in not only building strength but in the cleansing and healing process. Volumes have been written on the importance of exercise so I won't duplicate that; however, there is a form of exercise that is very effective in stimulating the flow of lymph called "rebound exercise." This form of exercise uses a mini exercise trampoline commonly known as a rebounder. This term was coined by Albert Carter who was a pioneer in discovering and teaching the benefits of rebound exercise.

By properly using a rebounder, it is possible to increase lymphatic flow, aid the cleansing process, keep the blood proteins circulating and strengthen every cell in the body without causing any physical trauma. Those may sound like strong claims to make for an activity so simple and easy, so let's see how it works.

First of all, a basic, fundamental law of developing strength is that in order to develop strength there must be an opposition. As one lifts weights, does push-ups, sit-ups or pull-ups, what force is being opposed? What is being worked against? The answer is gravity. The gravitational pull of the earth is the basic common denominator of all exercise. To develop strength one increases the opposition or challenges the muscle. As an example, in lifting weights one would increase the amount of weight or the number of repetitions. The key thought to remember here is, "challenges build strength."

The cells in our body have a remarkable ability to adjust to their environment. If a cell is stressed in a positive way such as exercise it will adjust to that increased demand by becoming stronger. If a muscle is not used, atrophy sets in and it loses its strength. This is not just limited to muscle however.

An example of this principal would be working in your yard or garden. If you rake leaves or hoe weeds over a period of time, what happens to your hands? They form calluses. In this process the individual skin cells adjust to the stress caused by heat and friction and become stronger. What happens if you work too hard or too long? You form blisters because there was too much stress, too much friction and too much heat. The cells were pushed past their rupture threshold and destroyed. So, stress is good to a point because it builds strength; however, too much becomes destructive.

Dr. Hans Selye, who is considered to be the father of stress research, identifies these positive and negative stresses as eustress and distress. Eustress is the tension necessary for growth that has positive physical and emotional effects resulting in increased levels of health. Distress is destructive stress that causes physical and emotional damage. This principal not only applies to physical, mental and emotional health, but to all other systems such as families, economies, organizations and nations. In all cases "challenges build strength" however too much stress becomes destructive.

There are two forces that have the same effect upon a physical body as gravity. These forces are acceleration and deceleration. When taking off in a jet you can feel the force of acceleration press you back in the seat. When the jet lands and reverses the thrusters, you can feel the force of deceleration pull you forward. Acceleration, deceleration and gravity are all measured in terms of "G" force.

Rebounding takes the forces of acceleration and deceleration and puts them in a vertical line. This arrangement will increase the effect of gravity on every cell in the body. As one bounces up and down there is an alteration between deceleration and acceleration. As one contacts the mat, slows down and stops, every cell in the body is positively stressed by the force of deceleration. Depending on how high one is jumping, and it doesn't take much height to be effective, he or she can weigh up to two times as much at the bottom of the bounce. This means that a person weighing 150 pounds would actually weigh 300 pounds at the bottom of the bounce.

As the exercise trampoline rebounds, the body is subjected to the force of acceleration as it is propelled upward. This increase in "G" force creates an environment of positive tension to which every cell in the body must adjust. This strengthens and tones muscle, internal organs, connective tissue, skin and bone without the trauma caused by exercising on a hard surface.

A form of exercise that does not cause trauma to the cells is the most ideal form. As you will remember, traumatized cells give off histamine and bradykinin. These substances have the effect of dilating the pores in the capillary walls causing the blood proteins to rush out. Our purpose in exercising is to raise the level of health, not cause more damage. By utilizing a rebounder or lymphosizer, there is no shock to the system or damage done to the cells, and you will increase strength, energy and endurance.

How does rebounding increase the flow of lymph fluid? As you will recall this system circulates through a series of one-way check valves. There must be more pressure below the valve then above it, in order for it to open and flow. When you are rebounding, the pressure is increased at the bottom of the bounce by decelerating, which causes the valve to open thereby increasing flow. At the top of the bounce you are weightless, and this takes the pressure off the top, which causes it to open. At the bottom of the bounce when the "G" force is increased, all the tissue in the body is compressed. At the top of the bounce, the body is weightless and the compression is released causing increased lymphatic flow. The lymph system pumps fluid and protein out of the tissue spaces each time the tissues are compressed or moved in any other way. Using a rebounder is one of the most effective means of causing that compression to increase lymph flow.

I might add, this process holds true for using a full-sized trampoline as well. A back yard trampoline with a safety net around it can be a wonderful way for children to experience these benefits.

A word of caution. Using a rebounder can increase lymphatic flow so effectively that some people may become dizzy or feel nauseous. This is because the toxins are being pulled out from the cells so rapidly that the system is overwhelmed. Start slow, and start low. It's not necessary to jump high to benefit from this activity.

CHAPTER 5

THE BREATH OF LIFE

We have already seen the importance of oxygen to the cell in maintaining healthy, effective functioning and preventing cellular breakdown. One of the easiest, most effective ways to increase your level of health is by employing basic breathing exercises. They are simple and effective, and may have a dramatic effect on your health. And they don't cost anything. Dr. Otto Warburg said, "Deep-breathing techniques which increase oxygen to the cell are the most important factors in living a disease-free and energetic life... Remember, where cells get enough oxygen, cancer will not, cannot occur." Dr. Sheldon Hendler MD, author of *The Oxygen Breakthrough*, says, "Oxygenation through deep breathing boosts the immune system and can rid the body of chronic illnesses.

In addition to the disease prevention and healing aspects of deep breathing, other benefits include greater relaxation, resulting in less stress, increased mental clarity, higher levels of energy and vitality, weight loss, enhanced detoxification, better mental attitude and a greater sense of emotional well-being. The more you understand the overall health-creation benefits that deep breathing offers, the more motivated you will be to actively engage this under-used and taken-for-granted gift.

Breathing Techniques

According to doctors Thomas and Caron Goode, directors of the International Breath Institute, the average concentration of oxygen in the blood during normal breathing is between 60 and 70 percent. There must be a minimum of 53 percent oxygen content in the blood to sustain life. When the oxygen level is 80 percent or higher, the result is a marked health improvement in all areas. The best way to accomplish this is through conscious, deep breathing.

One of the breathing techniques taught by the Goode's is called circular breathing. Place your hand on your abdomen. As you inhale through your nose, feel your stomach rise as you take in the air. After the stomach fills, continue the in-breath and let it rise up into your chest. As you exhale, relax and just let the breath flow out of the chest and then the abdomen. Without pausing, begin the inhalation process again. Continue this rhythmic pattern, letting each breath flow into the next. By focusing your awareness on the rising and falling of your breath, you will notice a decrease in tension and an increase in emotional calm and mental awareness. Doctors Tom and Caron Goode provide a number of excellent products and services and may be reached at www.internationalbreathinstitute.com.

Here are two more basic breathing techniques that will markedly improve your health. Pick one of these three and make conscious breathing a habit.

The first technique involves a strong inhale through the nose, filling the abdomen, followed by a forceful exhale through the mouth. This is repeated two more times. On the third out-breath, you exhale two more times. Inhale, exhale, inhale, exhale, inhale, exhale, exhale, and exhale. If this is done in conjunction with a brisk walk, so much the better.

For the second technique, place one hand on your abdomen. Inhale through your nose into your stomach and feel your hand rise. When the area below the diaphragm is full, continue inhaling. Once you have reached maximum capacity, stop for a couple of seconds. Then take three more additional quick breaths in short bursts through the nose. Next, purse your lips together and exhale slowly as if you were blowing through a straw. You will feel the resistance of this tighten your abdominal muscles as you continue to exhale. As soon as you have pushed all the air out of your lungs and diaphragm, stop for a couple seconds and then blow out three more short bursts through your pursed lips. Repeat this process for several minutes, rest and do it again. Fifteen minutes a day will produce remarkable results.

All of these techniques are very effective ways to deliver oxygen to the cells, which, as we have seen, is the most important nutrient your body can have. At the same time, these activities will stimulate the lymphatic system, which aids the cleansing and detoxification process.

Oxycising

One of the most effective ways to deliver that oxygen is through a series of simple breathing exercises called *Oxycise*. This system was initially designed as a weight-loss program. However, the benefits go far beyond just taking off those extra, unwanted pounds in a simple, effective way. This technique will assure the delivery of life-giving oxygen to the individual cells. Since obesity is such a problem for many people, and it increases the risk of illness, let's briefly look at this revolutionary new way to correct the weight problem.

Jill R. Johnson, developer of *Oxycise,* found through her research that fat is made up of carbon, hydrogen, and oxygen atoms. When one increases the oxygen delivery to the cells, it combines with the fat to cause oxidation. The result of this oxidation process is carbon dioxide, which is the greatest byproduct of the metabolic process. The carbon dioxide is then simply exhaled out. It is hard to believe that something so simple could be so effective. This isn't just another fad, and it's not a diet. It truly is a revolutionary new way of solving the weight problem, and the process will work for anyone.

An additional benefit of this program to the effective burning of fat is the building of strong, firm abdominal muscles. One of Ms. Johnson's students had been a state body building champion who was already in great shape. Using the *Oxycise* program exclusively for only three weeks, he took another one and a half inches off his waist. His conclusion was that the toning he got from this method in 15 minutes was equivalent to 400 crunches a day. If you have a weight problem, and you want to tone muscle, this program is a must.

Ms. Johnson has received hundreds of letters from people who have not only benefited from dramatic weight loss, but have also experienced numerous other health benefits as well. Many were surprised and delighted to find that the positive side effects of increased oxygen intake include an increase in energy levels, greater mental clarity, a higher resistance to flus and colds, as well as a greater experience of overall well-being. All of these positive benefits are great reasons to breathe consciously.

Science of the Breath

In addition to the wonderful physical benefits deep breathing provides, this "Science of the Breath" has been used for centuries as a means to enhance our relation to spirit. Taking the time to focus our awareness on the breath, and gradually follow it to its source, is a technique that has been used by numerous spiritual traditions down through the ages. It is no wonder that breath and spirit are linked. *Breath* is usually thought of as an activity necessary to sustain the life of the physical form. In many traditions, *spirit* is understood to be the source of life itself.

This link is far greater than most of us realize. When we begin to look deeper, it becomes apparent that the nature of breath and spirit are synonymous. We find that in many languages, the word for *breath* is the same word that is used for *spirit*. In the Aramaic language, the tongue Jesus spoke and in which he taught, the word *ruha* is the word that has been translated as *spirit*. However, if we look at its multiple meanings we find *ruha* is also the word used for *breath, air, and wind*. In English the words *spirit, breath, air and wind* all are translated from the Hebrew word *ruach*.[16] According to both Aramaic and Hebrew, it would be necessary to consider all meanings of a word to gain a wholeness of the truth. Thus we see that the references in scripture to the *Holy Spirit*, could also be translated as the *Holy Breath*

In some Eastern traditions, the *breath* is equated with the *life force*. In India, it is referred to as *prana*, in China, *chi* or *qi*. In Japan, this *life force* is called *ki*. As we understand Spirit to be the source of life, and how different cultures and religions equate *breath* with *life force*, the translation of *Holy Breath* takes on new meaning and a deeper significance. Later, we will explore the nature of this life force in greater detail. The more we understand that the gift of breath is truly the force of life, the more effective we will be in using it to create high levels of health and well-being.

CHAPTER 6

STRESS

In addition to the effect that physical trauma and certain foods have on dilating the capillary pores, negative mental stress, usually resulting from negative emotions, also has the same effect. The chemical reactions caused by negative stress and negative emotions dilate the capillary pores, increasing the exit of blood proteins into the interstitial spaces.

As we have seen, trapped blood proteins gradually shut off the electrical process of the cells resulting in a loss of energy. Have you ever had the experience of being in a stressful situation with your spouse, your children, your boss or other people at work and, after the stressful event passed, you have felt exhausted? Your electrical generators have shut down.

Often, we do not take the time to rest and let our bodies recuperate. When we are under constant stress, it will begin to take its toll. With your growing knowledge of the physical conditions caused by trapped blood proteins, you can begin to understand why ongoing stress causes physical degeneration and eventually breakdown.

The quality of nutrition, amount of exercise, and the degree of stress in our life all have an effect on the integrity of the capillary walls. This determines to a large degree, the amount and the rate at which plasma proteins escape and the effectiveness of the lymphatic system in removing them. Learning effective ways to manage stress, would eliminate much of the damage caused by blood proteins.

Part of our process into greater levels of health and wholeness is growing into a greater awareness of ourselves. The following activity will raise your level of awareness regarding your point on the path as you move toward high level wellness. It will help to set the stage for the upcoming exploration into the relationship that thoughts and emotions have on our health.

The Fully Alive Holistic Health Questionnaire

This Fully Alive Self-Test was developed by Robert A. Anderson MD, ABIHM and Robert S. Ivker DO, ABIHM both who are co-founders and past presidents of the American Board of Integrative Holistic Medicine. It is used with their permission.

Rate your level of frequency in which you participate in these activities, on a scale of 0 to 5.

0 = Never or almost never (Once a year or less)
1 = Seldom (2 to 12 times a year)
2 = Occasionally (2 to 4 times a month)
3 = Often (2 to 4 times weekly)
4 = Regularly (4 to 6 times a week)
5 = Daily (Every Day)

Body: Physical and Environmental Health

_____ 1. Do you maintain a healthy diet? (low fat, low sugar, fresh fruits, vegetables and whole grains)
_____ 2. Is your water intake adequate? (one half ounce per pound of body weight?)

_____ 3. Are you within 20% of your ideal body weight?

_____ 4. Do you feel physically attractive?

_____ 5. Do you fall asleep easily and sleep soundly?

_____ 6. Do you awaken in the morning feeling well rested?

_____ 7. Do you have more than enough energy to meet your daily responsibilities?

_____ 8. Are your five senses acute?

_____ 9. Do you take time to experience sensual pleasure?

_____ 10. Do you schedule a regular massage or body work?

_____ 11. Does your sexual relationship feel gratifying?

_____ 12. Do you engage in regular physical workouts lasting at least 20 minutes?

_____ 13. Do you have good endurance or aerobic capacity?

_____ 14. Do you breathe abdominally for at least a few minutes?

_____ 15. Do you maintain physically challenging goals?

_____ 16. Are you physically strong?

_____ 17. Do you do some stretching exercises?

_____ 18. Are you free from chronic aches, pain, ailments and diseases?

_____ 19. Do you have regular, effortless bowel movements?

_____ 20. Do you understand the causes of your chronic physical problems?

_____ 21. Are you free of any drug or alcohol dependency, including nicotine and caffeine?

_____ 22. Do you live in a healthy environment with respect to clean air, water and indoor pollution?

_____ 23. Do you feel energized and empowered by nature?

_____ 24. Do you feel a strong connection with and appreciation for your body, your home and your environment?

_____ 25. Do you have an awareness of life energy?

Total Body Score _____

Mental and Emotional Health

_____ 1. Do you have firm goals in your personal and professional life?

_____ 2. Do you have the ability to concentrate for extended periods of time?

_____ 3. Do you use visualization or mental imagery to help you attain your goals or enhance your performance?

_____ 4. Do you believe it is possible to change?

_____ 5. Can you meet your financial needs or desires?

_____ 6. Is your outlook basically optimistic?

_____ 7. Do you give yourself more supportive messages than critical messages?

_____ 8. Does your job utilize all of your greatest talents?

_____ 9. Is your job interesting and fulfilling?

_____ 10. Are you willing to take risks or make mistakes in order to succeed?

_____ 11. Are you able to adjust your beliefs and attitudes as a result of learning from painful experiences?

_____ 12. Do you have a sense of humor?

_____ 13. Do you maintain peace of mind and tranquility?

_____ 14. Are you free from a strong need for control or the need to be right?

_____ 15. Are you able to fully experience (feel) your painful feelings such as fear anger, sadness and hopelessness?

_____ 16. Are you aware of and able to safely express fear?

_____ 17. Are you aware of and able to safely express anger?

_____ 18. Are you aware of and able to safely express sadness or cry?

_____ 19. Are you accepting of all your feelings?

_____ 20. Do you engage in meditation, contemplation, or psychotherapy to better understand your feelings?

_____ 21. Is your sleep free from disturbing dreams?

_____ 22. Do you explore the symbolism and content of your dreams?

_____ 23. Do you take time to let down and relax, or make time for activities that constitute the abandon or absorption of play?

_____ 24. Do you experience feelings of exhilaration?

_____ 25. Do you enjoy high feelings of self worth and self esteem?

Total Mind/Emotions Score _____

Spirit: Spiritual and Social Health

_____ 1. Do you actively commit time to your spiritual life?

_____ 2. Do you take time for prayer, meditation or reflection?

_____ 3. Do you listen to your intuition?

_____ 4. Are creative activities part of your work or leisure time?

_____ 5. Do you take risks or exceed previous limits?

_____ 6. Do you have faith in God, spirit guides, or angels?

_____ 7. Are you free from anger toward God?

_____ 8. Are you grateful for the blessings in your life?

_____ 9. Do you take walks, garden, or have contact with nature?

_____ 10. Are you able to let go of your attachment to specific outcome and embrace uncertainty?

_____ 11. Do you observe a day of rest completely away from work, dedicated to nurturing yourself and your family?

_____ 12. Can you let go of self interest in deciding the best course of action for a given situation?

_____ 13. Do you feel a sense of purpose?

_____ 14. Do you make time to connect with young children, either your own or someone else's?

_____ 15. Are playfulness and humor important to you in your daily life?

_____ 16. Do you have to forgive yourself and others?

_____ 17. Have you demonstrated the willingness to commit to marriage or a long term compatible relationship?

_____ 18. Do you experience intimacy, besides sex, in your committed relationships?

_____ 19. Do you confide or speak openly with one or more close friends?

_____ 20. Do you feel close to your parents?

_____ 21. If you have experienced the loss of a loved one, have you fully grieved that loss?

_____ 22. Has your experience of pain enabled you to grow spiritually?

_____ 23. Do you go out of your way or give time to help others?

_____ 24. Do you feel a sense of belonging to a group or community?

_____ 25. Do you experience unconditional love?

Total Spirit Score _____

Total Body, Mind, Spirit Score _____

Health Scale

325 – 375 Optimal Health

275 – 324 Excellent Health

225 – 274 Good Health

175 – 224 Fair Health

125 – 174 Below Average Health

 75 – 124 Poor Health

   0 – 74 Extremely Poor Health (surviving)

CHAPTER 7

ELECTRICITY AND MAGNETISM

We have already seen how the plasma proteins interfere with the life process of the cell by leaking out faster than the lymphatic system can pull them off thus causing trapped blood proteins which results in shutting down the sodium-potassium pumps. The next step in this downward spiral of degeneration is that as the electrical generators in the cells shut down, the electrical fields around the cells are reduced. When the electrical fields are reduced, the blood proteins cluster and start to stick together like glue. When they reach this point of sticking together, it becomes very difficult, if not impossible, for the lymphatic system to pull them off.

So again, the problem is compounding. Trapped proteins clog around the cells, preventing oxygen and nutrients from getting to the cells and wastes from being removed. Your body moves from a dry, healthy state into a state of excess fluid, excess sodium and disease. The sodium-potassium pumps shut down and this reduces the electrical fields around the cells. In this state, blood proteins cluster and stick together. The life processes of the cells shut down, and the cells degenerate, mutate and die. Because the lymphatic system can't remove the clustered proteins, the "swamp state" continues to expand and so do the unpleasant organisms that live in the swamp. The downward spiral continues, and the location in the body or organ in which this process occurs determines the name of the disease. Once we reach this state, how can we reverse the condition and start the healing process?

In an interview with Dr. Samuel West he shared his experience of learning this secret when he attended a workshop presented by Dr. Plog who was the inventor of the laser acupuncture machine. In this workshop, Dr. Plog explained how he could make incisions without pain, extract a tooth without pain, and, in about 60 seconds, take the pain out of an accident. Dr. West asked, "Aren't you just moving out the blood proteins?" Dr. Plog answered, "We have known about the blood proteins in Germany for a long time. It's been discovered that when the energy fields are reduced around the cells that the blood proteins will cluster. We have also discovered that electricity will dissipate the clustered proteins." If you run an electrical current through the clustered proteins, the process will break them up so the lymphatic system can pull them off. This is one of the secrets to reversing the downward spiral of degeneration.

A remarkable experiment published in *Science World Magazine* dramatically demonstrated how electricity stimulates the healing process. A young man, age 14, had been born with a birth defect of a broken tibia. Over the years, doctors had tried a number of things to make this break in his leg heal, but to no avail.

Two scientists, one a physicist, the other a surgeon, designed this experiment. They placed an electrode on each side of the break and ran a weak current across the fracture. The leg was placed in a cast and the electrodes were powered by two D-cell batteries. Four months later, when they removed the cast, the break had healed.[17] What happened?

As the electricity trickled across the break, through the bone and the surrounding tissue, it broke up the clustered proteins. The lymphatic system was then able to pull them from around the cells, the electrical generators in the cells were turned on, the life processes were turned on, the healing process engaged, and the body healed itself of the injury.

To clarify what is happening, look at Figure 3 again. When electricity runs through tissue in a diseased state, it breaks up the proteins, and the lymphatic system is able to pull them off. The electrical generators in the cells turn on, the life processes of the cells turn on, and healing takes place. When the conditions of health are fulfilled, the body has an amazing ability to heal itself. When blood proteins are moved out of the interstitial spaces, the cell generators switch on, and the healing process engages.

There are now products using magnetism that will accomplish the same thing. When you place a magnet on an area where there are trapped blood proteins the magnetic fields work in a similar way. I have a friend who had arthritis so badly that he had both of his hips replaced. The pain in his knees was unbearable. He was taking six ibuprofen a day just to manage the pain. Then he placed two small magnets on each side of either knee. In two days, he was completely free of pain and no longer needed medication.

Another friend had been in an auto accident several years ago that severely damaged her spine. She had been in constant pain and nothing she did had been able to relieve it. A friend suggested she try a magnetic mattress and loaned one to her. Much to her surprise, within a couple of days, the pain was gone. In these, and many other cases, the magnetic field broke up the clustered proteins and allowed them to be removed so the healing process could take place.

Energy Healing Techniques

By now, we have a fairly good understanding of how the 50 trillion cells that make up our body generate electricity. There is a simple activity that will give you a first-hand experience of this energetic phenomenon, and a greater understanding of the healing techniques.

Place your hands together and then rub them back and forth with a quick, vigorous action for 15 or 20 seconds. Move them apart two or three inches and sense the energy field between them. Most people can feel this right away. Gently move your hands further apart and then back together, holding your awareness on the area in between your hands. You will be able to feel this "energy ball" between your hands. You might want to do the same activity and hold your hands up to the hands of someone else to see if they can feel it. This will give you a sense of the energy generated by the cells and increased by the friction.

The first technique entails a combination of pressure and massage to physically compress the tissue. This is followed by a quick brushing stroke along the skin, which generates static electricity. This self-generated electricity has the same effect of breaking up trapped blood proteins as an electrical current, or exposure to a focused magnetic field. It may be of value to do this not only at the site where the pain is occurring, but the surrounding areas as well. If the area is too sensitive, or too tender to touch, this technique will work without any physical contact. It is the same electricity being generated by movement that is causing the breakup of trapped blood proteins and the increased movement of lymphatics.

A simple technique that will help headaches, tight shoulders, and back and hip tension, consists of pressure, massage and a light, rapid brushing stroke. To perform this on yourself, put your left hand on your abdomen. This will plug into all the electrical activity being generated there, thus increasing the effectiveness.

1. Start with your right hand positioned toward the back of the neck and gently pull forward as shown in Photo 1.
2. Work your way down the shoulder and then back up the neck as shown in Photo 2.

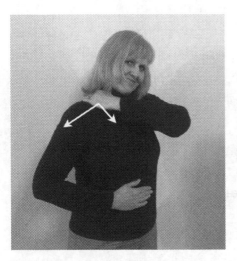 

Slight pressure pulling forward
moving toward shoulder

Slight pressure forward moving
back up towards the neck

3. Next, do a gentle massage on the muscles in the shoulder, neck and upper back as shown in photo 3.
4. Next, Then, starting on the neck, below the ear, with a flat hand, do rapid, light strokes. Brushing down and out, over the shoulder 10 times as shown in photo 4.

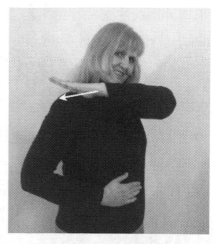

Gently massage the neck,
shoulder and back.

Starting at the neck, quickly
brush out toward the shoulder.

Switch hands on the abdomen and work the other side in the same manner. Depending on the problem, continue brushing down on the top of the arms and upper back, working both sides evenly, not just the side that has the tension. If it is too painful to touch the skin, do the brushing action down the shoulder without touching the skin. The rapid movement of the hand over the skin will generate electricity. When the pain goes away, continue doing the technique to allow a complete healing to take place. The general rule of thumb would be 60 seconds every half hour for the first day, then 60 seconds every hour the second day. Gradually reduce the time but continue to listen to the feedback your body is giving you.

The rapid brushing can be used to direct energy to different parts of the body. By brushing right below the rib cage, as shown in photos 5 and 6, you support the liver and the gall bladder on the right side, and the spleen and pancreas on the left. These techniques can be adapted to support other organs and healing in other parts of the body as needed. We will learn later, in greater detail, why mentally directing thought to an area of pain will increase the effectiveness of this process. For now, as you do these activities, keep in mind that thoughts are things. They have substance. They are electrical in nature, and energy follows thought.

A similar technique can be used by one person (the healing facilitator) working on another (the receiver). The facilitator stands to the side and places one hand on the shoulder for balance, as shown in Photo 7. With the other hand, they brush down the back. At the bottom of the stroke, the hand moves away from the back and circles up to the top to start the process again, as shown in Photo 8.

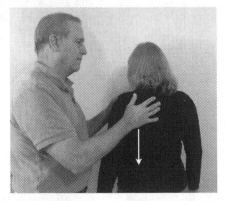
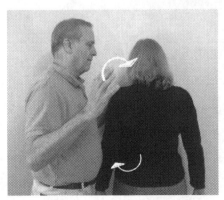

This circular motion generates electricity as the hand moves downward. As the hand leaves the contact with the body and passes upwards through the electromagnetic field of the earth, it also draws in additional energy. This is repeated on both sides even if the pain or discomfort is only on one side.

A similar process has the facilitator standing behind the receiver and brushing both hands down the back, as shown in Photo 9. At the bottom of the back, both hands move out and circle upwards and around to start the process again as shown in Photo 10.

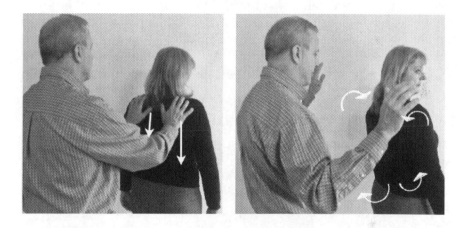

To gain a deeper understanding and more clarity on how to use these techniques visit newdimensionsinhealth.com and watch the video demonstrations there. There are a number of variations using these basic techniques and powerful, more advanced techniques can be learned through the Applied Lymphology Course at powerheal.com.

The main thing to remember is that the sodium-potassium pumps generate electricity and that electricity can be directed through the hands. The rapid movement of the hand over the skin generates electricity. This breaks up the trapped proteins and allows the lymphatic system to pull them out. By using the deep breathing techniques we learned earlier, we increase the effectiveness of the lymphatic system in pulling out the proteins and excess fluid.

This will allow oxygen to get to the cells and turn on the sodium-potassium pumps. When the generators are turned on, the electrical field around the cell is re-established and the healing process begins.

We learned earlier from Dr. Warburg that through the activity of the sodium-potassium pump, healthy cells generate between 70 and 80 millivolts. If the cellular voltage drops to 50 millivolts, the person experiences a loss of energy, chronic fatigue, and is more susceptible to illness. If the voltage drops to 15 millivolts, the cell becomes cancerous. By using these healing techniques, and applying deep breathing, we create an environment where cells can heal, flourish, and maintain a high level of health.

We also learned that a lack of oxygen causes pain. As the blood proteins are broken up and removed, the pain will leave of its own accord. However, it is important to continue doing these techniques, even after the pain has left, to give the body time to heal completely. The ideal condition of health and freedom from pain is the dry state. The more we are able to keep the blood proteins circulating, and prevent them from becoming trapped; causing the "swamp state," the sooner true healing will take place.

Over the years, I have witnessed and heard of truly amazing healings that have occurred as a result of using these and similar healing techniques. One person whom I'll call David shared his story of a miraculous recovery using these and other advanced healing techniques.

"I was in an automobile accident in 1992 which resulted in severe head trauma. Twenty-five percent of my brain was damaged to the point where it was considered dead. As a result of this, I spent the next nine years lying on the floor (a bed was too uncomfortable). I had to have help with basic, everyday activities such as eating and going to the bathroom. I was on 21 medications a day, just to maintain myself.

"In January, 2002 a friend called me and told me about a health and healing educational course. He said, 'I don't know for sure, but I think this might help you.' I bought the Applied Lymphology Course, learned the healing processes, and diligently began doing the techniques.

"The results were amazing! In one week, I was off the floor. By the second week, I was walking outside by myself. This was the first time I had been outside in nine years. By the third week, I was shooting baskets and by the fourth week I was mowing the lawn with a push mower. In fact, I was so happy to have my life back, I mowed my neighbors' lawns, as well.

"There is no way in the world I could place a value on what I received as a result of this course. This information is truly priceless, as is the gift of health."

Was this particular healing, and the many other injuries and diseases that have responded to these techniques, when nothing else worked, a miracle? Or was it the process of fulfilling the conditions of health, and the pain and disease left of their own accord? When we obey the laws of health, the result is health. When we violate those laws, knowingly or unknowingly, the result is pain, disease, and suffering. By applying the information in this book you will be on your way to optimal health and high level wellness.

For more information and to learn advanced healing techniques go to powerheal.com and check out the Applied Lymphology Course.

PART II

THE MERGER OF SCIENCE AND SPIRITUALITY

CHAPTER 8

ENERGY, HEALTH AND HEALING

How important is the role of electricity in health, healing and life? We are beginning to understand the body more and more in terms of energy, and scientific validation of energy medicine is a rapidly expanding field. Robert Becker MD, author of *The Body Electric*, has extensively researched the role that electricity plays in healing and the life process. During the course of his research, Dr. Becker noted that when he amputated the leg of a salamander, it would grow a completely new leg. However, when he amputated the leg of a frog, the frog would not grow a new leg. This puzzled Dr. Becker because the frog is just one step above the salamander on the evolution scale. What was the difference? Dr. Becker then measured the electrical potential flowing across the stump of the frog leg, and the electrical potential flowing across the stump of the salamander leg. This was the difference. Dr. Becker then decided to artificially stimulate the electrical potential flowing across the stump of the frog leg to make it match the potential of the current flowing across the salamander stump. The result of this stimulation process is that *the frog grew a new leg.*[1]

Dr. Robert Miller is a research chemist who has studied the relationship between an increase in growth rate, magnetism, and the energy from the hands of healers. His research on how the surface tension of water is affected by a magnetic field, compared to how it is influenced by the energy coming from a healer's hands, led him to conclude that the energy being emitted from the healer's hands is magnetic in nature.

One of Dr. Miller's experiments involved three groups of rye seeds with 25 seeds in each group. All three groups had identical growing conditions and were watered with regular tap water. The only difference was that the tap water used for the second group was treated by an experienced healer focusing the energy from his hands into the water. For the third group, the tap water was treated with magnets before being administered to the plants. What were the results? The first group that received the straight tap water had a germination rate of eight percent. The second group receiving the healer-treated water had a germination rate of 36 percent, a four-fold increase. The third group of rye seeds receiving the water exposed to a magnetic field had a germination rate of 68 percent, an amazing eight-fold increase. This experiment, and others performed by Dr. Miller, demonstrates that the use of magnets and other energetic stimulation can dramatically affect the germination and growth rate of plants.

In his book *Vibrational Medicine*, Dr. Richard Gerber cites numerous experiments performed with people who believed they had the capability of healing by the laying on of hands. Was there really any substance to the statements made by people who claimed they possessed this ability? According to the studies gathered by Dr. Gerber, the answer is a resounding yes. Phenomena such as a measurable increase in growth rate, acceleration in enzyme reaction rates, a significant reduction in the surface tension of water, a subtle but detectable shift in bond angles of water molecules, and a significant increase in hemoglobin values were observed in the studies conducted. The conclusion of the studies was that *the energy emanating from the hands is magnetic in nature*, and that *the gift of healing is a skill that can be developed.*

As a result of some of these experiments, Dr. Dolores Krieger of New York University developed a Master's Degree course entitled "Frontiers in Nursing: The Actualization of Potential for Therapeutic Field Interaction." It was found that after training, nurses involved in the course were able to increase a patient's hemoglobin through therapeutic touch. Dr. Krieger wrote a book based on her experiences entitled *Therapeutic Touch: How to Use Your Hands to Help or to Heal.* Dr. Krieger has trained thousands of professionals and laypeople to use these techniques.

Does this energy from the hands have other healing properties? How does its effect differ from the use of magnets? Dr. Justa Smith, a nun and biochemist working at Rosary Hill College, conducted experiments exploring the speed of enzyme reaction rates. She reasoned that since enzymes are the workers inside the cell, if their reaction time could be increased, it would result in an acceleration of the healing process.

In her experiments, different types of enzymes were placed in test tubes. As she compared results between the enzymes that were stimulated by an artificially induced magnetic field and the energy coming from the hands of a healer, she discovered an interesting difference. An artificially induced magnetic field would always increase the enzyme reaction rate. However, when the healers held and directed energy into the enzyme-containing test tubes, in some cases, the reaction rate would increase, in some cases it would decrease, and in some cases there would be no change. The healers would always direct the energy with the thought and intent of healing, although the healers didn't know that they were working with different types of enzymes.

This effect was puzzling. Why would the same energy cause an increase in some enzymes and a decrease in others? The puzzle was solved when Dr. Smith observed the difference in reactions from the viewpoint of the entire cell. The increase or decrease was always in the direction that would lead to greater cellular health. There seemed to be an innate intelligence within the energy received from the healer's hands that directed the effect that the energy had on the cells and hence, the entire organism.[2]

We've known for a long time that the body has the ability to heal itself. Drugs and surgery don't heal. Alternative healing modalities such as acupuncture, massage and homeopathy don't heal. Anything that has a positive effect, removes the blockages, and supports the body in a way that will allow the body to heal itself. As we view the experiments of Dr. Smith, that understanding is again confirmed. There is an intelligent, creative, guiding power that always works towards wholeness, whether it is in a cell or in the greater organism.

In the past, we've understood health and the body in terms of physical structure and chemistry. The next level of understanding will be to view the physical body, thoughts, and emotions in terms of energy. Dr. Gerber refers to these patterns of thinking, or paradigms, as Newtonian vs. Einsteinian. The Newtonian viewpoint sees the body as a big machine. The limbs are levers, the heart is the pump, lungs are billows, and the circulatory system is regulated by valves and driven by hydraulics. The next level, and perhaps a more accurate way to view the physical, mental, and emotional aspects of our being is through the Einsteinian paradigm. This viewpoint sees the human constitution as a dynamic, changing, interrelationship of energy. Gaining an understanding of this energetic viewpoint and its practical application is the objective of our next section. Keeping

Einstein's quote in mind that a problem cannot be solved at the same level of thinking that created it, the following material will hopefully stretch your awareness to new levels of possibility.

The Energy Fields

Much of our understanding concerning the energetic nature of man and the world has roots in various religious and spiritual traditions of the world. However, science is now discovering, validating and applying many of the concepts previously confined to the spiritual arena. Willis Harmon, a brilliant scientist, and former President of the Institute for Noetic Sciences, made the point that mature religion and mature science are completely compatible. They are mutually inclusive. Both religion and science are a search for truth and reality. In different ways they explore our relationship with ourselves, with each other, our environment, and our Creator.

As we look at the basic makeup of a human being, one of the perceptual shifts we must make is that all matter is, in fact, energy. For most of us this will be a new way of understanding life and the world around us. Some of this material may seem a little abstract and foreign to our way of thinking, so give it a little time to soak in. It will provide you with some of the keys to creating higher levels of health and knowledge to help you move forward on your path of healing and wholeness.

If we break down physical matter into its basic building blocks, we have atoms. Atoms are comprised of protons, neutrons, electrons and other components each possessing electro-magnetic properties. Breaking these down further, we find that the subatomic structure of matter is that of electromagnetic wave forms, each possessing its own unique wavelength and frequency. These various frequencies are the subatomic components of atoms, which are the building blocks of matter.

Let's bring this somewhat abstract concept of energy, frequency and vibration into more concrete terms. Imagine a bucket filled with rocks the size of your fist. Now, imagine slowly pouring gravel into that bucket as you gently shake it so that the gravel sifts down and fills the spaces around the rocks. When the gravel has settled into the spaces we now have within the confines of the bucket, rocks and gravel occupying the same space at the same time. Next, we slowly pour sand over the rocks and gravel, gently shaking the bucket, allowing the sand to filter down into the spaces left between the gravel and rocks. When this process is complete, we now have rocks, gravel and sand within the confines of the bucket, all occupying the same space at the same time. Although the rocks, gravel and sand are basically the same substance, each is a finer grade and therefore has different characteristics and uses. If we apply this analogy, and think in terms of energy, we would say that each is vibrating at a different frequency. This is an example of the Newtonian vs. Einsteinian paradigm which shows that matter of differing frequencies can occupy the same space at the same time in a nondestructive arrangement.

In this example, the rocks represent the physical body. It is the densest, vibrationally speaking. The gravel, being more refined, represents emotional matter or the emotional field. The sand, still more refined represents the mental matter that makes up the mental field. These three different expressions of energy, the physical body, the emotional field, and the mental field within the confines of the individual, all occupy the same space at the same time. In addition, these energy fields extend beyond the confines of the physical body.

We could make a similar analogy with water. At its most dense level, at the slowest vibrational rate, it is ice. Raise the vibrational rate through heat and it is liquid. Increase the vibrational rate even more and it enters a gaseous state and becomes water vapor, at which point it becomes so small that we can no longer see it. It is the same substance but at different frequencies. As the vibrational frequency raises or lowers, the way water manifests and behaves changes.

Figure 5 portrays the different fields that make up an individual's constitution. The fields extend beyond the physical form, and each finer grade of matter interpenetrates the others. The experiences in life that we have are first registered in the energy field and then transferred into the brain, which causes the physical response.

As an example, when we experience stress or distress in the emotional field, the effect in the physical body will show up as a change in hormones, an increase or decrease in the release of neurotransmitters and overall nervous system activity, suppression of the immune system, and numerous other physical effects. A key point to understand is that these physical reactions are the effects, not the cause.

This is a different way of understanding how our emotions and feelings are influenced. For most of us our experience, education and understanding is limited to the physical plane. The way we explain emotionally motivated feelings and behavior is usually through chemical reactions in the brain or body. An understanding of our energy constitution gives us a greater level of understanding and more resources with which to work.

The cause of stress or distress originated in the emotional field. This feeling was then translated into a physical response on a chemical level via the etheric field (which we'll explore later), and was experienced as an emotion such as depression, anger or, on the positive side, joy.

ENERGY FIELDS
Figure 5

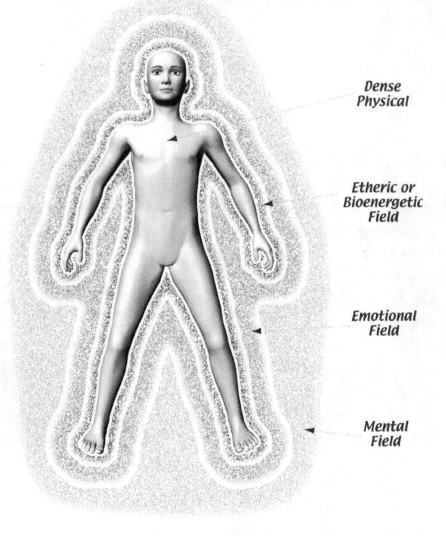

Dense
Physical

Etheric or
Bioenergetic
Field

Emotional
Field

Mental
Field

Energy Fields

Taking the rocks, gravel, and sand analogy a step further, we could note that some particles of gravel or sand will be larger than the norm and some smaller. Nevertheless, they are of like substance. Because of the size, each varying grade would have its own characteristics and uses.

The same principle holds true for the classifications of physical, emotional and mental matter. Some frequencies or grades of matter would be classified as emotional and yet have different characteristics, effects, responses and expressions than other grades in the same category. Mental matter that is vibrating at a lower rate will have similar, yet different characteristics and qualities, than substances of the same domain vibrating at a higher level. On the physical plane, the more refined grades of matter are known as etheric matter. This is physical matter vibrating at a frequency that is imperceptible to most people. However, it is still considered to be physical although much lighter and more refined, having its own properties and characteristics.

It is helpful to break down these gradients of matter, or rates of vibration, into different classifications. Each field, physical, emotional and mental, can be considered to be a level or a plane. According to some spiritual traditions, each plane has seven gradients of matter. We will refer to these gradients of matter as sub-planes. As we shall see, science is beginning to confirm this premise.

Figure 6 is a visual representation of how the planes and sub-planes correspond to vibrational frequency and affect our experience through the physical, emotional and mental arenas of life. Again, this may seem quite abstract; however, as we gain an understanding we'll see the practical application as we progress.

In clarifying the concept of sub-planes, we see the lowest vibrational rate is that of dense physical matter. The next sub-plane of the physical plane would be liquid, and third, the gaseous state.

The four higher levels of the physical plane are referred to as the first, second, third and fourth etheric sub-planes. Etheric matter is physical matter but it is vibrating at a rate that is beyond the ability of our five senses to perceive.

PHYSICAL, EMOTIONAL & MENTAL PLANES

Figure 6

PHYSICAL, EMOTIONAL & MENTAL PLANES

Higher Abstract Mind

MENTAL PLANE

Lower Concrete Mind
Operates on the 3 lower subplanes.

Logic, Analysis, Criticism
Evaluation, Contrast

Higher Emotional Plane
Feelings of being "In Love"
Appreciation & Gratitude

EMOTIONAL PLANE

Lower Emotional Plane
Anger, Resentment, Rage,
Depression, Lust, Envy

Fourth Etheric

Third Etheric

Second Etheric

PHYSICAL PLANE　First Etheric

Gas

Liquid

Solid, Dense Physical

Physical, Emotional & Mental Planes

Some people do have a more refined or trained sensory apparatus that is able to see or sense these different ranges of vibration. They may have different names for and interpretations of the energy on the sub-plane they perceive. This is helpful to keep in mind as we explore the work of other healers and teachers who work in this area. Different names for the same thing can sometimes be confusing.

Although there are distinct arenas of expression, they are on a continuum of vibrational frequency. Rather than just a linear understanding in terms of a continuum of different levels, we can also view this expression of energy as fields within fields. The matter of the mental field interpenetrates the emotional field.

Both of these finer grades of matter interpenetrate the etheric field and dense physical body just as the gravel and sand filled the spaces between the rocks in the bucket. Because we are dealing with energy, and the physical arena is the lowest expression of that energy, it is important to keep in mind that what happens in one field affects the others. Anything that affects the vibrational frequency of any substance along this continuum will have an effect on other grades of matter in different placements.

Research in quantum physics indicates that matter from the etheric level and above is operating in a dimension that obeys different laws and principles than matter of the lower physical plane. When we break matter down into its basic building blocks, the result is a structure comprised of atoms. Breaking the atom down further, we have subatomic particles such as protons, neutrons and electrons. At the subatomic level, these entities have characteristics of both a particle and a wave. This is a key point to remember. They appear to be, and have the characteristics of both energy and matter at the same time. When we think of an electron, we think in terms of a particle. However, an electron has no dimension. An electron can manifest itself as a particle or as a wave. This dualistic nature of both matter and energy is a characteristic common to all subatomic particles.

To understand the characteristics of the mental, emotional and etheric fields let's explore some of the newer discoveries and revelations regarding the relationship of matter and energy. If we consider the energy spectrum with physical matter at the bottom being the densest, and we gradually increase its vibration, we will move upward through the emotional and mental planes and beyond. This vibrational ascension could be taken all the way until the energy is in its pure, undifferentiated, formless state. Some in the scientific community have referred to this non-material state as zero point energy, aether, and virtual energy. In spiritual terminology it may be referred to *as primary substance, pure consciousness, universal prana* or *spirit*. Regardless of the name, this energy is everywhere and pervades everything. Some spiritual traditions would say that consciousness and intelligence are also aspects of this energy.

To get a sense of the immensity and power held in zero point energy, imagine traveling a billion miles away from earth into the nothingness of empty space. Let's take a cubic centimeter of that nothingness and measure the energy in it. The energy contained in the virtual energy state can be expressed in the measurement of 10 to the 95th ergs per cubic centimeter (an erg is a unit of measurement). To keep it simple, and provide a sense of what this really means in terms of energy, imagine the power of the sun. Now, multiply that a hundred million times. Now multiply that power by a hundred million (years). That is the amount of zero point energy contained in one cubic centimeter of empty space. To this energy add consciousness and intelligence. There are numerous other ways of expressing the magnitude of zero point energy and not all scientists agree on this. However, regardless of the details, the amount of energy at this level is mind-boggling.

Adam Trombley is an astrophysicist whose research in zero point technology has indicated to him that, "the materialization of an object in space represents only one quadrillionth of the energy available in that volume of space."[3] Physical matter is only a minute expression of the total energy available in the virtual state. The amount of energy stored in matter is tremendous, as evinced by the results of releasing the energy from a small amount of uranium in the form of an atomic explosion.

Regardless of the name, it is from this original state that energy slows into the lower vibrational rates and eventually condenses into physical matter. Energy that vibrates faster than the speed of light has different properties and characteristics than that which is vibrating slower than the speed of light. As we shall see, energy in this domain also seems to operate under a different set of laws.

A deeper understanding of this formula suggests that matter and energy are interconvertible and interconnected. Energy can be transformed into matter, and matter into energy. Sub-atomic matter is actually a form of condensed, particularized energy. Physical matter is condensed energy or as some have allegorically said, "Frozen light." As this energy slows down in its vibrational rate, it "precipitates" into physical form. Using our water example again we could say that water vapor condenses into clouds and then precipitates in the form of rain. Applying this analogy to the matter/energy relationship we now understand that whatever we see in physical existence is a representation of an energetic projection into time and space.

Dr. William Tiller is a professor of engineering at Stanford University. His pioneering research examines what happens in the domain wherein non-physical particles vibrate faster than the speed of light. In this domain, which he defines as "negative space/time," the energy exhibits what he refers to as "negative entropic-properties."

This is the opposite of entropy, wherein matter moves toward a state of greater disorder and chaos. Negative entropic means the energy or matter has a tendency to move towards greater and more complex levels of organization. There is an intelligence that guides matter toward a greater state of synthesis. An example of this principle is biological systems that have the ability to be self-organizing. They move toward a state of greater order, rather than dis-integrating or falling apart.

David Bohm, physicist and protégé of Einstein, was one of the world's foremost authorities on quantum theory. *Quantum* is a word that is synonymous with the concept of *wave-particle*. This is any substance that possesses the characteristics of both a wave and a particle, or properties of both energy and matter. Dr. Bohm explains this precipitation of energy into matter as energy moving from an "implicit" order to an "explicit" order. *Implicit* means "enfolded order" and *explicit* means "un-enfolded order." The apparent dissolution of matter as it moves from a physical state and is reconstituted as energy is the movement from an "explicit" order to an "implicit" order.

Bohm uses an example shown in Figure 7 wherein a cylinder is filled with a thick, clear, substance known as glycerin. A crank turns the glycerin-filled cylinder. The result is that the ink drop is slowly spread out in a line and eventually disappears into, or becomes enfolded within the glycerin. At this point, the turning of the cylinder stops, and is reversed. Gradually the ink reappears. It is reconstituted into the strung-out line and eventually back into the original dot.[4]

It could be said that the ink was enfolded within the implicit order of the glycerin. As the process was reversed, it emerged from the implicit order and un-enfolded into the explicit order, which was the original dot of ink. In an analogous way, energy can move from a virtual, formless, implicit, or enfolded state into an explicit state manifesting as matter. This perhaps gives us a different viewpoint of the First Law of Thermodynamics, which states that energy cannot be created or destroyed, but only changes form. The physical form is the explicit or outward expression of a far greater energy that is its source. The physical expression of energy is the lowest form, vibrationally speaking, that condensed energy takes on.

ORDER CAN BE HIDDEN OR MANIFEST
Figure 7

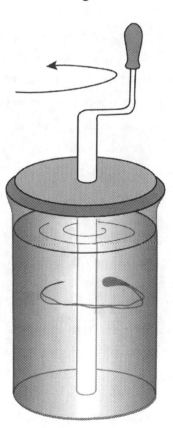

Cylindar of Glycern

Figure 8 depicts how zero point energy slows in vibration and increases in density. As we saw earlier, one way that is helpful in understanding this is to think of condensation and precipitation. Water vapor condenses into clouds and eventually precipitates as rain. As the vibrational rate of pure energy slows it takes on different qualities and characteristics. Eventually the energy condenses into matter on the mental plane. As the vibrational rate further decreases, the matter becomes denser and descends or precipitates on to the emotional plane. In some spiritual traditions this is referred to as the astral plane. As the precipitation process continues, the emotional or astral matter increases in density and moves into etheric matter. Eventually, it condenses and precipitates into physical matter taking on different forms.

Physicists have proposed the existence of a particle / wave known as a "tachyon" which exists only at speeds exceeding light velocity. It is thought that this may be the interface between this virtual energy state and physical matter. As you will note in Figure 8, when the vibrational rate of a tachyon slows, it becomes a photon and enters into the physical domain. As it continues to be stepped down, it moves into a state where it can be identified, measured and understood according to the principles that govern the laws of physical matter as presently understood.

This understanding of how energy operates and expresses itself at different levels, gradients, and rates of vibration, is a key to understanding the process of building physical, emotional, mental and spiritual health. The better we understand the vibratory principles of health, the better we will be able to work with them, rather than being the victim of the discordant mixing of inharmonious vibrations. The more we understand the laws the Creator made to govern the universe, the more effectively we will be able to work with them and move forward on our path.

ENERGETIC CONDENSATION CONTINUUM
Figure 8

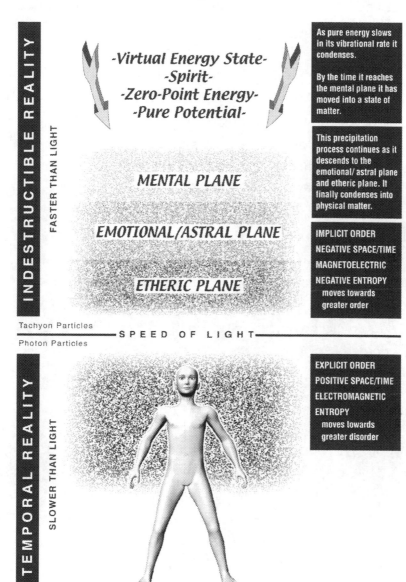

Virtual Energy State-
-Spirit-
-Zero-Point Energy-
-Pure Potential-

As pure energy slows in its vibrational rate it condenses.

By the time it reaches the mental plane it has moved into a state of matter.

INDESTRUCTIBLE REALITY

FASTER THAN LIGHT

MENTAL PLANE

EMOTIONAL/ASTRAL PLANE

ETHERIC PLANE

This precipitation process continues as it descends to the emotional/ astral plane and etheric plane. It finally condenses into physical matter.

IMPLICIT ORDER

NEGATIVE SPACE/TIME

MAGNETOELECTRIC

NEGATIVE ENTROPY
  moves towards
  greater order

Tachyon Particles

SPEED OF LIGHT

Photon Particles

EXPLICIT ORDER

POSITIVE SPACE/TIME

ELECTROMAGNETIC

ENTROPY
  moves towards
  greater disorder

TEMPORAL REALITY

SLOWER THAN LIGHT

MEASURABLE PHYSICAL REALITY

Energetic Condensation Continuum

For most of us, our understanding and reality are based on very limited perceptions and on information gathered through the five senses and intellect. From this perspective we are at the bottom of this energy continuum in physical reality looking up. The physical world which can perceived by our senses and that which can be identified and measured is referred to as the "real" world. This world is temporal and changing and is governed by certain laws that apply to reality at this level. However, as we ascend the energy continuum we find that there are different laws that govern the expression of energy and life at higher levels.

Although they may lie at different points along the energy continuum, we can see that the virtual energy state is similar to Bohm's implicate order, or Tiller's negative space/time domain. It is in this dimension that the etheric, emotional and mental fields operate and direct the working and expression of the physical world. The principles that govern this dimension appear to be the inverse of those governing the physical world in that they always move toward higher order.

Holographic Reality

A hologram is a three-dimensional image composed of light created by using a laser. Figure 9 shows a laser beam focused on an instrument called a beam splitter designed to separate the focused, coherent light in half. One half of the beam is directed toward the object being photographed and is referred to as the object beam. The beam first passes through a diffusing lens. As the diffused light hits the object, in our example a cup, the light is transformed into waveforms that are directed toward a photographic plate. The other beam is directed off to the side, reflected off a mirror, and passed through a diffusing lens toward the same photographic plate.

Both beams of light collide right before they hit the plate causing what is called an interference pattern. This same effect would be caused by throwing two rocks into a still pond and watching the ripples pass through each other as the rings expand. As the ripples collide, they create a pattern of waves or an interference pattern.

In the creation of a hologram, it is these waves of light that cause the interference patterns which are then recorded on the photographic plate. When we look at the plate, there is no image there, only a faint series of swirls. However, when light is passed through the plate, the cup becomes visible as a three-dimensional image suspended in space that can be observed from different angles.

HOW A HOLOGRAM IS MADE
Figure 9

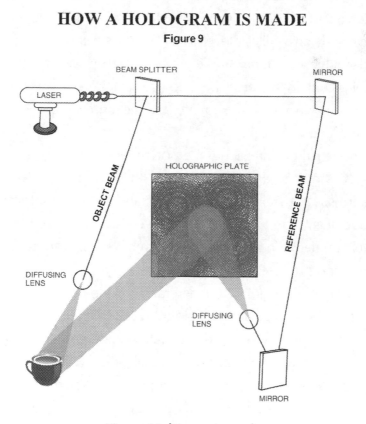

How a Hologram is made

The remarkable thing about holographic principles is that the complete image is contained in every part of the photographic plate. If we take an ordinary picture and cut it in half, we have only half a picture. However, if we cut the holographic plate in half, we still will have the whole image when the light shines through. Cut it in half again, and we still have the whole image. Drop it on the floor, shatter it, and pick up a piece. When the light shines on the fragment of the plate we still will have the whole image. The key point to remember is that *the information to create the whole is contained in every part of the hologram.*

The principles of holography give us an understanding of how experience and information are holistically stored in the mental, emotional and etheric fields as well as the brain, and throughout the physical body on a cellular level. The constitution of the energy fields is holographic in nature. As we grow in our understanding of the principles contained within the holographic nature of our energetic constitution, we will begin to acquire the knowledge needed to begin working with higher law.

Although there are a number of theories on how the brain operates, there is growing evidence that the brain recognizes waveforms, registers frequencies, and stores information holographically. Dr. Karl Pribram, who has been referred to as the "Einstein of the Brain Sciences," cites over five hundred studies that reinforce this premise.[5]

In view of this unfolding understanding, the question could be asked if the brain is actually a hologram or whether it is a physical mechanism that receives and translates holographic information coming from the mental and emotional fields. There is growing evidence that points to the understanding that past experiences and information are stored in the energy fields. People who have the ability to perceive these energy fields can often see and interpret experiences that are stored there. Events or activities cause this information to be transmitted to the brain where it becomes physical in its interpretation and expression.

David Bohm also suggests that the implicate order may actually be holographic in nature. This notion that the universe is holographically organized, answers much previously unexplained phenomena. One of these examples is that paired electrons, when separated a sizable distance, accurately mirror each other's movement instantaneously. What happens to one electron is instantly reflected by its twin. This instantaneous reaction is faster than the speed of light. The conclusion of research done in this area indicates that these paired electrons, although a great distance apart, are, in fact, a part of a greater whole. This is what accounts for their ability to seemingly defy the laws of nature and the physical reality to which we are accustomed. The holographic viewpoint suggests that regardless of the energy state or form that something takes on, everything in the universe is interconnected.

What does this profound insight mean in practical everyday terms? First, it means that Brotherhood is not just some nice religious idea - it is a scientific fact. We could look at the Lakota Sioux word "Mitakue Oyassin," which means "all my relations," with a deeper appreciation for the truth it expresses. We are in fact, interconnected with all of creation. It means that what happens to one individual affects us all.

I remember as a kid in school thinking how unfair it was when one person misbehaved in class and the whole class was punished. As much as I disliked it, that was a valuable lesson. What one person does effects the whole. Whenever there is a lack of personal responsibility resulting in the misuse or abuse of freedom, the result will be a loss of freedom for everyone. On a practical, social level, the actions of the individual affect the greater system of which they are a part. On the quantum level, regardless of the energy state or form something takes on, we are all interconnected. What we do to one another or to the environment we do to ourselves.

Remote Viewing

This idea that the universe is holographically constructed helps us understand phenomena that in the past would be classified in the realm of metaphysics or esotericism, such as remote viewing and medical intuition. Remote viewing is the ability to identify the characteristics, quality, shape, size, and makeup of things at great distances, without any prior knowledge or other information. Since the mid-seventies, research in remote viewing has been conducted by the Stanford Research Institute (SRI) with remarkable findings. Around this time, two of the physicists conducting research in this area were contacted by the U.S. Government's intelligence community who wanted to see if remote viewing could be a reliable source of information gathering. The projects started out with basic experiments such as identifying the contents hidden in containers in other rooms. Remote viewers not only did this with remarkable accuracy, but they identified the structure and workings of equipment of which they had no previous knowledge. One of the participants, Ingo Swann, identified the operation of the magnetometer located beneath the floor in a shielded vault. He then drew a close facsimile of the structure and inner workings of the complex instrument. None of this information had ever been published.[6]

Carrying the work further, those working in the field of remote viewing would project their consciousness into secret Soviet installations to identify contents, structure and the nature of the operation. Data gathered from other intelligence sources such as satellite imagery verified the accuracy of the findings. After the Cold

War ended, some of those who participated in these experiments contacted former KGB agents and members of the Soviet military to compare notes and verify their findings. The results showed that some of the participants had been able to identify target sites that had not been identified on a map until a later date. In many cases, there was an amazing accuracy in identifying the location, structure and contents of these secret military installations.

Carrying this experimentation further, Swann suggested that they do some remote viewing of Jupiter before Pioneer 10 made its journey there to see if information of the planet's conditions could be attained before the probe arrived. Much of the information reported by viewers ran counter to accepted scientific findings of the time. However, when the probe sent the information back from Jupiter, it did verify the accuracy of the observations and conclusions made by Swann. One of the things identified long before the space probe made its flyby, was a ring around Jupiter that had never before been noted. At first, this was thought to be totally incorrect but when the reports came back from the space probe, one of the discoveries made was that there was indeed a ring around Jupiter. With an understanding of the holographic structure of reality, we begin to see that distance and physical barriers are no obstacle to consciousness.[7]

Some people have the ability to tap into this universal hologram and identify physical conditions and medical problems at a distance. There is an emerging field of medical intuitives who are working with medical doctors in the process of patient assessment and diagnosis. Using holographic principles, the intuitive is able to access information about a patient's medical condition and relay important, undetected information to the physician treating the person. It doesn't matter if the patient is on the East Coast and the medical intuitive is on the West Coast, because, as we have seen, in the implicit order, time and space obey different laws. Twenty or thirty years ago this would have been considered nonsense or science fiction in most circles, and the work of the devil in others. However, we now understand these higher principles that govern the universe, and we are learning to work with them. The interconnectedness of all creation is a scientific fact. This knowledge has profound implications in many areas.

Sacred Unity

The new findings in quantum physics are indeed remarkable, and do have a profound effect on our understanding of the nature of reality. This understanding has been expressed in numerous religious traditions for centuries. If we look at the teachings of Jesus Christ in Aramaic, the language in which he taught, we find the holographic principle of unity and interconnectedness. The word for *God* in Aramaic is *Alaha*. According to scholar Neil Douglas-Klotz, in his book, *The Hidden Gospel,* this word, and Aramaic words in general, have several different meanings depending on the context in which they are used. *Alaha* can be translated into *Sacred Unity, The All, Oneness, The Ultimate Power and Potential,* and *The One With No Opposite.* According to Douglas-Klotz, wherever you read a passage in scripture where Jesus refers to *God*, you can substitute the word *Alaha* and increase your understanding of what Christ really meant. I have found it to be quite enlightening, although challenging to my past ways of thinking, to reread the New Testament and substitute *Sacred Unity,* as well as other Aramaic words and their meanings in familiar passages.

With our understanding of holographic principles and the energetic nature of creation, we can understand terms like *Sacred Unity* or *The All* from a scientific viewpoint and still appreciate the profound sense of sacredness they embody. These "new" discoveries are revealing ancient teachings in a new light. They are universal principles. The value of this understanding lies in our ability and willingness to adapt ourselves to live our lives in accordance with these truths.

The knowledge of this dynamic interrelation also gives us a clearer understanding of how the Law of Cause and Effect works. On a physical level, we are all aware of Newton's Third Law that states, "For every action there is an equal and opposite reaction." On an energetic level, this is also the case. The truth of this law was expressed by Jesus Christ in the statement, "As a man sows, so shall he reap."

Positive thoughts and intentions set the matter of the mental field in motion. The energy goes into the collective mental field of humanity, and is returned in the form of positive thoughts and actions. Likewise, negative emotions move out into the collective emotional field and return to their source. Whatever we put out into the universal hologram has an effect on the whole. The energy will be attracted to a similar vibration and will eventually return to its source.

This Law of Cause and Effect is known in the East as the Law of Karma. It is not a law of retribution or punishment. Like all natural laws, it is impersonal. It just works. *Gravity doesn't care if you're a good person or not. It just works.* As we grow in our understanding of how this interconnectedness on a quantum level works, we are in a position to use the law intelligently and make it work for us. We can consciously choose to send forth positive, healthy thoughts, emotions and actions and thereby enhance the quality of our life and the lives of others. By doing this, we will begin to offset and balance the negative repercussions of the misguided, negative energy we may have already put in motion.

These insights into the principles of holography have led both Dr. Bohm and Dr. Pribram to ask fundamental questions about the nature of reality, which we might do well to ponder. Does the reality of a hologram consist of the swirls *on* the photographic plate, the implicate order, or is it the three-dimensional image of light that we perceive visually, that is projected *from* the photographic plate? Is reality the explicate, outer expression of the physical forms which the senses perceive, or is it the waveforms that reside inside of the enfolded reality in the negative space/time state?

Understanding these holographic principles can also add deeper insights into our spiritual knowledge. A number of spiritual traditions refer to the physical reality we all experience as illusion or maya - that which is not real. This does not diminish the importance of the life we experience on the physical plane through our senses or the emotional and mental planes we experience through our feelings and intellect. It does indicate that there is something much greater that when experienced (not merely believed in) puts one's sense of physical reality in a much different perspective. As we proceed on the path, we too, may grow into an awareness of the greater reality that is behind the forms we see.

Keeping the nature of these principles in mind, with the understanding that etheric, emotional and mental matter all lie in the realm of Dr. Tiller's negative space/time, negative entropic, self-organizing model on the energy continuum, or David Bohm's implicit order, let's take a look at the conditions of health that we can choose to build into our lives that will enhance healing and move us more effectively along the path.

CHAPTER 9

THE ETHERIC OR
BIO-ENERGETIC FIELD

Although the etheric/bio-energetic field is imperceptible to most people, it is comprised of physical matter. There are people who have the ability to see this energy field in the form of an aura, and there are various forms of instrumentation, which have the ability to register its presence, measure its activity, and photograph its workings.

In the early 1940's, Dr. Harold Burr of Yale University was studying the electrical properties of life. As he was observing the electrical field around salamanders he noted that the field was in the shape of the adult animal. He also noted that the field had a positive/negative axis that aligned with the spinal cord and brain. Dr. Burr wanted to find out how early in an animal's development this electrical field came into being. He measured it earlier and earlier in the development of the salamander and discovered that the electrical axis originated in the unfertilized egg. Not only did the spinal cord and brain development follow this axis, but the electrical field actually preceded the growth of the physical animal. This led him to conclude that this bio-energetic field was the guidance system or template for the organization of physical development.

He also experimented with the energy field around seedlings, and noted that the field wasn't in the shape of the seed, but rather in the shape of the adult plant. As a result of his experiments, Burr concluded that *the electrical field gives spatial orientation and direction to the developing organism.* It was the formation of the energy field that first laid the pattern into which the physical organism would grow.[8] This is a key point to understand and remember.

At the same time, halfway around the world, Russian researcher Semyon Kirlian had begun developing a form of electrographic photography. This technique photographs the electrical field or aura around living objects. It can be used to identify and track changes in shape and color. Both Burr and Kirlian have noted that diseases like cancer caused significant changes in the electromagnetic fields of living organisms. The disease was often detectable in the bio-energetic field before it manifested itself physically.

These techniques validate the many properties attributed to the etheric field. One of the most important is the self-organizing properties it exhibits. This energy field is the organizing principle that serves as a holographic template to direct and guide the formation of the physical body. Physical matter, governed by the Law of Entropy, will tend to break down and move towards a state of disorder.

Figure 8 shows that etheric matter is vibrating faster than the speed of light and is therefore in the domain of negative space/time. It is governed by self-organizing principles, which means there is an intelligence that guides matter to higher levels of wholeness and more complex expression. Understanding that the etheric field is the template that guides and organizes the dense physical body toward higher states of complexity and wholeness is a key to greater levels of health and supporting the healing process. If there is damage or toxicity in the etheric field it will show up as a variety of physical problems. If the damage in the etheric field is corrected or mended, the physical body will automatically make the corrections, because it is being supported by the etheric blueprint.

If you take a picture of a leaf using Kirlian photography you will see a radiant aura of light surrounding the leaf. If you cut a third of the leaf away and photograph it again you will still see the complete energy field as though nothing had happened to the physical leaf. The etheric field is the energetic template that supports the physical, and if the physical expression is damaged the energy field still remains in place.

There is a phenomenon that some people with amputated limbs have experienced known as the phantom limb phenomenon. They may have lost a leg in an accident and yet at times they will feel pain, itching or some other form of discomfort in their foot. They no longer have a leg or foot and yet they are experiencing pain where it used to be. How is this possible? As with the leaf, the etheric blueprint is still there. The dense physical is gone but the energetic counterpart is still there causing an experience of discomfort. As we shall see, there are other ways to communicate information from different parts of the body, other than through the physical nervous system.

As you look at Figure 8 the main point to remember is that the etheric field, which is energy vibrating faster than the speed of light and in the domain of indestructible reality, is the guiding principle or template that organizes and supports the physical body. The physical body is in the domain of temporal reality and is an effect or result of forces originating at a higher level.

The etheric field is also known as the vital body in that it is the source of vitality. Just as an individual has a vital body or etheric field, so does the planet. The etheric field of the individual draws energy and life force from the planet's vital energy field. The vital or etheric field of planet earth is energized by the sun. This system takes cosmic energy from the sun, subtle energy from the atmosphere, and magnetic energy from the earth (all of which I refer to as subtle, nutritive energy) and feeds it into the physical body through various organs, meridians, nerve plexus, and energy centers. The etheric field of an individual is the intermediary by which subtle, nutritive energy is stepped down and translated into a physical response, such as a chemical reaction or a nerve impulse.

The etheric field, also referred to as the etheric body, is composed of multiple lines of force or energy currents, which carry vital energy throughout the system. The points where these lines of force cross, form centers or vortices of energy. There are seven major centers, which are scientifically verifiable, and 21 minor points where these lines of force cross. These centers are aligned with major nerve plexuses in the physical body, and serve as points of energy exchange between the etheric and physical body. If there is a lack of life-giving, nutritive, subtle energy flowing into the etheric field, there will be an absence of vitality in the physical body. If there is a blockage in the transfer of energy through the centers, then it will affect the corresponding nerve plexus, physical organs, and endocrine gland associated with that center.

Additionally, there are smaller lines of force known as *nadis*. The nadis are actually the etheric counterpart of the nervous system that sub-stand the neurons. In a sense, they can also be thought of as an etheric nervous system. These nadis radiate out from the centers and deliver energy to the brain, nervous, and endocrine systems, the skeletal structure, and, finally, the individual cells. The nadis are another means whereby subtle, nutritive energy is stepped down and delivered to the dense physical body.

The Meridian System

The other interface between the dense physical body and the vital body is the meridian system of classical Chinese acupuncture.

This system delivers subtle nutritive energy or life force (also known as *chi* in the traditional Chinese system or *prana* in the Ayurvedic system) to the organs and cells of the physical body. Within the past thirty years, Western medicine has conducted research to explore the function and nature of the meridian system. What has been discovered is that there is a passageway between the nervous and circulatory systems that is used by the meridian system to deliver subtle, nutritive energy to the body which appears to reach a molecular level.

In his experiments, researcher Dr. Kim Bong Han injected an isotope of radioactive phosphorous, known as P32, into an acupoint of a rabbit, and followed the course of its movement. He discovered that the P32 was taken up into a fine tubule system approximately 0.5 to 1.5 microns in diameter that followed the classical acupuncture course. When this same procedure was followed by injecting the substance into the skin, venous or lymphatic systems, none of the P32 could be detected in the meridian network. This finding indicates that the meridian system is independent from the circulatory and lymphatic systems.[9]

Dr. Pierre de Vernejoul, a French researcher, performed similar experiments with humans. He injected radioactive technetium 99m into the acupoints of human patients. He followed the movement through the tubules by using gamma camera imaging. He also found that the radioactive substance followed classical Chinese acupuncture lines.

Through his research, Dr. Han found that there were actually four different superficial and deep networks of the meridian system. He also referred to this system as a duct system and found that the terminal ductules actually reached to the level of the cell nuclei. It is through this network of tubules that the subtle energy, or chi, is delivered to the cells. Although these duct systems operate at different levels, they are interconnected much like the circulatory, lymphatic, and nervous systems.

What are the practical applications of this knowledge of the meridian system? There are a number of different instruments that will measure the flow of energy in a selected meridian and the organ associated with that meridian. By measuring the energy flow it is possible to identify weaknesses in the system and organ and treat them using homeopathic or other natural remedies before the problems identify themselves through different symptoms or manifest as an illness.

In an effort to reduce health care costs a large Utah-based, self-insured company conducted a study using this technology with their employees. The results were dramatic. Participants experienced a 75% reduction in the severity of symptoms for the adults and a 93% reduction for the participating children. The annual gross savings per participant was $3,878. This was broken down into a savings of $1,393 for reduced medical and prescription expenses. A savings resulting from reduced absenteeism and increased productivity amounted to $2,485 per employee. Those in the study rated the overall improvement in the quality of their life from 0 to 100% averaging 45%, and most have continued to enjoy better health and lower health care costs beyond the one year study.[10]

By using new technology that measures the flow of subtle energy through the meridian system, a system that most traditional doctors don't even recognize, the overall levels of health increased, illness decreased, cost decreased, productivity increased as did the quality of life.

As with Dr. Harold Burr and his experiments with salamanders, Dr. Han wanted to find out how early in the stages of development this network of tubules began to form. In his embryological studies with baby chicks, he found that the meridian ducts were formed within fifteen hours of conception. This is long before the internal organs begin to form. Since the formation of the meridian system precedes the formation of any organs, it would suggest that this system would guide or influence the formation and spatial organization of the internal organs. We have seen that the holographic template of the bio-energetic field directs the guidance and formation of the biological system. Given the fact that the formation of the meridian system precedes the construction of the biological structure, it appears that the meridian system acts as the interface between the etheric field and the physical body.

Obviously, if there is congestion or blockage in the etheric body or the meridian system, then the transmission of needed energy to the physical body will be diminished. Healing techniques such as acupuncture aid in removing the blockages and restoring the flow of healing energy. As we learned earlier, when energy shuts down, the healing process shuts down, and our level of health is reduced. The conditions of health that are especially helpful to maintaining the well-being of the vital field are sunshine, nutrient-rich, live foods, and the avoidance of fatigue, worry and other vibrationally coarse, energy-draining emotions.

Since the etheric body receives information and impressions from the mental and emotional fields, it is sensitive to the impact that positive or negative thoughts and emotions have on it. It can also be guided and directed by our intention. As it receives experiences from those fields, it translates the messages into the physical body by means of chemical responses, neural transmissions, hormonal reactions, and sometimes subtle structural movement, as seen in craniosacral therapy.

There are three key points to remember about the etheric body. First, it is the template that guides the organization and design of the physical body. It has self-organizing properties, which cause it to direct matter toward an organized pattern of wholeness. This is obviously a very important role in the process of healing. It is on this level that most energy healers work. Second, it absorbs subtle energy, or chi, from the environment and uses it to nourish the physical body. Third, the etheric field is the intermediary between the physical body and the emotional and mental fields. It translates information from these two fields into the physical body via the brain and nervous system.

For our purposes in this discussion, we will refer to the sum total of the physical/etheric, emotional, and mental energies as the personality. One of our objectives as we move along the path of personal and spiritual growth is to develop each field to its fullest capacity and then learn how to integrate and harmonize each field within the others. As we purify thought and emotion the vibrational rate of matter composing each field is raised and refined. The vibrational rate of each field begins to synchronize with the other fields. Although this vibrational rate is higher or lower, depending on the field, it can be thought of as the same note being sounded at different octaves. This is the process of personality integration and coordination. It is a necessary step on the path toward true health, wholeness and spiritual development.

CHAPTER 10

THE CENTERS AND THE CHAKRA SYSTEM

Although the etheric, emotional and mental fields are comprised of matter vibrating at different frequencies, each within its own domain, there is an exchange of energy between them as well as a flow of information. This exchange happens primarily through a system of energy centers that receive and translate the energy of a higher frequency down to lower vibrational rates, and eventually have correspondence with an endocrine gland on the physical level.

These centers are the interface between energy and matter in the human system. In addition, each center has a relationship with a nerve plexus and a physiological system in the body. If there is a blockage in the transfer of energy through the centers, then it will affect the corresponding nerve plexus, physical organs, and endocrine gland associated with that center. As mentioned earlier, there are seven major centers, also known as *chakras*, and 21 minor centers. For our purposes we will focus primarily on the seven major ones.

Chakras in Spirituality

For most of history these centers have been associated with different religious traditions or spiritual teachings. In the Bible, John refers to these centers as "the seven seals on the back of the book of life." In the Sufi tradition some call them "latifas," or "the subtle ones." The Kabala refers to these centers as "the seven centers in the soul of man."[11] The word "chakra" in Sanskrit means "wheel" which is descriptive of their rotating motion. Noted medical intuitive, Carolyn Myss, draws a correlation between the seven major centers of the Hindu tradition, the seven sacraments of the Catholic Church, and the seven levels comprised of ten sefirot on the Jewish Tree of Life. These centers affect health on all levels. They not only reflect our level of consciousness but their activity is influenced by the consciousness of the individual. Although there are seven different centers it is still one system.

Different people will ascribe different meaning to the functions of a chakra as it corresponds to our level of consciousness. Depending on the teacher or tradition there may be some discrepancy with the information imparted. It is important to consider that our point of development on the living continuum or our spiritual path will have an effect on the energetic activity of these centers and their function at that time. It is important to remember that this system, like all other systems of living is in a dynamic, ever-changing and adapting process.

Although these centers first appear in religious traditions as do many forms of truth, we are finding that as instrumentation continues to be refined in its ability to measure subtle energies, the existence of these centers is entering scientific validation. As research progresses, their function is being understood and practically applied.

Chakras in Science

Dr. Hiroshi Motoyama has developed an instrument that measures the activity of a center. In an experiment, he designed a light-proof room that was shielded from all electrical interference. Using his apparatus for measuring the functional conditions of meridians, and their corresponding internal organs, known simply as an AIM device, he placed electrodes 12 to 20 centimeters from the center's location to see if there was any increased electrical activity when a subject mentally focused his attention there. He found that if the center was one that a meditator had previously practiced energizing, there was a measurable increase in electrical activity. If there had been no thought directed to that point, the AIM was unable to detect anything. In later research, Dr. Motoyama was able to document a relationship between a center, the corresponding gland, organs and nerve plexus.[12]

Dr. Valerie Hunt of UCLA, used EMG electrodes to measure the electrical activity of the skin corresponding to a chakra location. The normal cycle per second (cps) of the brain is 0 to 100 cps with most activity occurring in the 0 to 30 range. For muscles, it is 225 cps and for the heart it is 250 cps. Dr. Hunt found that the electrical activity on the skin that was aligned with a center was between 100 and 1600 cycles per second.[13]

Although the measurement of these centers is still in its infancy, there is enough empirical evidence to scientifically validate their existence, functioning, and importance in the maintenance of a person's health.

These centers act as receivers of energy from the environment to an individual, and transmitters of energy from the person to the environment. As they take in nutritive, subtle energies from the surrounding environment, the energy is transduced, or stepped down into a frequency or form that can be assimilated and used by the physical body. This nutritive subtle energy is composed of light and associated cosmic energy from the sun, magnetism from the earth, and numerous other forms of energy circulating throughout the atmosphere.

We learned earlier that physical matter is a stepped-down form, or a condensation of energy, that has moved from an implicit state of virtual energy into an explicit order of physical expression. The chakra system is the mechanism whereby this process takes place within an individual. Figure 10 shows how the centers of each field or body are superimposed over, and aligned with, those in the other fields.

ENERGY FLOW THROUGH CHAKRAS & ENERGY FIELDS
Figure 10

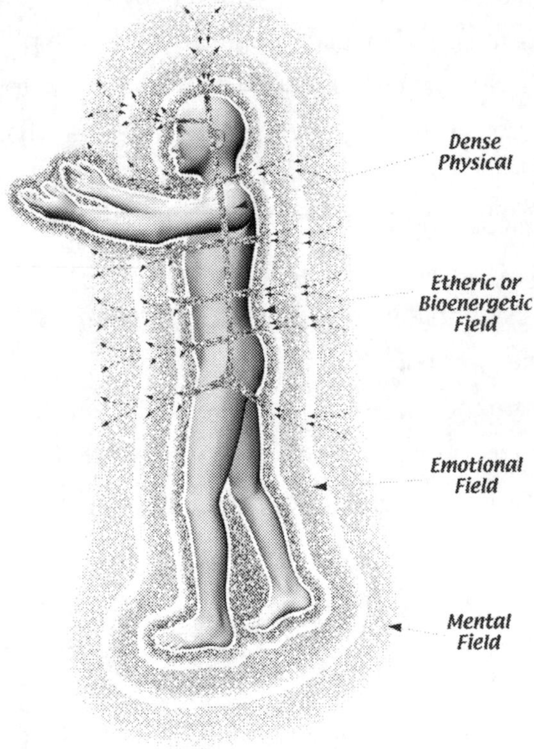

Energy Flow through Chakras and Energy Fields

The centers in the mental field feed into those of the emotional field, and those in the emotional field transfer energy into the etheric field. From here, it is further stepped down via the glandular system and distributed throughout the physical body.

Each energy center has a physical counterpart in the form of an endocrine gland in the physical body. Figure 11 shows the name of the center, the corresponding gland, and physiological system that it governs. The overall health of the gland and hormonal production is an indication of the level of activity within the corresponding chakra.

SEVEN MAJOR CHAKRAS
Figure 11

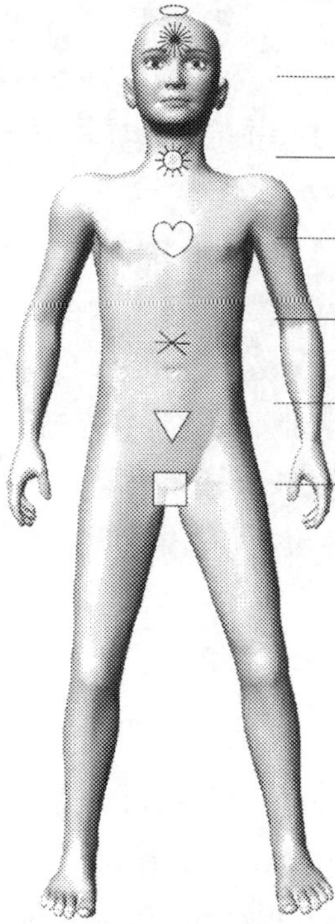

Center	Endocrine Gland	Physiologic System
Crown	Pineal	Central NS
Brow	Pituitary	Autonomic NS
Throat	Thyroid	Respiratory
Heart	Thymus	Circulatory
Solar Plexus	Pancreas	Digestive
Sacral	Gonads	Reproductive
Root or Base	Adrenals	Central NS

The Seven Major Chakras

When we see increased hormonal activity, or depleted, weak, poorly functioning glands, it is a reflection of the amount of activity or blockage within the associated chakra. With this basic understanding, let's move into an investigation of each center.

The Crown Center

The Crown Center is located at the top of the head and is associated with the cerebral cortex and pineal nerve plexus. The physical correspondence of this center is the pineal gland located behind the corpus callosum and above the brain stem. The physiological system to which this center is associated is the central nervous system. The vibrational frequency associated with this center is the color violet and the tone is B. As it is tied to the cerebral cortex it affects the higher thought processes and the functioning of the general nervous system. As there is an activation of this center the activity between the right and left hemispheres of the brain is synchronized.

The pineal gland is active in early childhood until the "will to be" is firmly established. Then, in most people it becomes inactive. It lies dormant until a person reaches a certain point of development on the spiritual path. It then resumes activity. It is the inflow of soul energy that stimulates it into activity. At that time the Crown Center serves as the organ for distributing the energy of will.

Brow Center

The Brow Center is located between the eyebrows just above the eyes and is associated with the hypothalamus-pituitary nerve plexus. The pituitary gland is its physical externalization. The two lobes of this gland correspond with the horizontal distribution of the lobes or "petals" that make up this center. The vibrational frequency associated with this center is the color indigo and the tone is A. The organs and structures it affects are the eyes, ears, sinuses, nose and spinal cord. The physiological system with which it is associated is the autonomic nervous system. The autonomic nervous system governs all the body's involuntary functions such as breathing, digestion, circulation and elimination.

One of the main functions of the brow center is to oversee and monitor the entire chakra system. Whereas all of the other centers are located on, or pass through the etheric spine, the brow center is located in front of the forehead. The brow center acts in the capacity as a director of the other centers below it. Through this center one directs intention. It is through focused intention that we are able to influence the direction of our life and the results we create.

Part of this process uses the creative imagination and visualization to direct and regulate the flow of energy. This direction of energy can be used to create specific results internally, and in the outer world. The brow center also plays the role of the observer as "the mind's eye." It is from this point, "the mind's eye," that we see ourselves, so it is tied to our self-image. The self-image is the internal guidance system for our life. By directing the intention from the brow center and using visualization, we are able to change our self-image and thereby influence the direction and quality of our life.

When this center is weak, underdeveloped, or inactive, we do not have the ability to act effectively upon our world. A simple goal-setting process whereby we experience a series of small successes that gradually build proves to be an excellent activity that strengthens our intention and develops this center.

The Throat Center

The Throat Center is located at the neck, reaching upward to the medulla oblongata and downward to the shoulder blades. The nerve plexus with which it is associated is the cervical ganglia medulla. The physical externalization of this center is the thyroid gland. The vibrational frequency associated with this center is the color blue and the tone is G. The physiological system with which it is connected is the respiratory system. Other glands and structures it affects are the parathyroid gland, the mouth, vocal cords and the cervical vertebrae.

This center also is related to the parasymphatic nervous system, and has a particular effect on the Vagus nerve. This nerve is the tenth cranial nerve, which leaves the brain stem and runs down the neck to supply the heart and lungs with energy. This nerve serves as a very powerful connection between the heart and the brain enhancing communication between the two.

Through this connection, we see the relationship of the throat center with the respiratory system through which the rest of the body receives oxygen and subtle nutritive energy.

One of the primary functions of the throat chakra is that it acts as the center of creativity. As energy moves it must be directed and used or else it will stagnate. The energy flowing through this center must be directed toward some creative outlet. Whereas the brow directed the intention behind creativity, the throat is the center of the creative process. This is the center of intelligent, mental activity. We would expect to find much activity of the throat center in most "intellectuals," and people who have developed professional careers.

The vocal cords and mouth are the instruments of the creative process through the spoken word. Communication is likewise an important role of the throat center. It is an expression of the degree to which intelligence governs an individual.

In some schools of thought, this center is associated with the will. Whereas the crown center deals with the spiritual quest and divine will, the throat center is more related to personality will such as how we actively communicate our wants and desires. If there is an inability to communicate our will is thwarted, or perhaps it is because of a weak will that we may be unable to communicate our needs. As we develop the mental aspect of this center we are able to more effectively exercise our will and communication.

The Heart Center

The Heart Center is located between the shoulder blades and is associated with the heart nerve plexus. The physical externalization is the thymus gland. The vibrational frequency associated with this center is the color green and the tone is F. The physiological system it corresponds to is the circulatory system. The life force itself is anchored in the heart and carried throughout the body via the bloodstream.

This center distributes subtle nutritive energy to the bronchial tubes, the lungs and breasts, and the entire circulatory system. Through its effect on the circulatory system, it distributes nurturing oxygen and subtle energy to all the other parts of the body. The nurturing effect of this center is expressed through the breasts, the only organs associated with the nurturance of another being. As this center opens, there is a natural unfolding of the desire to serve and nurture others. The converse is also true. By serving with love, we support the development of this center and all that is associated with it. Studies have found that people, who do volunteer work, or some kind of service-oriented activity, live longer and enjoy higher levels of health.

One of the reasons the thymus is so important is that it plays a key role in the function of the immune system. One of its functions is to store, process, and program lymphocytes to do specific jobs. Much of this programming takes place during certain developmental stages of childhood. This can determine the overall integrity of the immune system throughout a person's life.

In most cases, the thymus gland atrophies later on in life. For the most part this has been thought to be a natural occurrence. However, we are now beginning to consider that it may be the lack of nutritive energy in the form of available love that is the cause. When the flow of love is blocked, or its presence is nonexistent, the nutrients needed for healthy development and functioning are not available and the thymus shrivels up. Consequently, the overall effectiveness of the immune system is impaired.

As we have seen, researchers have established the connection between our emotional state and our physical health. Consciously directing positive emotion to the heart has a very powerful healing and strengthening effect. Research at the Institute of Heart Math has shown that *the heart generates an electrical field 60 times greater than that of the brain.* Energy follows thought, so wherever we direct our thought, energy will flow. This is a key point to remember.

As we begin to understand love in terms of being a subtle, nutritive energy necessary to fulfill the principles of health, it becomes clear how the energy distributed by this center affects our health. Love flows through this center and is directed by a conscious act of the will toward ourselves as well as others.

The Solar Plexus Center

The Solar Plexus Center is located between the umbilicus and the sternum and is associated with the solar nerve plexus. The vibrational frequency associated with this center is the color yellow and the tone is E. The physical externalization of this center is the pancreas, which is responsible for regulating digestion and blood sugar levels. This center distributes energy to the organs of the digestive system, such as the stomach, liver, pancreas, spleen, gall bladder, as well as the lumbar vertebrae. These organs are responsible for taking the nutrients from the environment and transforming them into fuel as well as building materials used to make up the physical form.

On a basic emotional level this is the center of personal power. The degree to which we have control over ourselves and our environment, and what happens to us is a basic function of this center. It is also where the greatest range of emotions is felt. Thus, the solar plexus has a powerful affinity with the emotional field.

Lower grade emotions such as hate, rage, lust, resentment or anger, move through this center. These lower emotions, such as anger, can be expressed either aggressively toward others, or turned inward if we feel powerless. In any case, the vibrational rate of these lower emotions translates into chemical and hormonal responses that have a direct, negative effect on the overall functioning and health of the body, mind and spirit.

More refined emotions such as the experience of being "in love," appreciation, affection and gratitude have a direct, positive effect on the state of solar plexus energy. These emotions are, for the most part, higher solar-plexus-based and not of the heart as so many think. The love associated with the solar plexus is personal and somewhat possessive in nature whereas the love at the heart level is of a higher nature which is selfless, unconditional, inclusive and impersonal. These higher solar plexus emotions are the kind of refined, positive emotions, whose vibrational rate transfers easily to the heart, thus aiding and strengthening that organ and center.

One of the objectives of using this center is to transform emotions of a lower nature into a higher expression, to transform desire into aspiration, affectionate love into divine love, and selfishness into selflessness. The physical benefits of these positive emotions are many.

One example of this is the research done by the Institute of Heart Math. When we experience the emotion of frustration, the heart activity shown on an EKG is erratic and jagged, indicating an unhealthy, stressful state as shown in figure 12. When we focus our attention on the heart area and concentrate on the feeling of appreciation, a more refined emotional vibration on the EKG reading changes to a smooth, even, healthy flow.

Figure 12

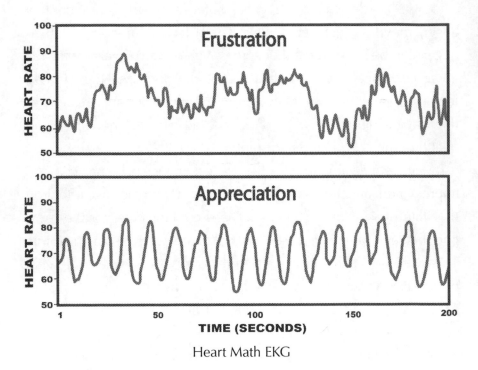

Heart Math EKG

The Heart Math exercise called "Quick coherence technique," utilizes the process of focusing one's awareness on the heart and creating an experience of appreciation. This has the effect of transforming a "lower" solar plexus emotion of frustration into a more refined, higher and healthier emotion. This exercise helps to lift the energy from the solar plexus to the heart and the effect of this is a measurable reduction and dissipation of stress.[14] To learn more about the excellent trainings provided by the Institute of Health Math, you may contact them at www.heartmath.com.

The solar plexus center is a clearinghouse for all the energies that are generated below the diaphragm. One of its roles is to transmute these lower energies through a purification process, and transfer them into the heart center. One of the lessons of this center, and part of this purification process, is to learn to use personal power for selfless service, rather than a way to build our ego and feed our selfish personal desires. This is no easy task but is a necessary part of progressing on our spiritual path.

On a higher level, this center synthesizes the physical, emotional and mental fields by harmonizing and blending the vibrational rates in unison. Even though each field is vibrating at a different level, just like notes on a musical scale, they are of the same key at a different octave. As the vibrational rates synchronize with each other, yet maintain the identity of their different levels, the fields are brought together and integrated with each other. There is a sympathetic resonance between the fields. Although each field is distinct, they are integrated into a unified whole. When this point is achieved, the person has an "integrated personality." A very important point on the living continuum has then been reached.

The Sacral Center

The Sacral Center is located in the lower part of the lumbar area and is associated with the sacral nerve plexus. The vibrational frequency associated with this center is the color orange and the tone is D. Its external expression is the gonads in which the reproductive cells develop. It distributes energy to the reproductive organs, the large and small intestines, the urinary bladder, appendix, and the lumbar vertebrae. Being associated with the sex organs, this center is involved with the act of physical procreation.

This center is associated with basic security needs such as food, clothing, shelter and sex. Sex is the instinctive urge towards union or fusion. This can be expressed on a physical level between man and woman and at a higher level it is the drive to unite spirit and matter. On a higher level, this center can be seen to work with the whole process of creation. There is conception, a gestational period, and birth. This process is true for the creation of a child, as well as the process of bringing an idea into form.

The Root or Base Center

The Root Center is located in the base of the spine and supports all the other centers. It supplies nutritive energy to all of the physical tissues throughout the body. The vibrational frequency associated with this center is the color red and the tone is C. It is associated with the sacral-coccygeal nerve plexus. Its physical externalization is the adrenal glands. The root or base center is associated with basic survival issues, which can be seen in the fight or flight response for which the adrenal glands are responsible.

This is also the center that grounds us to the physical world. It is responsible for our ability to function successfully on the physical plane. This center is the source of "the will to survive." Under activity in this center can weaken the will to live. Over activity can lead us to feel a sense of paranoia and a tendency to react defensively to situations that pose no real threat.

Balancing the Chakras

As we consciously choose to build in the conditions of emotional and mental health, the centers automatically develop and open to function at an optimal level. It is strongly suggested that we not engage in activities or practices that are designed to stimulate a particular center. Too much energy focused in a center, causes over-stimulation, which may create problems and detrimentally affect the organs in that area. Instead, concentrate on building the physical, emotional and mental principles of health. Then, the chakric system will unfold safely in its own time. When there is too little or too much energy available, there will be an imbalance in the energetic system and problems associated with the corresponding organs in the physical body. The practice of selfless service and the cultivation of edifying thoughts and deeds are two actions that will help the centers to unfold at their own rate in a safe, healthy way.

Progress on our spiritual path and the level of health we experience on the living continuum is a result of the degree to which we have purified ourselves of vibrationally course, lower emotions and infused higher qualities into our energetic makeup. The level of mental and emotional frequency experienced at a given vibrational level will produce a corresponding level of chakric activity. Depending on our point on the path and the degree to which the chakras are activated and balanced, there will be a correspondence of physical health or disease to that part of the body associated with that center.

CHAPTER 11

BELIEF SYSTEMS

We find today that more and more is being communicated about the importance and power of belief systems in our lives. In the area of health and medicine, pioneering doctors such as Larry Dossey, Deepak Chopra and Bernie Siegal have documented the power of thought and belief in building health or creating disease. In the personal growth and business arena, people such as Tony Robbins, Brian Tracy and Stephen Covey express the power of belief in building success or limiting one's potential. So, what are beliefs?

Simply put, belief systems are energetic patterns of thought in the mental field and patterns of feelings in the emotional field. The experiences of life create the holographic patterns discussed earlier relating to the mental and emotional fields. Positive emotions, negative emotions, feelings of success, love and acceptance, feelings of failure, being unwanted and rejected, all are encoded in the energy fields as patterns of thought and emotion. These energetic patterns are then translated to the physical level via the etheric body and stored in the brain, nervous system, and cellular structure. Although these energy patterns have become integrated into our constitution, for the most part, we are not conscious of them. They are stored at a subconscious level. Nevertheless, they have become a part of our internal apparatus, and will affect our quality of life and overall health.

The energy, experiences and information stored in the subconscious are very potent forces. To use these forces to our advantage, rather than being the unconscious recipient or victim of them, it is necessary to know how to identify and clear the negative patterns and harness the positive one so they can move us in a positive direction. If these forces are misunderstood, misused or misdirected they will thwart our effectiveness and limit the quality of our life. The energy stored in the fields has the potential to move us into the lower half of the wellness continuum and create a state of dis-ease without our even being aware of what is happening. It also has the power to propel us upward to greater states of wellness and a much fuller experience of life when activated and directed.

Before we move forward it will be helpful to clarify some terminology. When we use the word "conscious," we are referring to that part of us which is aware of present experiences, or those which we can call up from memory, upon command. It deals with those experiences of which we are aware, and information that is relevant to daily living. It is the place where the will is exercised. When the word "unconscious" is used, it means everything of which we are not consciously aware. This includes the subconscious and the superconscious aspects of the mind.

Superconscious Awareness and Subconscious Recording

The "superconscious" is that reality which exists in higher dimensions, where we have to yet develop the ability to experience at will or access the information. Principles based on higher law, experiences beyond our normal comprehension, divine knowledge, tapping into the universal hologram and soul contact would fall in the category of the superconscious. This is a level of reality that is beyond mental cognition or recognition. Never the less, the means of perceiving this level is latent within each of us. Our path up the living continuum is the process of learning how to grow into a greater awareness, to access the superconscious, and use the things learned there in daily living, for greater growth and service.

Prophets, seers, mystics, yogis and other advanced spiritual beings have the ability to perceive these higher levels of reality. Through their teachings and scriptures they translate parts of this reality to those who are receptive. Most of us interpret these teaching through our present level of understanding but as we progress in our spiritual growth, we will eventually come to experience these higher levels of reality for ourselves.

Most of us have heard about those who have had near death experiences. Most of them tell about the great feeling love they felt there. They talk about how they now have a better understanding of who they are and what they need to do, how it has made them want to become a better person, kinder, more loving, that their new mission is to love and help everyone with whom they come in contact. Because of their experience, they have gained a greater awareness of themselves and the positive energy around them. They had a glimpse into superconscious reality.

The subconscious is the total composite of all experiences we have had throughout our life. The experiences are stored in our mental and emotional fields, and corresponding parts of the brain. They are, nevertheless, part of the sum total of our past experiences and therefore have an effect in our present existence and level of health. Because these stored experiences are below our level of consciousness we are not aware of the effect they have on our behavior and health. Noted medical intuitive, Caroline Myss points out the fact, "Your biography creates your biology." Dr. Bruce Lipton in his book the Biology of Belief explains how this subconscious programming creates beliefs that affect us all the way down to the level of our DNA. There is no question that past experiences, have an effect on the levels of health we experience today.

Perhaps the best way to think of the subconscious apparatus is that it works very much like a camcorder, in that it picks up and records everything we see, hear, think, feel, taste, touch or smell. The five senses are the camera through which the information flows. The job of the conscious mind is to choose where the camera will be pointed. The energy fields are the tape on which everything is recorded and stored.

Every experience we have ever had since the day we came into this world, everything we have ever seen, tasted, touched, smelled, heard, thought or experienced emotionally, is stored in the energy fields. This process begins at conception and continues through pregnancy. If the mother is anxious and fearful, those energy patterns will affect the child. If she feels joyous, confident and loving, the child will experience those emotions. Either way, they will be a part of that child's energetic programming. Although this is a life-long process the period from pregnancy through the first eight years of life set the stage for the rest of the life.

This programming goes into the energy fields and establishes an energetic pattern of thought and emotion. As the energy of thought and emotion move through these lines of least resistance, the patterns are strengthened. These patterns of thought and emotion build structures out of the substance, which comprise the respective energy field. Remember, each field is a finer grade of matter, but matter, nonetheless. Mental matter aligns and coalesces to form the patterns of thought in the mental field, and emotional matter aligns and coalesces to form the energetic patterns in the emotional field. The forms constructed out of mental and emotional matter are known as "thought-forms."

Remember the hologram. The interference patterns produced a three-dimensional image of light. It was the energetic pattern that gave rise to the form. These energy patterns represent the interference patterns of the hologram. The thought-forms, which they build, are similar to the image of light. In this case, the image is constructed of the mental or emotional matter from which the energy field is made. These patterns and forms become our belief systems, and they become a part of our energetic constitution.

Belief System Formation

Belief systems are energetic patterns of thought and emotion. They are also the result of forms constructed from the mental and emotional substance of which the energy field is made. These patterns of thought and emotion do translate into the physical mechanism via the brain and nervous system. This results in chemical reactions, hormonal activity, and other physical responses. The flow of information or experience is from the mind to the brain, and then the nervous system. The brain is the physical receiving station for information coming from the non-physical energy fields. As we have already seen, information is carried from the mental and emotional fields into the etheric field through the centers. From there, it is distributed into the nervous system and cellular structure via the nadis and meridians.

Dr. Lipton explains in his book the Biology of Belief how the receptors on cells receive and respond to vibratory information coming from the subtle energy fields. He states, "Biological behavior can be controlled by invisible forces, including thought."[15]

These belief systems influence and, to a large degree, determine our perception. From an understanding on just a physical level, sensory perception is typically understood to be a function of brain and nervous system activity. However, perception is also the result of the patterns and forms contained within the energy fields. Perception, on one level, is how we see and experience the events life sends us. It is the lens through which we experience life, physically, emotionally and mentally. On a higher level, perception is the meaning we ascribe to the experiences that reach our conscious awareness through our sensory experience.

How we see things, and the way in which we interpret the experiences life sends will, to a large degree, determine how we act and react to the situations we encounter as we go through life. If a child is the recipient of healthy emotional nutrients, by being raised in a loving, supportive environment, and is made to feel valuable and worthy, then a healthy sense of self-worth becomes part of that child's energetic disposition. The child will view herself that way and respond accordingly to the situations that life sends. If a child is rejected, or made to feel guilty, insignificant or unloved, that energy pattern becomes recorded in the energy fields. Those are the feelings, many times unconsciously, she will have about herself and that is how she will perceive herself. Wherever these children go, and whatever they do, those patterns, those belief systems, will be the filters through which they experience the world.

These belief systems and patterns exist, and are stored in the mental and emotional fields. As the vibrational rate of this energy is stepped down, this programming has a very powerful effect on the nervous system and biochemistry of the physical body. When a thought or action is repeated over and over, it strengthens the neural pathways, so that it becomes an automatic response. Hence, the thought or feeling will manifest itself as a physical behavior. In time, that experience becomes a part of the cellular memory. A certain pattern of thought or emotion will release select neuro-peptides, which affect cellular function. The cells will respond according to the messages sent, and the chemicals released will have an effect on perception. The perception causes a further release of neuro-peptides, affecting the cell, and thus a continuous feedback loop is created. The chemistry feeds the perception, and the perception stimulates the chemistry.

We would naturally assume that since the conscious mind makes the decisions, it would be the controlling factor in this arrangement. What we find is that over time, the programming that goes on the recording tape of the energy fields influences the decisions that the conscious mind makes without its awareness. Most of our decisions are based on the programming or scripting stored in the subconscious. As we become aware of this process, we can learn how to change the programming and create the desired results we want to experience.

These belief systems can be so powerful, and influence our perception to such a degree, that in many cases it is very difficult to see things that don't fit the pattern. A minister shared a study he had read regarding people's upbringing and their perception of God. He found that people who grew up with a very authoritarian, strict, harshly disciplining father had the perception of God as being an angry, judgmental and wrathful God. People whose father had been loving, supportive, caring and kind, perceived God to be a loving, caring, kind God. In many cases, people had a difficult time even trying to imagine a God who didn't fit their already established image.

We automatically and unconsciously screen out information that is not congruent with the mental and emotional patterns that are a result of our past programming. In traditional psychology, this is referred to as "selective perception." As a result of this, if someone is presented with something they cannot understand, they will automatically ascribe it to, or associate it with, something they can understand, or they will discount it completely.

New information must be congruent with, or have a place to fit into our present reality or mental model. This is one of the reasons it can be challenging for people when they are first exposed to these concepts of viewing life and its experiences in terms of energy. There is no file in their personal computer (mind) for the information to fit into. However, in order to grow and progress we must learn how to expand the files and when necessary create new ones. The best approach when one is exposed to new ideas is to hold an openness to possibility coupled with healthy skepticism.

A paradigm is a belief system or pattern of thinking shared by a group of people. Dr. Thomas Kuhn coined the word "paradigm" while working with scientists. One of the observations he made was that if someone had a belief, a mental picture of how something was supposed to be, an expectation of how an experiment was supposed to turn out, then, often times, they couldn't see things any other way. Their belief determined their perception. Even if hard data contradicted their preconceived ideas about an outcome, many times they were unable to see it. There would be a tendency to unconsciously twist the facts to fit the preconceived belief.

The history of science is filled with the resistance of the old guard to new ideas that do not fit the governing paradigm. Columbus was ridiculed for his belief that the earth was round. Bruno was burned at the stake for claiming that the earth was not the center of the universe. The physician William Harvey was disgraced when he taught that the heart pumped blood throughout the body through arteries and veins. Ignaz Semmelweis was fired from his hospital post for requiring his staff to wash their hands. Radical ideas at the time are now facts that we now take for granted.

As the new thought-form belief system gains acceptance and power, it gradually supersedes or overrides the old ones. Through this conflict between the old and the new, a higher level of harmony may be synthesized and a greater understanding realized. This rarely comes without a struggle, but it is through this challenge that the truth of the emerging ideas is strengthened and legitimized.

The Power of Misinformation

Unfortunately, the reverse of this is also true. Purposeful misinformation can create belief systems that have no basis in truth and yet, over time, can be used to manipulate and control people. Hitler's minister of propaganda, Joseph Goebbels used what he called "the big lie technique." "It doesn't matter how big the lie," he said, "If you tell it enough, people will eventually believe it."

One of the activities of purposeful misinformation that contributes to the growing health crisis is manipulative advertising. Those who study the effects of advertising on health and behavior point out that psychologists who design the ads understand the power of creating an image to influence belief and perception. By manipulating perception, it is possible to influence beliefs, and beliefs control behavior. This process is quite effective with young children, as they do not have the discriminating capacity that adults have. There is no question that adults succumb to this as well, whether or not they understand the process.

Considering that the average child sees 40,000 commercials a year, the effects of manipulative advertising targeting kids includes an increase in obesity and complications of type II diabetes, due to the increase of high calorie fast food and high sugar and fat junk foods that have little or no nutritional value.

Additional problems caused by the deliberate programming of belief systems include eating disorders based on young girls' perceptions of themselves, and how they are trained to think of how they "should" look. The unspoken message is that, if you don't look like Barbie, there is something wrong with you. This false and image-based belief is used to sell diet foods, cosmetics and clothing. It contributes to the dissatisfaction of young girls with their body and the consequent self-esteem issues associated with it. Advertising can also contribute to family stress in that some of these ads are ingeniously designed to subtlety teach children effective ways to nag their parents to buy a certain product. The beliefs communicated to children about what they need to be happy, healthy or successful will have long-term effects on their health, behavior, and quality of life.

Another place advertising is used to mold beliefs and influence behavior is the sale of pharmaceutical products. Watch an evening of television and see how many commercials communicate the message, "If you have this problem, take this drug." This is the "education" we are being programmed with. Yet we wonder why the use of drugs among youth is so prevalent. In the past few years, drug companies have been required to list the side effects caused by certain medications. However, one of the effects of this approach is that it can be used to desensitize people to these side effects. The warning might say, "If you have a hang nail take X for fast, effective relief." Side effects may include nausea, hair loss, high blood pressure, vomiting, blindness, hearing loss, heart attack and kidney failure. Ask your doctor if X is right for you.

Discerning Fact from Fiction

Part of the message included in this commercial is that the side effects are just a normal part of treating disease. As this belief becomes instilled, people just naturally accept this as the way it is and it's all right. Over time, this programming has a numbing effect, which impairs peoples' discernment and leads them to accept the presented reality of, "That's just the way it is." Often times the programming from these ads is so powerful that if a person's doctor doesn't prescribe the medication the person will shop for a doctor until they find one who will.

These are just two examples of how effective advertising (others downloading their program or agenda into your own personal computer) will gradually affect your own beliefs, which in turn influence perception. Once the belief is programmed in, then it will determine your perception and behavior. We are controlled without even knowing it. This is true in the sale of a product by a company, or the sale of an idea to people by their government.

This latter point happens more often than most of us are aware. As commander of Hitler's Air Force, Hermann Goerring said, "The common people don't want war but they can always be brought to the bidding of the leaders: All you have to do is to tell them they are being attacked and denounce the pacifists for lack of patriotism."

I remember listening to taped conversations between President Johnson, secretary of defense Robert McNamara and other high level politicians about how they were going to present the Gulf of Tonkin incident to the American people. This was the incident that triggered the Viet Nam War. Presenting this incident in the right context took some doing by these politicians who we elected and placed our trust in, because as these conversations revealed these attacks of American ships by the North Vietnamese *never* occurred.

The whole pretext for Congress giving President Johnson a blank check to escalate the Viet Nam conflict was fabricated. General Goerring's formula worked and 58,000 GI's died for a politician's lie. If this seems a little harsh I invite you to check this out for yourself at npr.org. Click on *archives* and type in *President Johnson, Gulf of Tonkin* and listen to the actual recordings there. This is but one example of how politicians manipulate public perception to support their agenda.

The more we understand this process of manipulating perception and influencing beliefs, the greater becomes our ability to discern the difference between truth and falsehood. Learn to look behind what you see and hear. Part of the process in our journey to wholeness, lies in learning to identify the beliefs we have that are based on that which is not true, causing warped perspective, and destructive behavior. This is not always an easy or comfortable thing to do, but a very necessary part of the growth process. As we do this, awareness grows, consciousness expands and things begin to fall into harmony.

Abraham Maslow, the psychologist who developed the Hierarchy of Needs, made a wonderful observation with regards to understanding this principle of programming, perception and belief systems when he commented, "If a person is trained as a hammer he sees the whole world as a nail." That training, that programming, is the filter through which the world is seen.

An example of this is the field of medicine. Because of their training in allopathic medicine, which emphasizes drugs and surgery many people have difficulty accepting alternative treatment methods. Although it is changing, it is still fairly common to hear medical doctors say that what you eat has very little or nothing to do with your health, alternative modalities are a waste of money and that energy work is just nonsense. Keep in mind that this bias goes the other way as well. There are many trained in alternative therapies who are unable to see the wonderful contributions made and the value that allopathic medicine brings to the process of healing.

This type of bias is a major contributing factor to what has been termed "the spirit of separateness." This is the perception that because someone does not share the same belief, viewpoint or understanding, that they are separate and apart from you. This applies to religious beliefs, cultural differences, political ideologies, race, national identity, professions, clubs and anything that people externally identify with.

An understanding of this is essential as we aspire to move up the living continuum in the pursuit of truth. The way we perceive something to be and the way it actually is may be two different things. Beliefs are not necessarily truth. They may mentally align one with truth. They may result in actions that are based on correct principles. However, beliefs can also be stumbling blocks that prevent us from moving to higher levels of understanding and experience. They can distort perception and limit our ability to engage in the world. Errant belief systems are so powerful that they can motivate us to vehemently defend the very bonds that hold us prisoner without our knowing. The goal is to understand natural law and universal principles and then to live in accordance with them. The great religions of the world reveal many of these truths. Most of us, however, with our limited understanding, only perceive a part of the greater whole.

A great example of this is the story of five blind men, each touching a different part of the elephant and describing what an elephant was by what they experienced. One touched the side of the elephant and said, "An elephant is like a wall, solid and flat." The next one, grasping the trunk said, "You're wrong, an elephant is long and strong like a snake." The third one, holding the leg said, "You're both wrong, anyone can tell that an elephant is round and straight like a tree." The next one, holding the tail said, "No, no, no you are all wrong. An elephant is long and skinny like a piece of rope." The fifth blind man, who was a little fanatical, was holding the elephant's ear exclaimed, "You're all a bunch of idiots. Anyone with any brains could tell an elephant is flat and floppy like a banana leaf." Based on their limited perception of the whole, they explained the "truth" of what an elephant was, based on their experience and understanding. Their experience became their belief system of what an elephant was.

No doubt, some of them became frustrated when their friends adamantly disagreed with what was so obviously true to them as we do when our friends have the same problem. If they were open to other possibilities, they could learn and gain a greater understanding of a greater expression of truth. Their old belief systems would be expanded to include a greater understanding. However, if they were locked into their belief system, their own rigidity would prevent them from growing. Holding on to their version of truth would have prevented them from moving into a greater awareness.

All of us have beliefs based on past programming that limit our growth and experience of life. The process of moving forward on the path requires a discerning openness and a spirit that is willing to learn through new experience. It also requires a willingness to move past our present beliefs systems into a greater understanding. The blind man holding the leg of the elephant would have to be open to investigating other possibilities. To do this, he might have to let go of the leg in order to touch the ear, side or tail of the elephant. Even though he has to let go of the leg he still has the value of that knowledge. As he grows through experience, his understanding of what is true deepens.

This isn't to say we randomly discard all the beliefs we have. Many are in alignment with natural law and universal principles and these tools serve us well. It is good to stand on your beliefs. At times, it may be necessary to defend them. However, it is also wise to realize they are *only* beliefs not necessarily the complete truth. Find the balance between healthy skepticism and openness to possibilities.

As we look at the energy continuum in Figure 8 we see that most of our understanding of reality is based in the physical level, with a limited understanding of the astral plane, and some experience in the lower mental plane. A person who has the ability to perceive the greater reality which is beyond, a person who has developed a higher and more complete spiritual awareness is going to have a considerably different perspective from those who are not as far along the path. If one knows, not merely believes, but knows the unity of creation, realizes we are all interconnected and that what I do to my brother or my enemy, I do to myself - then counsel such as love your enemies, do good to those who harm you, bless those who curse you and other truths expressed in the Sermon on the Mount make perfect sense. For those of us who perceive the physical plane as reality and who operate under a belief system based on very limited sensory perception, that we are all separate individuals who must look out for "number one" - this advice is ridiculous.

Through our limited sensory perception and intellectual abilities, we are only touching a very small part of the cosmic elephant. A very small part of what *is*. The greater reality is above the mental plane. Although the mind is a valuable tool in understanding the nature of things at the mental level and below, it is unable to comprehend that which is greater than itself. Belief systems can move us forward, and they can also hold us back. Part of the process of becoming whole and ascending the wellness continuum is to recognize beliefs for what they are, learn to discern the true from the false, and bring our lives into alignment with universal principles and natural law.

A wise man was once asked about his concepts of spirituality. His response was, "Concepts of spirit have nothing to do with spirit. They have to do with concepts. Beliefs of God have nothing to do with God. They have to do with beliefs." Concepts and beliefs are mental constructs that can take us closer to truth or hold us back. We will learn some techniques for reprogramming limiting beliefs when we investigate the power of the imagination or mental imagery but ultimately we must move past beliefs into direct knowing. This knowing can only happen with the illuminating experience caused by a higher power greater than our mental understanding.

Although people may have different understandings of this higher power and use different words with different meanings to describe it, I am going to use the word "Soul" when I refer to this power beyond mental comprehension. This event of soul-knowing and understanding greater than mental cognition is summed up in the Vedic Scripture of The Bagavad Gita which states, "True Self can only be known when, beyond the five senses, the mind and the intellect, the soul perceives itself, by itself." There are other ways "to know" and as we move up the living continuum, we eventually move past beliefs into a greater awareness of life and a deepening growth in the experience of consciousness itself.

CHAPTER 12

THOUGHT FORMS

We have seen that mental and emotional fields are comprised of substance and are magnetic in nature. One of the basic laws that govern this arena is that "energy follows thought." When we think a thought over and over, that thought actually begins to take on a form created out of mental substance. This may also be understood in terms of electromagnetic waveforms. When we visualize something or nurture a mental image in our mind, that image actually starts to coalesce into a form of mental matter or a thought-form (TF).

The process of thought and imagination produces chemical reactions in the brain. However, the chemical reactions are only a byproduct of this activity. The image visualized is not a result of the neurological activity or chemical reactions in the brain. As *The Neuropsychology of Achievement* by Sybervision reveals, the image is, in reality, much like the hologram that we spoke about earlier. It is a three-dimensional image suspended in space composed of mental substance. The more thought is directed towards this image, the clearer and more vividly it is defined, and the more it is imbued with emotion, the stronger and more dense it becomes.[16]

Over 50 years ago in his study of success, Napoleon Hill made the statement in his classic book, *Think and Grow Rich,* "Thoughts are things, that when mixed with definiteness of purpose and a burning desire, will transform themselves into their riches or other material objects." Again, we see the process of stepping-down energy. An idea is intuited above the mental plane. It is stepped down, becoming a thought clothed in mental matter. The mental blueprint of the idea is formed. Emotional matter is added in the form of desire, which provides the motivation to bring it into physical expression.

This is how thought-forms are constructed. A thought-form is an actual form built out of mental substance, composed of electromagnetic waveforms. They have substance. As some research has shown, thought, consciousness and intention can affect physical reality. Once a thought-form has been constructed it stays until acted upon by some other force.

As an example, if you nail two pieces of wood together, you will have constructed a form out of physical matter. That form will stay intact, unless some other force such as a crowbar acts upon it or the wood deteriorates and eventually rots away. So it is with forms built out of mental matter. Once they are created they remain having an effect for as long as they exist. They will stay active until an outside force acts upon them. They affect our perception in that they contribute to the filtering process through which we perceive the world.

Holding Us Back or Moving Us Forward

In many cases, thought-forms and beliefs are synonymous. Whether it is an individual belief system or an organizational, racial, national or cultural paradigm; the role that perception plays in our life has a tremendous effect on our quest for higher consciousness, awareness and truth. These forms built of mental matter remain in the energetic field or aura. It is through these forms in the surrounding field that the one in the center perceives the world. These forms dramatically affect how we experience the happenings and events in the world around us.

Thought-forms that are in alignment with universal law, principles of health and higher values will move us up the living continuum more effectively. Misaligned, unhealthy thought-forms generated by faulty programming will cloud or skew perception and limit our understanding. The result of this will be distorted emotions and misguided actions. If an idea that is good and pure is presented but must go through distorted patterns and thought-forms in the aura of the perceiver, by the time it arrives the pure idea will be distorted. The perceiver will interpret and respond to the distorted idea rather than the true, original presentation.

Faulty programming, errant belief systems, and distorted thought-forms must eventually be identified, corrected and brought into alignment with correct principles if we are going to become whole and continue moving upward.

Does Truth Elevate Us To Its Level or Do We Lower It To Ours?

Let's look at our wellness continuum or point-on-the-path mountain metaphor again. If our understanding is at a lower point on the continuum, and we are presented with an idea that is much higher than our current level of understanding, the tendency will be for us to pull that idea down to a level that fits into our limited understanding. Hopefully, the presented idea or truth will instead serve to uplift our understanding to a higher level. However, the natural tendency in the past has been to make the truth fit into our limited understanding rather than expanding our awareness.

Nowhere is this more evident than in the field of religion. The truths and principles such as love, brotherhood, selflessness, humility, faith and wisdom, on which major religions are founded, are universal and timeless. The essence, goodness, power and purity of the true teachings presented by Jesus, Buddha, Krishna, Mohammed and others were guideposts for humanity at a particular time, and they continue to serve as Beacons of Light.

Take for example the teachings of Jesus Christ. When practiced and lived, they do transform lives. Those teachings have been interpreted by a multiplicity of different denominations and put into practice through a wide range of behaviors from the highest expressions of selfless love to the most abhorrent cruelty. So what happened?

How does one take the basic messages expressed in the Sermon on the Mount, - "love your enemies, walk the extra mile, turn the other cheek, and do good to those who despitefully use you," - and then initiate actions like the Crusades and the Inquisition? Many have asked that and rejected Christ, His message and His gift, because of what others have done, supposedly in His name.

The level of love and selflessness taught by Jesus Christ is incomprehensible to most people whose understanding is basically selfish and "me" oriented. In some cases, this truth has lifted many to a higher level of understanding, and inspired them to live in accordance with divine law. In other cases, this teaching has been distorted and twisted to fit the selfish motive held by so many people at the time. Individually and collectively, we interpret information according to our current level of understanding.

Often, what people reject is their own misinterpretation of a presented truth. They identify that misrepresentation with the form, e.g. the denomination or religion in which it has been presented. They reject the form, but the real issue has been the dislike they have for *their* interpretation of the presented truth, not the real essence of that truth. How true it is, that we see things not as they are, but as we are. It has also been said that what we see in others, is a reflection of what is actually within ourselves.

I have friends who are Catholic, Protestant, Jewish, Mormon, New Age, Buddhist, and Agnostic. I find it fascinating to hear how they have progressed from their religion of origin to their present point on the path. What did they embrace that had value? What was it that they rejected? It seems that when they were young, the quality of their experience was largely based on how the teachings had been presented and lived by those who taught them. According to their level of understanding, certain thought-forms and belief systems had been put into place. In many cases, they rejected their religion of origin and moved to something higher as their understanding developed. In other cases, as they grew spiritually, their understanding of a presented teaching within their religious framework grew with them to a higher level. In either case, progress was made. Progress is good. A wise man once said, "To be born into a certain level of truth and understanding is good. To die at the same level is most unfortunate." How true. No progress had been made.

The important concept to understand is that we interpret that which is presented to us according to our level of understanding and experience. As a presented truth moves through our belief systems and the thought-forms in our auric field, it can be distorted like sunlight moving through water. As we aspire to higher levels of awareness and understanding, we learn to discern and leave behind certain false beliefs. Those beliefs have served their purpose, and it's time to move on, expanding on our new discoveries of Truth. This process of formulating a greater understanding based on experience and insight, incorporating it into our life, and growing by making that truth a part of who we are is how we build the path on which we walk. When new information is presented, remember, we run it through our filters and it becomes colored as a result of those filters. In other words, we interpret that experience according to our current level of understanding.

Creating Your Reality

We could apply this understanding to a currently popular belief system that states, "We create our own reality." This statement or belief can be interpreted on two different levels. First, since we can learn to choose our programming and thereby affect our experience of the world in which we live, we do indeed create our own reality. "Reality" according to this definition, is how we experience life. On one level this is true. Our thoughts, choices and actions affect our programming, which in turn affects our perceptions. For most of us our sensory perceptions are "reality" unless we are aware of something greater. This is a personal reality that is relative according to our experience.

On a higher level, perhaps contained within the implicit order, Reality IS, Spirit IS, Truth IS unchanging and constant. They have nothing to do with our perception. Sensory perception perceives only a small part of that energy or primary substance which has condensed or precipitated from the implicit order. These higher qualities exist and play their part whether or not we are aware of them. They are constant and unchanging. It would be more accurate to say that we create our own illusion, based on past programming and misperception, and call it reality. God works according to absolute laws and principles. Man works in relativity. The objective is to learn how to identify, modify, and correct the personal programming, the faulty thought-forms, and limiting beliefs that are contrary to what true reality is. As we aspire to understand the higher laws and principles and learn to align our thoughts and actions accordingly we ascend the living continuum. The higher we ascend, the more we become aligned with natural laws, universal principles and absolute truth.

If I am climbing a mountain and its cloudy and raining, my view and experience is a result of where I am in elevation. Someone who is above the clouds, standing in the radiant sunlight looking out over the vast illuminated expanse, will be having a completely different experience. The person at the top will have a greater understanding of the whole than those at lower levels making their ascent. Just because I'm experiencing mist and fog in my life doesn't mean that the sun isn't there all the time. The more one understands and embodies greater truths, the more clearly he will see them in all their different forms and various paths. If complete truth is the summit, the different paths will converge the higher they ascend.

Past programming is a part of our individual makeup and affects each of us. Having a basic understanding of this process is essential to learning how to work with universal principles and natural law rather than working against them, to heal us, rather than harm us. The wonderful thing about this is that once we become aware of how the laws work, we can choose the correct programming, or belief system. By learning to consciously choose our beliefs and how to direct our thought and intention, we are using the process of active believing and inspired faith. We are using the law of "energy follows thought," and so we are constructing thought-forms and beliefs that are in alignment with universal laws.

Learning, then applying and living the principles put forth in scriptures, will gradually bring our programming, or belief system, into alignment with higher reality. Prayer and meditation help us establish the connection with the power that is greater than our mind. This puts our guidance system on course and allows us to work with forces that are greater than ourselves rather than being victims of their effects. Intended belief and inspired faith, backed by actively living these higher principles, begins to build the bridge that leads from believing into knowing.

CHAPTER 13

IMAGINATION AND TRANSFORMATION

One of the most effective ways of redirecting energy and creating correct belief systems and thought-forms that serve us is through the use of creative imagination. We have seen how the energy and movement of thought and emotion will create patterns and thought-forms in the energy fields. These fields record a vividly imagined experience just as an actual physical experience. The imagination using visualization or mental imagery is a tool whereby these patterns and thought-forms are constructed with deliberate intent.

One of the reasons that imagination is so powerful is the link between mental and emotional fields and the physical body. When something is vividly imagined, and this process is repeated over and over, the thought pattern is transferred to the nervous system where it becomes a physical action. For instance, when you are watching a movie, logically you know that it isn't real, however your body starts reacting, your heart rate increases, adrenaline is released, your body parts move and jolt.

Mental Training Affects Physical Results

For years as an athlete, I have personally used visualization techniques. In over 45 years of athletic experience, including trampoline, aerial acrobatic freestyle skiing, and high diving at 80 feet, I have never broken a bone in my life. I attribute much of this to first learning the skills mentally and then translating them into physical action.

I set the goal of performing a full, twisting, double back somersault on skis long before I became adept at aerial skiing. During a year I took off from college to travel and work, I drove a truck on a rather long, boring route. During that drive, I spent many hours mentally rehearsing this skill in my mind/body. I could mentally see myself performing the skill. I would create the kinesthetic feeling in my body of what I thought it would feel like. I would hear the sounds of the skis on the snow, and the whoosh of the air as it went by.

The imagined sensory detail was so real, that I remember on several occasions feeling the knot in my stomach that I usually get before I perform a skill for the first time. My clothing was soaked in perspiration from vividly focusing on the skill. Several years later, when I was actually ready to perform the skill physically, I landed the first one on my feet, and skied out of it like I had performed it a hundred times.

For years top athletes around the world have used this technique of using their imagination, mental imagery, to affect their physical body and improve their performance. Numerous studies have been conducted regarding this phenomenon. However, only recently have we begun to discover how thought directly affects the nervous system.

One study involved basketball and mental imagery. In this study, there were three groups, consisting of 20 people in each group. Each person stood on the free throw line and shot 25 times. The average amount of baskets made by each group was nine shots out of 25. For the next 30 days, the first group did nothing. The second group came into the gym, and each person practiced shooting as many baskets as they could for 20 minutes each day. The third group would practice in their imagination for 20 minutes a day. In their mind, they would see the ball arching through the air. They would hear it swish through the hoop and bounce on the floor. They would mentally feel the ball in their hands, and their muscles tense as if poised for the shot.

At the end of 30 days, each group was tested again. The first group that had done nothing at all showed no improvement. The second group that had practiced physically 20 minutes a day showed an improvement of 24 percent. The third group that practiced only in their imagination, showed an improvement of 23 percent.[17]

These results appear to be remarkable. However, research in brain and neurosciences is showing us how thoughts and emotions have a direct effect on our nervous system. By using mental imagery, and practicing in our imagination, the brain is able to strengthen neural pathways, which direct the muscles to new movements and faster reactions.

Healing and Imagery

Drs. Carl and Stephanie Simonton have pioneered research using the imagination as a means of fighting cancer and other diseases. As an example of these imagery techniques, patients might visualize white blood cells in the form of a Pac Man video character, gobbling up cancer cells. Dr. Candace Pert, in her book, *Molecules of Emotion,* shares her experience of focusing on the frontal lobes of the brain, and releasing a flood of endorphins to help modulate pain caused by a headache.

Since the subconscious mind cannot tell the difference between something that actually happened, and a vividly imagined experience, mental imagery can be effective in re-patterning a negative emotional response. When we vividly imagine an experience in rich, sensory detail, it has an effect on the nervous system, which in turn affects our actual experience and behavior.

One technique that is quite effective in healing past emotional pain is to mentally replay the harmful event in your imagination in a way that you would have preferred it to be. As an example, suppose that someone has done something or said something that has hurt you emotionally. When the event happened you had a response that caused neurological activity and chemical reactions. Each time you think of the event, it triggers the same neurological activity and chemical reactions, which result in the unpleasant emotional experience.

You obviously can't change what happened but here is how you can change the physiological and emotional responses of the body. Close your eyes and rewrite the script. Imagine the situation playing itself out the best way possible. Instead of hurtful words or actions coming from the offending person mentally replay the scene with them expressing kind, positive words and expressing actions of goodness, or whatever would have been the ideal, appropriate response. As you *see* the positive experience, as you *hear* the kind words, and as you kinesthetically and emotionally *feel* the result of the goodness being expressed, you will gradually start to change the information that your nervous system is sending.

Just as mentally practicing basketball, changed the messages the nervous system was sending, so will replaying a usually emotionally upsetting event with the new, correct perspective. It is a wonderful way to take a negative and potentially destructive experience and not only defuse the destructive aspects, but create a positive experience out of a negative one. As we've seen, unresolved emotional trauma and stress can cause physical illness and emotional pain and limit our quality of life for years. This simple technique can be used to change the negative response and its effects into a positive experience, and enhance the healing process.

We can use our imagination to enhance our quality of life, improve our athletic performance, clear past emotional trauma, develop character or fight disease. Mental and emotional energy translates into physical results in the nervous system and our biochemistry.

Energy Follows Thought

The second reason for learning how to use imagination effectively is that "energy follows thought." This universal principle applies both internally to our physiology and externally to our environment.

Wherever we choose to focus our mind will determine the direction in which we will move. Thoughts create events and thoughts influence the experiences we attract to ourselves. Belief systems and thought-forms have power over health and quality of life. Consciously using imagination will dramatically increase the power and effectiveness of our mental tools and our mindset. Remember: if misused, imagination will have a detrimental effect. If we continually visualize a negative situation or event, we will draw that experience to ourselves. Energy is impersonal. It works according to principle. It is up to us to make sure it is directed in alignment with the laws of health.

Although thousands of books have been written on this subject from a philosophical or metaphysical viewpoint, we are now beginning to understand these principles in scientific terms. Thought is electrical in nature. When it is directed by will it follows the line of focused intent. The more focused the thought, the more powerful is the electrical field it creates.

Thought Generated Electrical Current and Magnetic Field

It is a scientific fact that when an electrical field or current is created in any way, it simultaneously creates a magnetic field. I remember an experiment I did in grade school that demonstrated this. We ran a wire from one pole of a dry cell battery to a screw in a piece of wood. Another piece of wire came from the other battery pole, wrapped around a nail, and continued on to be attached to a short strip of metal, anchored to the same piece of wood. This piece of metal was arranged like a telegraph key that could be depressed to the screw anchoring the first wire. When the metal was pressed to the screw the circuit was completed.

As the current flowed through the wire around the nail the nail became a magnet that could be used to pick up small pieces of metal. When the electrical current was broken the nail lost its magnetic effect and released the metal it was holding. This simple experiment was a fun way to show that when there is an electrical current flowing it will generate a magnetic field. The stronger the electric current flows the more powerful the magnetic effect will be.

When we mentally visualize a goal or an event we are energetically and electrically creating that event or experience in our mental and emotional fields. That act of visualization begins to coalesce mental matter and the process of focused thought creates an electrical charge or current. The more clarity the visualization has the more effectively it will draw together the thought-form. The greater the mental focus guiding the stream of thought the more powerful the magnetic field will be. As a result of this electrical field, a magnetic field is simultaneously generated. Thus, we magnetically attract to ourselves that on which we concentrate.[18]

An electrical current will generate a magnetic field and when a mechanical armature is passed through a magnetic field, it generates electricity. Electrical generators work by passing an armature through a magnetic field. This is how the electricity you use in your home is generated. We see that there is a dynamic interplay between magnetism and electricity. Understanding these principles can be quite advantageous to our personal growth and healing process.

Magnifying Thought

We have seen the power that electricity and magnetism have on creating rapid, powerful healing. One way to magnify the power of thought and increase its effectiveness is to have your physical body become the armature that passes through the magnetic field. This can be accomplished through the use of a small exercise trampoline or rebounder. This technique was first discovered by Dr. C. S. West, when he observed someone gently bouncing up and down. He thought of this interplay of electricity and magnetism. Here is his insight:

Considering the fact that the Earth is a giant magnet, with north and south poles surrounded by a magnetic field, perhaps it would be possible to use that field to generate electrical energy. By standing on a rebounder and gently bouncing up and down, our body becomes the armature passing through the magnetic field of the Earth. As this is done, the process magnifies the electrical power of thought. We know electricity dissipates trapped blood proteins. Wherever that thought is focused in the body, it will direct electricity to that point and increase its power. The result will be that we are literally able to break up the clustered plasma proteins through the power of magnified thought. This will allow their removal by the lymphatic system. Oxygen will then be able to reach the cells, turning on the electrical generators, and engaging the healing process.

Using these techniques, people in pain for years have experienced relief and a reversal of those conditions. With the knowledge of how to magnify thought, they have been able to stimulate and direct the healing power, and heal themselves. This technique also enhances the effectiveness of affirmations, beliefs, expectations, intentions and other activities whereby the power of thought is consciously employed to produce specific results,

The Law of Attraction

We mentioned earlier in our discussions on thought-forms that when we visualize something the image is not in the brain. There is electrical and chemical activity in the brain. However, the image is a three-dimensional holographic structure of mental matter suspended in space. The greater the clarity with which we focus on this image, the greater the electrical charge that is generated. That electrical current simultaneously creates a magnetic field. This is the scientific explanation and validation for the belief that whatever we think about will be attracted to us. By continuously directing mental energy in the creation of a thought-form, one will actually attract those circumstances into play that will create the experience or event.

This principle works on both an individual level and it works collectively. Keeping these principles in mind, what do you think happens when millions of people all over the world watch violent movies? What are the images going into their mind? What are the collective thought-forms being created? What is the effect of this collective magnetic field set up in the energy fields of the planet?

Is it possible that the insane violence we see playing itself out in various ways around the world is the effect of these thought-forms built by the collective imagination of humanity? If you really understand this principle, you already know the answer to these questions.

Considering what we've learned about the power of thought let's take a look at this issue of violence and its cause. In July of 2000, the AMA, the APA, the American Academy of Pediatrics, and the American Academy of Child and Adolescent Psychiatry issued a joint statement to Congress. This statement said, "Well over 1,000 studies point overwhelmingly to a *causal* connection between media violence and aggressive behavior in some children."

Energy follows thought. Violent images in a child's mind may result in aggressive or violent behavior. If this is the case, will reducing the violent images result in less violent behavior? A study done by Stanford University involving two San Jose elementary schools, demonstrated that it does. In their study, they noted a 60 percent decrease in verbal aggression and a 40 percent decrease in physical aggression just by having kids cut down on their television time.

By observing playground behavior and through interviews, researchers assessed the baseline level of aggressive behavior in 192 third and fourth graders. Using a curriculum designed to reduce television and video games researchers got two-thirds of the students to eliminate all television for 10 days. Half the students agreed to continue the experiment for 20 more weeks and to keep TV and video games under seven hours a week. At the end of this period their *aggressive behavior dropped 40 percent* confirming that negative internal images produce negative actions and positive healthy mental images produce wholesome behavior.[19]

Imagination and Prayer

Let's take another look at the power thought, focused intent and imagination, combined with prayer can have in stimulating growth and healing. You will remember the study that Dr. Miller performed with magnetically charged water and its effect on the germination rate of rye seeds. Dr. Miller wanted to see whether or not thought and prayer would have an effect of the growth rate of rye seeds at a distance. He designed an experiment to measure that effect. He built an instrument called an electromechanical transducer to measure the growth rate of seedlings in thousandths of inches per hour and recorded the movement on strip graph paper. His participants were the same people who had provided the healing hands for the other rye seed experiment. The part of this experiment that is of particular interest is that the healers were located in Baltimore, and Miller's lab was in Atlanta, a distance of six hundred miles. They were requested to hold the seedlings in their thoughts throughout their regular prayer meeting which always began at 9 PM.

To monitor for consistency, the growth rate was measured for several hours before the prayer began. The strip graph showed a consistent rate of 6.25 thousandths of an inch per hour. Dr. Miller left the lab and locked the doors to assure there would be no other variables involved. The next morning, he noted that precisely at 9:00 the evening before the tracing of the graph began to move upward. The tracing indicated that the growth rate had increased to 52.5 thousandths of an inch per hour, *an increase of 840 percent*. Following the prayer time the growth gradually declined but never returned to the original level. When asked what they did the healers responded that while they were praying they visualized the seedlings filled with energy and light. Remember, this happened at a distance of six hundred miles indicating that thought directed by the imagination and prayer is not limited by distance. This is one of many experiments that validate the power of thought, imagination, and prayer.[20]

Much of the scientific research that has validated the power of prayer has indicated that the most effective way to pray is not for a specific result but for the highest and best good of all concerned. This is a different approach then the clarity of a specific goal.

By holding the person or situation in the light in your imagination you will help to direct additional energy into the prayer to be used according to the best good. The way you word it may depend on your spiritual tradition but the basic idea is, "Thy will be done" as you add your energy of directed love and light to the person or situation and release the results.

As we have seen with physical strength, the more you use a muscle the stronger it becomes. The same principle holds true with our imagination. To strengthen your ability to use this powerful tool, practice visualizing in rich, sensory detail. Practice seeing, hearing and feeling a goal, both physically and emotionally, as if it already had been accomplished. Or practice visualizing the dry state of cells with no fluid around them in your body. Remember, energy follows thought. Be conscious of where you direct it and how you use it.

The imagination can be a valuable tool used to enhance healing and personal growth. In any goal setting technique the use of the imagination will dramatically increase its effectiveness. The more sensory rich detail one can experience, the more they can see, hear and feel in their mind, the more effective they will be in re-patterning limiting beliefs, building thought forms and training their nervous system. A simple guideline is the term VAK which stands for **V**isual, **A**uditory and **K**inesthetic.

Rather than just writing out a simple goal such as "I have just won this award," a more effective way is to write a VAK statement that includes a visual, auditory and kinesthetic declaration of what one will experience once they have achieved the desired goal such as:

1. I see the finish line disappear as I run past it and hear the roar of the crowd while I feel my heart pounding and legs throbbing.
2. I feel the trophy in my hands as I accept the award, hearing the congratulations and seeing the smiling faces of approval.
3. I see my body in the dry state as I inhale white healing light to the place of injury and hear my cells thanking me for the needed oxygen, detoxification and real food.

For these statements to be effective you must see, hear and feel in your mind as though it is already true. The more clarity of sensory detail you can put into the end result the more effectively you will engage the resources and forces of your subconscious mind. Practice writing out 5 goals in this way. Being able to VAK in your imagination will greatly enhance many of the following activities and exercises.

Review the self-help healing techniques on page 66 - 68 and mentally direct your thoughts to the area as you do the physical activities of pressure, massage and a rapid light stroke.

CHAPTER 14

SELF-IMAGE

As a result of our past programming and experience, all of our thoughts, images, visions, words and pictures come together to form a composite image of who we believe ourselves to be. These images housed in our mental field form our self- image. Our self-image is a thought-form of how we mentally see ourselves. Each individual has these internal pictures or movies of themselves, living and performing at different levels in various arenas of life. *The self-image is a thought-form that is the controlling mechanism for directing our behavior and performance.* This is a key point to remember. *Our external actions will always match the internal pictures.* The activities we observe on the outside are a reflection of how we view ourselves on the inside.

An example might be a someone who is overweight and has tried everything they can think of to take off the extra pounds. If the subconscious image they have of them self is one of being too heavy, it doesn't matter how hard they try to change, or how much conscious effort they put into losing weight. If being overweight is the image they have of them self, then, as soon as they move away from that image by losing weight, the controlling mechanism of the self-image will automatically start to regulate behavior that brings them back into compliance with that thought-form. The external expression will always match the internal pictures.

We have seen how thought has a magnetic effect. This can be used to move us forward on our path of growth, or it can keep us stuck where we are. As we move away from the belief, the created image of who we are, into a new persona or expression there is a tension created. This can be thought of as stretching a rubber band. The more it is stretched, the greater the tension that is created. The greater the incongruence between the belief system and those activities that define who we are and the new person we are becoming, the greater the tension and discomfort caused. The result is that the tension usually pulls us back into the belief system of our former self-image, and those activities that are consistent with it. The magnetic effect of the thought-form has a very powerful effect in keeping our actions consistent with it.

As we have seen, energy follows thought. We also understand that the etheric body is the template for the physical body and if something happens in the etheric field it will eventually affect the physical body. The mental matter which comprises the mental field has an effect on the emotional field and how we feel. The matter and energy from the mental and emotional fields have an effect on the etheric field. It is then translated into the physical body via the nervous system.

The self-image works very much like the governor on a car. You may have a sports car with the ability to go one hundred and sixty mph. However, if there is a governor on the car's engine that automatically shuts it down at fifty mph, it doesn't matter that the car has the potential to go faster. It doesn't matter that the driver has the ability to safely drive faster. We can put on new tires, use a higher octane fuel and modify the car any way. Yet, no matter how much money, energy and effort have been put into improving the performance of the car, the governor will always shut it down at fifty.

Many of us are living our lives the same way. Let's go back to our living continuum. Perhaps we are at "not sick," we are getting by; life is okay, but not great. However, we decide we want to move into the high-performance living zone, to create higher levels of health, financial freedom and a higher quality of life. We make the effort and "try hard," but every time we start to move outside our comfort zone and start to perform in a manner that is not consistent with our self-image, the controlling mechanism, the governor, will start to adjust our behavior so that we move back into compliance with internal pictures. We may try harder and start to become successful again only to find that, for some reason or another we sabotage ourselves. Things that seem beyond our control come in and prevent us from moving forward. The patterns keep repeating themselves and in most cases we're not even aware of the process. The self-image is one of the many forms taken by limiting beliefs.

In the course of my work I had occasion to meet a woman who had grown up in a very emotionally and physically abusive situation. Over her life she had experienced a number of injuries and illnesses to the point where she was now disabled, dependent on a number of medications and living on a basic survival level. It was such a sad story that my heart really went out to her but as I listened there was something else being said.

The way she spoke of her disability was that is wasn't something she had, it who she was. I was clear to me that there were a number of things that could be done immediately which would make a very significant difference in her health as well as her life. I told her that I'd be happy to work with her clearing the limiting beliefs, straightening out her nutritional situation and doing some craniosacral work. All of which would have a significant effect. I would do it on a donation basis or for no cost at all. I never heard from her.

As I reflected on this situation it dawned on me that, for whatever reason this woman really valued the identity of being disabled. That was her self-image and who she had come to believe she was. As strange as it might seem to most of us she was more interested in getting something like insurance that would support her in that identity and pay for her medication than truly healing herself. Until her self-image, the internal pictures of how she saw herself and the belief system of who she was changed she would continue to be her disability. I'm sure there were other factors involved that I was not aware of but until the self-image changed and belief systems shifted nothing was going to change.

A Mental Template Directing Action

We have seen how the etheric body serves as a holographic template for the physical body. In a sense, the self-image is a thought-form that acts the same way. It serves as a mental template that directs our behavior and performance. Dr. Denis Waitly summed up the power and importance of the self-image in his program, "*The Psychology of Winning,*" when he said, "All a person will ever aspire to in life will be based on the all-important self-image. The self-image is the fundamental key to understanding behavior and performance. If you want to change your behavior and performance, change your self-image first. Then you will automatically change your personality, your behavior and your performance."

This dynamic tension created by the magnetic effect of the self-image can either pull us forward or draw us back. If the old self-image is the dominant factor the tension will increase as we move away from it. The reverse is also true. As we construct a new self-image out of mental substance, that thought-form creates a magnetic effect and begins to draw you towards itself. As your new self-image grows in strength and clarity it begins to bring your behavior and performance into compliance with itself. If the new self-definition is not adequately formed or is unclear it will not have the power to accomplish lasting change. To make this principle work you must build a new self-image. Clarity and intention are the two key words in doing this.

How to Change Your Self-Image

How do you change your self-image? How do you re-pattern limiting beliefs? One of the most tried-and-true techniques is through the use of the creative imagination. Energy follows thought and thought-forms are built from mental and emotional matter. As we have seen, they are most effectively assembled by clear intention. The subconscious mind cannot tell the difference between something that is real and something that is vividly imagined. On the physical level the nervous, endocrine, and immune systems respond to thought, which in turn affects every other part of the body.

To begin changing your self-image, visualize a mental image of your ideal self, having reached a goal that is important to you. The more clearly you can see, hear and feel the end result, the more it will start to change the internal pictures and replace them with new ones. This process not only changes the mental pictures, but also builds a new thought-form. This, in turn, produces the desired effects and moves you in a positive direction.

One of the suggestions I have found helpful, especially when working with children, is to act "as if." In presenting self-esteem building and high-performance living programs to schools around the country, a common question asked by parents and teachers is "How do you help a child overcome his negative attitudes about himself, his feelings of inability, or the belief that "I can't"? Telling a child they shouldn't have a negative attitude, that their feelings are wrong, or responding to a certain belief by stating the opposite, is invalidating the child's experience. If one feels something and it's real to him, then having someone tell him that he really doesn't or shouldn't feel that way makes him feel even more inadequate.

I have found it helpful to acknowledge the person's experience or belief and then add the "what if"? "I know you feel like you have problems reading, but what would it be like if you could read well? How would you feel if you were a good reader? Let's pretend you're a good reader. Can you hear your mom or dad telling you how good you are? Can you see yourself reading a story to your little brother? If you read him a story and he was really happy how would you feel"? As those images start to take hold, they will begin to change the internal perception. It doesn't change overnight, but by validating the child's experience first, and then helping them create a different image, the inner resistance will shift as you move forward with applied practice.

I have used this approach while teaching kids gymnastics and the use of the trampoline. When they are learning a new skill involving some risk it's natural to be afraid. The common response is "I can't." My response is, "That's right, you can't but you're ready to learn it so we're going to do it. Let's pretend you already know how to do this skill. What does it feel like? What do you see? What do you hear?" These images start the mental programming so there is less resistance to moving forward. The student's experience of fear has been validated, and a way to move past it has been provided. Depending on the person involved, "let's pretend" or "act as if" is a way to use the imagination that can be an effective way to change the self-image. The result is a change of behavior.

I have found that most people use this process in terms of visualizing a new self-image based on material success. That's fine, and there is nothing wrong with that, but here is an invitation to play at a higher level. What would it be like, what would you experience and look like if you were living your life in complete alignment with spiritual principles as a divine being made in the image and likeness of God? If you were living and expressing the teaching, qualities and virtues demonstrated by Jesus Christ, Buddha or the many saints and prophets of differing religions, but all with a love of God, how would you see yourself? What would the image look like? How would it feel? What would you hear? What would the quality of your life and relationships be like? How would you conduct yourself in business and your professional life?

Again, remember, the more sensory-rich detail you can use, the clearer you can see, hear and feel the desired experience, or spiritual quality the more effective you will be in overriding and re-scripting past programming. As these inner pictures change, so do the commands to the nervous system, thus moving a person in the direction of intended change.

Most of us expend a considerable amount of effort trying to change our circumstances but we resist changing ourselves. Our external circumstances can never change until we do. Inner beliefs drive actions. These in turn create outer results. So change the internal pictures first, build the thought-form with the imagination and appropriate action will follow.

In any situation there is the way we perceive ourselves, the way others see us and the way we truly are. The first step is to observe yourself. How do you see yourself as a parent, spouse, employer, employee, mentor, learner, healer, victim or whatever the various roles you play? If you have someone you trust, who will give you honest feedback; ask him his perception of you in 2 or 3 different roles.

In your imagination start building a new thought-form of your ideal self. How would you look, act, feel, perform, sound if you were living your life as this person. Just as you wrote out your VAK statements in the goal setting process do the same with the image of your ideal self. See, hear and feel what it is like now that you have achieved in your imagination the realization of your ideal self. Do this visualization several times a day. As the thought-form grows in strength it will begin to over ride the old self-image. Begin to think and act the way you would once you have become the person you aspire to be. This doesn't happen over-night but if you do it consistently the changes will inevitably happen. One thought to keep in mind. This image is only a thought-form that will guide and enhance your behavior and performance. *It is not who you are.*

CHAPTER 15

THE MAGIC OF MEANING

As we grow, and move up the living continuum, we learn that the meaning we ascribe to an experience affects our perception of that event, as well as the effect that the experience has upon us. The following is an example of how meaning effects health and one's quality of life.

In 1972 by the Massachusetts Department of Health, Education and Welfare observed that the majority of people who suffered a heart attack before the age of 50 did not have the four physical risk factors associated with a heart attack. They didn't smoke. They didn't have high blood pressure. They didn't have high cholesterol, and they didn't have diabetes. Those are the four physical red flags that indicate you may be a candidate for a heart attack. The Department wanted to find out what would give them the ability to predict if a person would suffer a heart attack. They conducted a study to isolate the key elements that would give them that insight. They finally found the one factor that was predictable: job satisfaction.

Another interesting fact that relates meaning to health is that more heart attacks occur at 9:00 AM on Monday morning than at any other time. Is it the fact that it is the beginning of a new work week that is the cause of heart attacks, or the stress and physical response caused by the meaning that people ascribe to Mondays?

E+R=O

As we begin to understand the power that meaning has in our lives, we begin to learn how to use that force to our advantage. When something happens it's not so much the event that matters but our response to it that makes the difference. For the most part events in life are not necessarily good or bad. It is the meaning we ascribe to events and how we choose to see them that determines our experience. This is summed up in a short formula expressed as E+R=O.

"E" stands for an Event. Many events that happen in our lives are beyond our control. Or, perhaps we are not conscious of our role in creating the event never the less it still *seems* beyond our control. "R" stands for the Response. We can't necessarily control the event, but we can learn to consciously choose our response. The response we choose will determine the outcome, which is the "O". The **Event + Response = Outcome**. The best way to influence the response is to become aware of and consciously choose the mental and emotional programming that is going onto the "tapes" we play in our thoughts. It also requires us to accept responsibility for our thoughts, actions and the results we create.

The power of this process is described in courses taught by Creative Healing and the Institute of Recovery Sciences. These educational programs teach people who suffer from chronic pain to change the meaning of the experience, and thereby alter the brain and nervous system's response to it. When the nervous system receives stimuli, such as a pin-prick to the finger it transmits that message to the brain. The brain interprets the sensory message as pain and relays that experience to the nerves and tissue at the location of the injury. With practice, we can learn to substitute a different meaning for the experience so that the brain interprets the nerve signal differently. The result is a diminished experience of pain, or no pain at all.

Changing Meaning, Changes Experience

The power to change meaning, and thereby alter one's experience, has a direct effect on the cells and nervous system. When we perceive an unexpected event as a threat, the sympathetic nervous system reacts and mobilizes our body into the fight-or-flight mode. The hypothalamus and pituitary activate our adrenals and pump adrenaline in to our system. This produces cortisol. This chemical puts us on edge and narrows our focus to deal with the threat. The immediate psychological effect is that it limits our ability to learn and restricts our perceived choices.

When we choose to interpret that same event as a learning experience or an adventure, our body's response releases ATHC, interferons and interlukens. These chemicals put our body in a state of optimal awareness, receptivity, and performance. By changing meaning, which is a choice, we instantly change the effect of our body's biochemistry. Its effect is immediate. In Neuro Linguistic Programming, this process of ascribing a different meaning to an event to alter one's experience of it is known as "reframing."

Reframing is changing the internal pictures created by an event or action in our mind to change our experience of the event. One example of using reframing to alter the intensity of an emotional experience is to change the mental pictures in our mind. If we have an argument that upsets us, we can mentally alter the appearance of the person we had the argument with. We might picture them with Mickey Mouse ears; add a Bozo nose and some goofy-looking hair. We could make the picture black and white or in color, brighter or darker. We could zoom the image farther away from ourselves, or bring it in closer.

Each one of these mental acts will produce a certain response in our nervous system, and the chemical activity in our body, thereby altering the physical effect the experience has on us. Try it, and observe how your feelings shift as you change the images.

Two Levels of Meaning

The meaning of an experience can be the result of a personal interpretation we choose to place upon it, or it can be the discovery of a deeper truth contained within the event or experience itself. By altering the meaning, we can alter the effect that the event has upon us. Thus we have the event, our experience of the event and a choice or interpretation of the meaning we ascribe to it. This is usually based on our past experience and limited understanding.

As we move up the living continuum we become aware of deeper meanings and hidden causes. Yes, we can change our interpretation and thereby alter our experience. However, when we understand that in some cases it is the soul or our higher self that is the cause and that the event is a needed experience to further our progress, meaning moves to a higher level.

A number of years ago, I was a part of a panel discussion held at a holistic health conference. One of the questions I asked the audience was, "How many of you became involved in holistic health, intentional personal growth, or a deeper spiritual search as the result of a serious illness?" About a third of the audience raised their hands. I then asked, "How many of you would say that the overall quality of your life has been significantly enriched as a result of what you've experienced in your quest for better health?" For the most part the same people raised their hands.

After the session several of the people came up to share their experiences. One woman had almost died as the result of her illness. She concluded her story by saying, "It was the best thing that ever happened to me because I never would have found the insights and realizations about my spiritual life had I not been faced with this crisis."

When there is a deeper cause to what is happening, our objective is to learn how to discern the underlying truth and adapt our life to work with it. We see that there is an inherent truth or essence to an experience. However, most of us interpret an event based on our present level of understanding. This is a result of our past programming. As we begin to work from a soul-inspired level, we begin to understand meaning in a much deeper way. We learn to trust the greater intelligence guiding the process as it unfolds and yet play our part as best we can.

If you are experiencing a serious illness take some time to journal and ask yourself what is the deeper meaning of this experience? What is the payoff or what are the benefits I am receiving from this situation? What is the gift in this condition? Ponder and meditate on these questions and you may be surprised at the things you discover. Don't rush the process. Just be present with it.

CHAPTER 16

EXPECTATIONS AND THEIR EFFECT

Since thoughts are things composed of mental substance we can begin to understand how our thoughts have an effect upon an event or experience. In fact, thoughts in the form of expectations have a powerful effect upon our own and other peoples' actions and behavior. An expectation is a thought-form that is magnetic in nature and works with the law of attraction. The form of the thought gives structure, definition and direction. As we have seen, thought is electrical in nature and whenever an electrical current is generated it will simultaneously generate a magnetic field. The magnetic effect of the frequency attracts or initiates activity in accordance with the mental construct. There have been over 450 studies done, demonstrating the effect that expectations have on the actions and behavior of others.[21]

Marilyn Schlitz and Stephen LeBarge, from Stanford University, conducted a study to see the effect that remote viewing would have on the autonomic nervous system of a group of volunteers. Two groups were formed. One group was designated to be the observers and the other was those being observed. The group being observed had the function of the autonomic nervous system monitored and recorded by instruments designed to detect subtle physiological changes. Unbeknown to those being tested, those in the observer group would stare at them from another room via closed circuit television at various intervals. The purpose of the experiment, which was not revealed to the participants, was to see if observation at a distance would affect the physiological functions of those being observed.

The people observing would cease staring for a period of time, and then resume the activity. Upon assessing the data that was being recorded from the response of the autonomic nervous system in those being viewed there was a substantial and measurable difference during the times when viewing occurred and when it did not. These findings led the researchers to conclude that observation and consciousness play a significant casual factor in influencing the outcome of a so-called "objective" experiment.

Richard Wiseman, a researcher from Cambridge University, was skeptical about the nature and reported results of the above study. He duplicated the experiment. In his experiment, the autonomic nervous system of the observed people showed no difference in activity when they were being observed and when they were not. Dr. Wiseman contacted Dr. Schlitz and reported that he had duplicated the experiment but had obtained different results. The researchers decided to perform the same experiment together. The only variable would be the person conducting it.

When Schlitz repeated the experiment, there was a notable difference in autonomic nervous system activity. When Wiseman performed the same experiment, in the same lab, with the same volunteers, there was no notable change. The researchers concluded that *the only variable* that changed between the two studies *was the expectation of the person conducting the experiment.*[22] In addition, there have been a number of studies in the field of education documenting that teachers with high expectations for their pupils achieve better performance from their students than do those teachers with lower expectations.

Expectations also have a direct effect on the nervous system and body chemistry of the person directing the thought in the form of an expectant belief. When thought is directed as a positive expectation the message that is delivered to the systems in the body is that the condition that is expected already exists. As a result of this command the nature and information of the messages carried through the nervous system change, hormonal activities change, the information being carried to and accepted by the cells is altered, and immune system responses all shift to come into alignment with the direction being communicated through the expectation.

Effects on the Nervous System

The Institute for Recovery Sciences uses expectations to help clients gain control over their chronic pain. By retraining their nervous system through the use of expectations, people are able to alter the nature of the messages being delivered. The expectation affects how the brain will interpret the message that is being communicated by the nervous system. An experience that would normally result in pain, can be altered by a person's beliefs or expectations, so rather than experiencing pain, the experience can be neutral or even positive. Expectations, properly used, can have a powerful effect in creating health and reversing chronic conditions.

I met a woman who had gone through a terrible auto accident, crushing her leg. After four surgeries the pain was still constant. Medication was of little help and she had to have her leg in a brace. The doctors said that they had done everything they possibly could that she would have to wear the brace for the rest of her life and just learn to live with the pain.

Depressed and angry she was resistant to taking a course using these techniques. How could thought, belief, meaning and expectations possibly have any effect on her pain where medication and surgery had failed? Fortunately for her, a friend insisted that she attend. The third day, she had one of those flashes of insight as to the power this work had and the effect it could have. She completed the course with a dramatic reduction of pain and an increased level of healing. When I heard her speak several years after her ordeal she said, "I play tennis, I run, I ride horses and I have my life back. I don't even know where the brace is." Numerous people who have gone through these courses have had equally amazing results.

One of the foundational teachings of this program is that the nervous system has the ability to modify the nature of its experience in accordance with that which it clearly understands. In a sense, the nervous system is plastic in that new information beliefs and expectations can mold its structure and change how it responds.

On Having No Expectations

There is another side to the understanding of expectations. Some schools of thought will suggest that we practice having no expectations. Expectations can skew perceptions and when unmet lead to disappointment.

A number of years ago I had the experience of being in a difficult business transaction with some friends. I knew how I would treat people, especially friends in this type of situation, and that's how I expected to be treated. However, it didn't work out that way. This unconscious use of an expectation on my part prevented me from acting according to the way things were rather than the way I thought they should be. In this case, the expectation led to disappointment and strained relationships. Having no expectation in this case would have allowed more clarity on my part. Setting a positive intention with respect to the desired outcome would have been a more effective, proactive way to deal with the situation.

There is much to be said about living our lives from a perspective of detachment from outcomes and specific results. This isn't to say that you don't have a clear direction with goals and objectives and that you're not making maximum effort. However, the intent is to do your best and let go of the result trusting a higher power.

On one level, we are going to make things happen the way we want them to happen and when we want them to happen. This "make it happen" approach has its merits but there is much truth in the saying, "If you want to make God laugh, tell him your plans." Besides, there is a higher level available from which to live and work. Do your best, let go of the result, and learn to work with a higher power trusting a greater guiding intelligence.

Most of us can think of times when we really wanted something to work out a certain way and when it didn't we were disappointed. Later on, as we looked back on the experience we saw how things did work out for the best even though it was disappointing at the time. Sometimes, life has a way of redirecting us in ways we're not aware of for our greater good. Detached effort without expectations has its place and dedicating the fruit of our actions to a Greater Power has a marvelous freeing effect.

As we begin to understand the energetic nature of thought and how it interfaces with the brain and nervous system we can begin to see how and why expectations have the effect they do. We are engaging the power of expectations all the time. The question is, are we doing so consciously? Are we actively using expectations as a tool, to create intended results, or passively being the recipient of their effect? They can either be the result of past programming and haphazardly formed, or they can be developed with conscious intent to produce specific results.

CHAPTER 17

POSITIVE MENTAL ATTITUDE

Most of us have heard about the power of positive thinking and the importance of having a positive mental attitude. An attitude is our mental and emotional disposition and outlook based on past programming, beliefs and expectations. It can also be the result of conscious intent. As we consciously choose our thoughts, we are able to rewrite the software of the mind. By learning to choose our interpretation of an experience we begin to alter the meaning, thus affecting the emotional and physical response.

Look For the Good

By choosing to develop a positive attitude we choose to look for the good in any situation that life offers. We may choose to look at difficulties as challenges that build strength. We may choose to focus our attention on what is good, true and beautiful, and to bring those qualities into relationships and daily encounters. Even if we are working in a situation we don't enjoy, or with someone we don't really like, we can choose to bring a high quality of living into the situation. Many times the situation is uplifted by people with the intent of seeing or creating something of goodness regardless of the external circumstances.

This intent and action will positively shift the energetic nature of the mental field and influence the quality of thought-forms being constructed. It will elicit positive biochemical activity and nervous system response. This not only has an effect upon us but it also has a direct effect upon others.

What We Send Out Comes Back

Our thoughts and actions send energy into the world. True to the law, the world will respond by sending back energy and experience of a like nature. This is the Universal Law of cause and effect, action and reaction, sequence and consequence. This is the Law of Karma, which states, "As ye sow, so shall ye reap." If you don't like what life is sending you, take a good look at what you're sending life.

The question of free will vs. destiny, has been one with which mankind has grappled for centuries. An understanding of the law of cause and effect gives us some insight to this question. Seeds in the form of thoughts or actions that have been planted in the past will eventually grow into their fullness. A man *will* reap what he has sown. This is our destiny, for we have all planted seeds in the past. Consciously choosing the quality and nature of the seeds we are planting in the present will determine what we reap in the future. This is free will.

By understanding the law and choosing to work with it, we can greatly affect our experiences. By choosing to have a positive attitude and looking for the good in life we have a very powerful effect on our health and the quality of life we experience.

CHAPTER 18

SELF-ESTEEM

The next emotional condition of health to develop is a strong sense of self-esteem or self-love. Self-esteem is a strong sense of self-worth or personal value based on feelings of meaning, purpose and significance. These qualities are built through meaningful achievement and affirming relationships. Perhaps the most powerful condition of health to build high self-esteem and a clear, healthy emotional field is unconditional love.

The word "love" in our society has been used in so many ways that there are many different understandings of what it really is. Some connotations are lofty and true, while some are quite base and perverse. Love in its essence is spiritual energy. Love is a free flowing, outgoing radiant, magnetically attractive force that soothes and heals. Love is harmless in thought and action. Love is not a sentiment or affectation, although those feelings are the result of the energy of love as it moves through the emotional field. Love is not proud, critical or judgmental. Love is understanding, accepting, and affirming. Love breaks down barriers and fuses diversity in union. Love is an act of the heart. As the heart center opens it has a healing effect on the entire system. The result of this is a commitment to nurture the spiritual growth of ourselves and others.

The nature of Love is selflessness. This is expressed through our thoughts and actions when our intention is to support others and do what is best for them. In order for a person to express and experience this quality of love, the emotional field must be clear, well-developed, and composed of a higher, more refined grade of matter. In the progression of development, an individual must first have a healthy sense of self-love before they can give love selflessly. The commandment to "Love thy neighbor as thyself" can only be fulfilled if you have genuine love yourself. One can't give what one doesn't have.

Emotional Nutrients

Unconditional Love is communicated through feelings of being understood, accepted and affirmed. As we grow up, these qualities are hopefully reflected back to us from the primary adult caregivers, in most cases, our parents. These emotional nutrients are essential for healthy development and growth. When these growth needs are not met, especially in early childhood, the necessary ingredients for building a healthy emotional field are not available. We saw this in our example of correlating the need of building materials for a house with nutrients needed to build a healthy physical body. In the same way we must have the necessary building materials for developing healthy emotions.

It is clear that the house won't be stable if it is missing essential building material. So it is with our mental and emotional health as well. If the programming a child receives is negative it poisons the field and creates a toxic, painful emotional state. The way most people cope with this is to shut down emotionally so they don't feel anything. They may erect a barrier to protect themselves. However, this not only numbs one to the experience of negative emotional energy it also blocks the emotional nutrients necessary for health. The result of this toxic emotional state is that it poisons the quality of life and eventually leads to physical disease.

In extreme cases this leads to a person who is incapable of caring. The emotional field is so poisoned or so poorly developed that it can't register the experience of a more refined emotion such as the quality of appreciation or care. The result of this tragic numbness is being reflected more and more by the growing number of violent crimes committed by children without a conscience. There is nothing that has been built into their lives or emotional constitution that registers right and wrong. They have never received love and respect, so they don't know what it is. Therefore, they are not capable of giving it. In extreme cases we see people who have been so poisoned by negative emotional programming that they go on a rampage killing innocent people and then themselves.

Growth Needs vs Deficiency Needs

When these growth needs of love, care, affection, attention, understanding, acceptance and affirmation are not built into the emotional field the result is a deficiency in the conditions needed to build emotional health. This is similar to deficiency conditions in the physical body. When there is a deficiency in vitamin C, the result is scurvy, a deficiency in vitamin B causes Pellagra, and a vitamin-D deficiency leads to rickets. Negative programming and absence of emotional nutrients are the primary causes of mental and emotional "dis-ease" and of outward expressions of violence, substance abuse and other forms of abuse directed inwardly or toward others.

There is much evidence that points to the fact that an absence of these *growth needs* or emotional nutrients is the cause of addiction. When the parent or significant adult does not meet these growth needs, the emotional field in the child lacks the substance necessary for healthy development. The child is starved for nutrients. As a result, the child experiences feelings of emotional hunger, of emptiness and abandonment. These feelings culminate in what has been referred to by John Bradshaw as "the hole in the soul." This "hole" is an inner void that continually drives a person and demands to be filled. The problem is that it makes no difference how much external stimulus one pours in - it always leaks out.

Many experts have come to believe this is the underlying cause of addiction. It doesn't matter whether the addiction is drugs, alcohol, tobacco, sex, overeating, shopping, work or television. They all have the same basic underlying cause. The inner void demands to be filled and compulsively drives a person towards that end. The physical addiction takes the edge off the emotional grating that a person feels. In some cases, it can shut us down and numb our ability to feel the pain. In other cases where we are already living life numbly, getting drunk or high is the only thing that allows us to feel anything.

As our understanding of this grows, we can begin to see how much physical disease is emotionally based. We know the foods, substances and other activities that damage our health, and yet we are compulsively driven to use them. The emotional need then becomes a physical addiction. The consequent damage follows, and the real cause is never addressed. In our society some businesses understand this and purposefully design their products and advertising to fuel this addiction.

Alcohol companies often target people that already have a tendency towards alcoholism and tobacco companies target young people in "search of an identity." If people don't have a strong, healthy sense of self or identity they are easy prey to those who will provide that image for them with their products. The damage that alcohol, drugs and tobacco have on the physical body is indisputable.

Is it possible that the negative emotions creating and releasing toxic chemicals and sending erroneous messages to the cells are equally as damaging?

As we consciously choose to develop and communicate unconditional love through expressing understanding, acceptance and affirmation, our own personal growth and wellness is enhanced. As we consciously choose to incorporate these qualities into our lives, we also help to fulfill these conditions of health in others. We are building healthy relationships that will strengthen the energetic quality of the mental and emotional fields. This is essential to everyone and it is especially important for our children.

Understanding

The first of these mental and emotional nutrients is understanding. This means taking time to connect by listening. True listening is actually a giving of oneself through the mental attention that is directed towards another. It is an expression of respect and a giving of value to the other person by recognizing that the part of themselves they are sharing is worthy of attention. Through genuine listening, there is an exchange of emotional energy. Through this exchange of emotional energy, a deeper understanding occurs. There is an energetic bond that is being built and an exchange of emotional nutrients.

True understanding is genuinely hearing, seeing and experiencing what the other person is saying, thinking and feeling. It is apprehending the meaning behind the words. It means suspending judgment or analysis, and being receptive and accepting of another's experience. We could say that true understanding is an exchange of emotional energy. This form of listening is called empathetic or empathic listening. Like any skill it is one that can be cultivated and strengthened by conscious effort.

How often do we find ourselves in a conversation thinking of how we want to respond, instead of hearing what the other person is saying and experiencing? Is that really listening? Is true communication really taking place? When we listen with the intent of converting or winning an argument what is being communicated? Is this valuing the person or judging them? In this case there is no real connection and no exchange of healthy emotional energy.

True understanding makes judgment impossible. It communicates to the other person a sense of value and worth. Understanding is the basis of right human relations which is an expression of selflessness and support. It is essential for healthy individuals and a healthy society. As Steven Covey so eloquently stated, "Seek first to understand, then to be understood."

Acceptance

The second way to nurture and communicate love is through acceptance. This means we take time to consider what another person perceives and feels to be true. We accept others for who and what they are, just as they are. Acceptance can be a willingness to receive, or an ability to tolerate. It can be an active giving or a passive, yet discerning, receiving.

The act of acceptance is learning to separate others from their actions and beliefs. When people are expressing themselves and we are accepting them, it doesn't mean that we have to agree with them. However, as we grow in our understanding that our thoughts and actions are the result of past programming, we can learn to accept other viewpoints as being valid for them just as our viewpoints are for us. By accepting others, we validate them for who they are. This intent can strengthen our ability to love. It's not always easy to accept someone who has differing viewpoints; however, it is a challenge that can build strength within us.

Before we can truly accept others we must first accept ourselves. This does not mean that we stop aspiring to constantly improve. It does mean that we recognize our assets and liabilities as they are. We then accept that this is where we are as a result of past experiences, and that in spite of all our mistakes and flaws "we're okay." We can't move in a meaningful direction until we first accept who we are. The act of consciously choosing acceptance builds a strong sense of self-worth in our self and others while helping to clear the emotional field and open it to the healing inflow of love.

When we love or dislike someone they are reflecting back to us something that we love or dislike within ourselves. This serves as an opportunity to identify and clear thought-forms in our field, or certain traits about our self that block the flow of love. Through the act of consciously choosing acceptance we can begin to clear our emotional field, thus allowing a greater flow of love to move through us. As we grow in spiritual strength the act of acceptance allows us to take a negative, lower energy into ourselves and transmute it through the intent of focused love. This action can heal and strengthen all concerned. It certainly is an act of a spiritual warrior.

Affirmation

The third ingredient to building self-esteem and communicating unconditional love is being affirmed. This means that we play an important, contributing role in the lives of others. We give of ourselves in a meaningful way. This is a key in building positive, healthy relationships, through which value and worth are reflected back to us. We are affirmed by knowing that we are an important and necessary part of a greater whole. This includes our many friendships, our family, our country and the world. Meaningful work that contributes to the well-being of others, or a higher purpose, creates a greater sense of value in life. Affirming ourselves, and building value in the lives of others, is something we can consciously chose to do daily.

These three qualities, as well as others, are effective ways to communicate and experience unconditional love that builds a strong, healthy emotional field. For the most part, mental and emotional diseases are results of an absence of the love, care, affection, and attention that children need from their parents or significant adults to assure that growth needs are met. Unconditional love is the most powerful antidote for mending "the hole in the soul."

Love and Physical Health

More and more doctors are coming to the belief that unconditional love plays a key role in the maintenance of physical health as well. Dr. Bernie Siegal, a professor of medicine at Yale, works with terminal cancer patients. He has made the observation that unconditional love appears to have a very powerful stimulating effect on the immune system strengthening one's ability to fight disease. Lack of unconditional love, or conditional love (I'll love you if...) seems to act as a depressant on the immune system, lowering its resistance. Dr. Siegal said, "I feel that healing is related to the ability to give and receive unconditional love. I am convinced that unconditional love is the most powerfully known stimulant of the immune system there is." This is something we can choose to build into our lives.

Caroline Thomas, a researcher at Johns Hopkins Medical School, wanted to find out the relationship between personality traits, emotional attitudes and disease. Between 1948 and 1964, she studied thirteen hundred medical students. The students were given a number of physical and psychological tests and were interviewed extensively about their personal history and family relationships. Over the years, as the older physicians began to succumb to different diseases, a pattern emerged. Dr. Thomas noticed that the people who had developed cancer had reported being emotionally distant from their parents and had memories of inharmonious family relations early in life. The negative emotions that resulted from these early childhood experiences had been bottled up with no avenues of expression or release.[23] As we have seen through our study of the energy fields and the chakra system, energy must flow or it will stagnate with unhealthy consequences.

In another study conducted at Harvard, it was found that many people who suffer from cancer and autoimmune diseases often have three psychodynamics present. These three are guilt, depression, and low self-esteem, a lack of self-love. The target organ of unreleased emotion is the immune system.

Immune System Suppression

What is the physical result of these negative emotions? Depression, grief and fear suppress the thymus gland. As we have seen, the thymus gland acts as a controlling mechanism for the regulation and distribution of energy throughout the body. It is the controlling gland for the immune system. Lymphocytes or white blood cells are manufactured in the bone marrow and then transported to the thymus where they mature under the influence of growth hormones. They are then transported to the lymph nodes and spleen where a second generation of T-cells are formed.

The T-cells are programmed to distinguish self from not-self and to destroy foreign cells. This immuneological surveillance system is responsible for identifying, attacking, and destroying invading bacteria, viruses and cancer cells. When the thymus gland gradually shuts down as the result of experiencing negative emotions that have been bottled up for years the ability to manufacture lymphocytes and T-cells is diminished and so is the effectiveness of the immune system.

As we understand the power that negative emotions have on our immune system and our quality of life it becomes imperative that we learn how to deal with them. When we understand that many of the emotional patterns we are unconsciously running, or should we say, are unconsciously running us, we can see the need to learn how to re-pattern the flow of energy and heal ourselves on an emotional level. When we accept ourselves for where we are on the path with our flaws and all, we can look at therapy in a different light. Rather than approaching it with the attitude of "I'm broken, and I need to be fixed," we can look at different therapies as resources and an opportunity to grow.

As parents, it is up to us to model a healthy way of working with our emotions. Avoid the use of negative emotions such as guilt or shame as a means to discipline children. It may be effective in the short run, however, when negative emotions are used to discipline or control they become a pattern locked in the emotional field and the long-term damage will far outweigh any short-term benefits of convenience. The past programming of negative emotions such as guilt and shame can be very difficult to overcome, and dramatically inhibit the quality and experience of our life. As parents, when we model human relations based on respect, cooperation and caring communication we begin to break up the destructive cycle of patterns that have been handed down from generation to generation.

CHAPTER 19

FORGIVENESS

One of the key components in cultivating unconditional love and allowing its distribution and expression is forgiveness. The act of forgiveness is also an essential process for clearing the emotional field of destructive, toxic thought forms and developing it in a healthy, vital manner. There is a growing body of evidence in the field of psychology that demonstrates the unwillingness or inability to forgive and related attitudes of resentment and bitterness are among the deadliest dynamics in the human psyche.

Often, when we have been wronged, injured or victimized, the last thing we want to do is to forgive. For most of us, our current belief about forgiveness is that it is a weakness. The truth is that it takes tremendous courage and strength to forgive. Mahatma Gandhi summed it up when he said, "The weak can never forgive. Forgiveness is the attribute of the strong." For the most part, the present consciousness of humanity extols the false values and virtues of revenge. This just perpetuates the flow of negative energy and increases its destructiveness. Much suffering could be prevented, and emotional pain healed, if more people had the strength and courage to forgive.

To Give Forth

Forgiveness is not necessarily about pardoning a wrong or forgetting what happened. If we examine the word "forgiveness" and break it down, it means "to give forth"-- to give forth love, to give forth compassion, to give forth understanding. "Resist not evil but overcome evil with good" is an example of proactively giving forth.

An article in Parade Magazine described people who had lost children or parents through murder, and how they responded to the killer. All felt rage and desire for revenge at first. For many people those emotions were gradually changed by a different viewpoint.[24]

One man, whose grandmother had been brutally murdered by a 15-year-old girl, shared his emotional change of heart when he learned of her emotionally traumatic history of abuse and neglect over the years. He contacted her in prison, and went to visit her. Over the years, they have exchanged over 400 letters. He didn't pardon or forget but he did understand. As a result, he has been able to heal some of the emotional trauma within himself, clear the blockage of love in his life, and move to a new level of freedom. By holding on to the anger and hate, even though conventional thinking says he may have been justified in doing so, he would have continued to damage himself physically and poison his life spiritually.

The best definition of forgiveness I have ever heard comes from Dr. Guy Petit who uses a forgiveness process as a part of his practice. Dr. Petit says, "Forgiveness is the cancellation of all conditions in my mind and emotions that block the flow of love, independently of the behavior of anyone else." That is a very powerful statement and affirmation, which accepts total responsibility for a person's commitment to love.

Forgiveness and Physical Health

What are the physical results of forgiveness? One of Dr. Petit's experiences included a woman whose blood pressure was extremely high. He worked on identifying issues that needed to be released through forgiveness. In a few sessions of clearing the blockage and releasing the past, the patient's blood pressure moved down into the normal range with no medication.[25] We already have a good understanding of what happens to our immune system and body chemistry with stress and negative emotions. Often times many adverse effects can be prevented by cultivating forgiveness.

Don't wait for physical problems to happen. If there are people in your life that you need to forgive, become aware of it and start the process. This is not necessarily easy, but it is well worth the effort. Choose to give forth unconditional love. If it is appropriate, you may want to contact the offending party and start building the bridge of greater understanding. This can result in healing and positive growth on both sides.

The Courage to Heal

If you have hurt others, or have been perceived as the origin of an offense, rather than defending your position, listen to what is being said, sense what they are experiencing, do your best to understand from their viewpoint, and then work from that position. If appropriate, acknowledge your part, and take responsibility. Far from being weak, this act of giving forth love requires real courage. My experience has been that when dealing with inappropriate actions or misunderstandings which have caused hard feelings, and my intention is to remedy the situation, I've said, "I'm not clear on what caused the misunderstanding or bad feelings, but I'd like to heal it." If one is genuinely sincere, in most cases, the other person will usually acknowledge some part in contributing to the problem and help to clear the air.

The several times that I've had the opportunity to do this, it has been a little uncomfortable to initiate the process. However, when I entered with the intent of healing, in most cases the results were positive. Practice forgiveness. "Give forth" of yourself. This healing process may be helpful even if you weren't at fault, or were not the cause of the problem. It's not always appropriate, but when it is, accepting responsibility for your part, and moving forward with the intent to heal, can be very beneficial. There is a question posed in *A Course in Miracles* that says, "Would you rather be right, or would you rather be happy?" By actively engaging in the forgiveness process you may not only prevent a physical illness from occurring but could also dramatically increase the quality of your life and strengthen your relationships.

A Time for Reconciliation

This principle of initiating the forgiveness process is actively put into practice through an act called the "Reconciliation Walk." This project was sponsored by organization known as Youth With A Mission or YWAM. This missionary organization organized this project with the purpose of starting to heal a 900-year-old wound caused by the Crusades. For three years, a group of several hundred Christians retraced the route of the Crusaders asking forgiveness from the Muslims, Jews and Orthodox Christians for the atrocities that were committed against their ancestors.

The damage caused by the Crusaders has left a wound that has yet to heal even to this day. Much of the antagonism that exists between Muslims, Jews and Western Christians can be traced to the actions of the Crusaders. In the course of their marches, the Crusaders pillaged and plundered their way through Europe, Turkey and other countries. When they conquered Jerusalem on July 15, 1099, they butchered every man, woman and child, Muslim, Jew and Christian, in the city.

The hatred this legacy caused is still reflected in the psychological barrier of fear and distrust that pervades the region. To this day, the word for Crusader in Turkish means "man of the cross." It still carries the image of a crazed butcher justifying his actions under the banner of the cross. The prevalent perception of Western Christians is still associated with this image.

To take the first step in healing this wound, small teams of people participating in the Reconciliation Walk traveled through the cities, towns and villages visiting with local officials and people asking forgiveness, and presenting the following statement.

> "Nine hundred years ago, our forefathers carried the name of Jesus Christ in battle across the Middle East. Fueled by fear, greed and hatred, they betrayed the name of Christ by conducting themselves in a manner contrary to his wishes and character. The Crusaders lifted the banner of the cross above your people. By this act they corrupted its true meaning of reconciliation, forgiveness and selfless love.

> "On the anniversary of the First Crusade, we also carry the name of Christ. We wish to retrace the steps of the Crusaders in apology for their deeds and in demonstration of the true meaning of the cross. We deeply regret the atrocities committed in the name of Christ by our predecessors. We renounce greed, hatred and fear, and condemn all violence done in the name of Jesus Christ.

"Where they were motivated by hatred and prejudice, we offer love and brotherhood. Jesus came to give life. Forgive us for allowing His name to be associated with death."

Because those who participated in this walk have truly been motivated by a spirit of love and brotherhood with no strings attached the message has been well received by most Muslims and Jews along the route with a genuine forgiveness and healing taking place. Often, after the initial skepticism and suspicion have been overcome, the Christians have been invited into peoples' homes to stay for a few days. Some reported that in spite of the religious, cultural and language differences, they experienced more love and a deeper sense of sharing with these total strangers than at home in their own congregations. As a result of the commitment and sacrifice by these people, bridges of love, understanding, acceptance and genuine respect have been built and a gaping chasm of a 900-year-old wound has begun to heal.

The people who initiated this action were not personally responsible for the damage done 900 years ago. Nevertheless, they had the wisdom and compassion to see the generational pain resulting from of this atrocity and the courage to take the initiative to do something about it. They took responsibility as true followers of Christ today for the damage that so-called Christians had done in the past. The result is that they enriched their lives and the lives of those whom they touched. There are many places in our world where similar courageous actions would greatly aid in the reconciliation of different peoples, ethnic groups and races. This would both prevent further damage from being done and it would begin to foster a genuine spirit of goodwill and brotherhood that would make the world a better place for all.

Although we can't change the past, we can begin to heal the present. In our own country this reconciliation and healing is something that needs to be done with those who have been wronged. As a nation, we enslaved the black race and engaged in the systematic extermination of the original inhabitants of this continent. By acknowledging the wrongs done, asking forgiveness, and moving forward with the intent to heal, we can be effective in solving many problems without perpetuating a victim consciousness in those who have suffered. When we see the positive effect that the reconciliation walk had in demonstrating the healing power of forgiveness, it is clear that those principles could have the same affect in healing the wounds caused by our forefathers.

As we look at forgiveness in the context of what we've learned about the energetic nature of thought and emotion, we are able to perceive a deeper understanding of what is happening in this process. Energy follows thought, and when that thought is directed with clarity and intent, it takes on a form constructed of mental substance. When that form is imbued with emotional energy, it literally takes on a life of its own. A thought-form charged with the energy of hatred creates a "presence" that is toxic to everyone who comes within its sphere of influence and it can affect emotional fields as well. This thought-form becomes a living entity and can grow to the point that it begins to drain energy from its creator. This can be observed in people who become obsessed with their own ideas to the point of fanaticism.

The act of giving forth love is a conscious choice which stops the flow of negative emotional energy. This results in a devitalization of the negative thought-form. Without energy, the form dies. It takes an act of will to redirect the mental energy and turn off the flow of negative emotional force.

The Transformative Power of Giving Forth

I had an experience several years ago of the transformative power of giving forth goodness. I had been involved in a presentation for several thousand people. The success of the program had been dependent on the sound system. The night before we were to perform, a rainstorm occurred and moisture got into the sound system. That morning, one of the new and inexperienced employees came in to set everything up. He made the mistake of turning on the power. There was a rather unpleasant noise of "poof," accompanied by a light-colored puff of smoke. We knew he had just fried the system.

The owner of the system who had contracted for the event let us know that a brand new $5,000 amplifier had been ruined. He and his team frantically began to get things working before the opening presentation, which was our performance. The time ticked away, and we waited. Fifteen minutes to go, ten minutes to go, five and then two minutes to our presentation time. At a minute before the scheduled starting time, I tracked down a different microphone to make an announcement that we were having a few technical difficulties and that the program would be delayed a few minutes. I politely thanked the audience for their patience and asked them to bear with us for a few minutes.

To me, this seemed to be a very reasonable course of action, considering the situation. However, the sound director didn't respond that way. He jumped all over me for making the announcement. "What are you doing, telling them that there are problems with the sound," he yelled. "This isn't my fault." I was taken off guard by his response, and a little stunned by the blast of his anger. He continued to yell, foaming at the mouth for another twenty seconds and then stomped away.

I had an automatic response of wanting to verbally defend myself and retaliate. As the anger started to well up in me I took a couple of deep breaths and reflected internally redirecting my attention. This helped to diffuse its power. I don't remember exactly what I said but it was something in the form of an apology. I remember thinking that the poor guy had just been stressed out.

Even then, I was still rattled inside by the experience and could feel the anger boiling. Fortunately I had enough experience with a meditative process that allows one to connect with an inner source of peace and to redirect emotional energy so I chose to change it. I started sending this person light and prayer. Basically, I did the best I could to send forth goodness and quell my own inner emotional turmoil. That process continued for about ten minutes or so. I kept shifting focus from the anger that I wanted to wallow in and the fact that this guy was a jerk and an idiot to, "He's a brother in pain. Keep sending him love and light."

Within fifteen or twenty minutes, this fellow, who had become as "fried" as his sound system came back to me and profusely apologized for the way he had acted. The sound was working and he told me, "If you need *anything,* ask me, and I'll take care of it." For the rest of the event, the sound director was my best friend and proved to be a tremendous help in a number of situations.

I sometimes reflect on that experience and think of what would have happened if I had matched his anger in my response. No doubt, it would have escalated and turned into a lose/lose situation of one person trying to harm the other and get the last punch in. We've all seen those situations and the damage they cause. It doesn't always work out this way, but my experience has been that by giving forth goodness and letting go of the results there is a positive flow of energy created that can counter the negative and initiate healing.

What can we do to enhance this power of forgiving by giving forth love? First, a willingness to release the past creates a space for something new. This may be easier when someone brings a positive experience as a replacement for the past negativity. This is what happened as a result of the Reconciliation Walk. Those participating had a genuine remorse for the past and a sincere intent to heal and replace hate and fear with love and respect. Even if the offending party does not participate the willingness to let go and refocus your attention can begin to take the toxic emotional charge out of the past experience.

Dr. Troy Giles, president of Complete Wellness Systems uses a very simple forgiveness technique in his practice. He has his patients make a list of things under three headings.

1. Things I did I wish I hadn't done.
2. Things I didn't do I wish I would have done.
3. Things that were done to me that caused harm.

The first two heading are about forgiving our self and the third is about forgiving others. The patient lies down and thinks of an issue on the list. They then take a deep breath and hold it as long as possible while continuing to think of the event that needs to be forgiven. There comes a point of tension when the body must absolutely have air and the physical tension created over rides the trauma of the harmful event and reboots the system. In most cases this will diffuse the emotional charge associated with the offending event and allow an experience of forgiveness to replace it.

Second, the act of reframing the hurtful event or offense in the imagination begins to break down the old form and create a new one to take its place. As we take a past event and reconstruct it mentally in a form we would have preferred the new form gradually assumes control. As we learned earlier, one technique is to take the event and mentally replay it so that it turns out the way you would have preferred it to be. Then deeply feel love, compassion and empathy towards the person while understanding all have weaknesses. When we do this visualization consistently in rich, sensory detail, it has the effect of re-patterning the nervous system. The message that is being sent is changed and so is the response. When done on an individual level, the new, positive thought-form creates an improved level of health in our biochemistry, and constructs new neural pathways. This changes our experience in the present and diffuses the power of the past event. When done on a collective level it begins to devitalize the old thought-form and create a new one that is in alignment with the principles of health.

Third, the process of giving forth love or compassion in a counseling session, a forgiveness encounter, or any situation where true communication and heartfelt connection are desired can be enhanced by the following practice. Focus your attention on your heart center. Then, using the creative imagination extend a line of light from your heart to the heart center of the person you are sharing with and hold that awareness. Next, direct your awareness to the top of your head and project a shaft of light from your crown center to source, God, or whatever your understanding of the greatest good is. Imagine the beam of light coming down from Source into the crown center of the person with whom you are communicating. There is now a triangle of light connecting you with the other person, via the heart center and with Source, via the crown. Once this has been established continue the communication with the intention of the highest and best good of all concerned and release any preconceived results.

Fourth, consciously choose the meaning that is given to the perceived offense. When you choose the meaning you ascribe to an event or action the response to the event and the affect it has on one is also changed. Over time, you may find a deeper meaning than was originally perceived. Personal growth and deeper understanding may be a result that would not have been possible any other way. In this case, the practice of appreciation would be an effective form of giving forth. There may be a deeper meaning to the hurtful experience of which we have not been aware. By practicing appreciation and looking for the gift in the difficulty we minimize the negative effect by countering it with a positive flow of healthy emotion. This intention will build strength within us to generate the needed change.

Forgiveness is a powerful force, although, as we have seen, not necessarily an easy one to wield. Consciously choosing to use this force engages the Law of Cause and Effect in a beneficial way. As we forgive those who have trespassed against us we too are forgiven. If we have knowingly or unknowingly sown any negative or destructive seeds in the past our actions and thoughts in the present will help to off-set the consequences. The more we give forth to life the more life gives forth to us.

CHAPTER 20

PURPOSE

Without a doubt, the power of purpose is one of the most powerful forces for directing, enhancing and strengthening our life. Just as we learned that meaning can be experienced on two levels - the meaning we ascribe to an event and the understanding that there is a deeper reality that is the cause behind the event we see or experience - so is the experience of purpose found on several different levels. Our experience of purpose will vary according to the point of personal growth and spiritual development. To simplify: there is selfish purpose, selfless purpose, and the purpose of the soul or divine purpose.

At its most basic level, purpose is the "why" we do what we do. For the majority of humanity, it is based on "I want." I want this, I want that, I want a partner, I want money, I want…, I want…, I want… There is nothing really wrong with this, however, there is no end to the "I wants." The primary motive for this is the desire for happiness, which is inherent in all of us. It is the belief that if "I have" then I will be happy. There are enough books written on how to get what you want, and there are plenty of examples of people who have everything except happiness, so we won't belabor the point.

Eventually, people reach a point where they realize that there is something more besides aspiring to fulfill the "I wants." Instead of looking for purpose in acquiring things there begins a search for greater fulfillment and deeper meaning. This is often experienced as a crisis, and marks the beginning of our spiritual quest. From that point on, there is a gradual shifting away from the values based on "I want" to bring them into alignment with a higher purpose.

Personal Purpose to Soul's Purpose

As we progress upward on the wellness continuum in our spiritual growth we learn to let go of the things that no longer serve us and live by a higher set of guiding values and principles. The purpose of our being changes and our motive gradually moves from "I want to have" to "I choose to grow" and eventually to "I choose to give" or simply, "I serve." Eventually, our personal purpose grows into an alignment with the higher purpose of our soul. Sometimes this comes about when our soul creates circumstances to redirect our path and bring our actions into alignment with our deepest purpose. It's been said that some people only look to God when their foundations are being shaken, only to learn that it is God who is shaking the foundation.

My own personal experience is that when one's higher-self or soul moves in to influence the lower-self or personality's direction, it is experienced as a crisis. In the preface I shared a story about how spirit showed up as a pain in my knee that was a way of redirecting my life. According to six doctors there was nothing wrong with my knee. I just couldn't use it. The seventh doctor after assessing the knee on a physical level concluded there was nothing wrong so he used intuition to assess the bigger picture. There was nothing physically wrong with my knee, but he sensed there was something wrong with my life and it was showing up in my knee.

As I look back on that experience it was a wonderful lesson in being willing to accept guidance from a higher source. The part of me that loved the adventure and thrill of professional acrobatic skiing was disappointed. However, I had been consciously aspiring to walk the spiritual path for a while and I had some understanding of the process. I knew that when we turn our life over to a greater power and aspire to put our life in alignment with God's greater purpose the rules of the game change. Had I not understood this it would have been a very difficult and painful experience because of my past tendency to hold on to the familiar and to try to go back. It was extremely beneficial for me to be aware of the meaning behind the event so I could work with it rather than resist.

As you reflect on your life and present condition ask, "What is my purpose? Why am I on this planet at this time? Do my actions reflect the higher values that are hopefully guiding my life? Am I aspiring daily to live according to the highest truth I know? Is my job or profession in alignment with my soul's intent?

We have looked at the relationship between heart disease, stress, and doing a job we dislike. We now understand that mental and emotional stress has a shock-like effect resulting in a condition causing disease. We have also seen that positive stress is necessary to build strength. Often, the difference between positive and negative stress lies in our viewpoint, how we choose to look at a situation, and the meaning we ascribe to it. However, there is no greater stress than being out of alignment with your purpose and that tension will precipitate a crisis.

Earlier, I shared the experience of asking an audience how many of them had been involved in holistic health as the result of a serious illness and if that had turned out to be a positive experience. Several people reported that even though it was difficult, painful, and life-threatening, it had been the best experience of their life because of the change and growth that had resulted.

The Crisis of Breaking Through

For the most part, we experience life through the mental and emotional filters created by our belief systems. We live according to our family, our cultural and our societal programming, and we create our own purpose accordingly. That's fine; however, there is something beyond that. Sometimes it does take a crisis to break through the old programming and pave the way for a higher understanding. Sometimes, old forms do need to be destroyed in order to allow for a greater expression of life.

Each of us has a part to play in a plan greater than our personal lives. Each of us has a unique contribution to make to life that only we can make. Finding that purpose and direction can be a real challenge. Yet if the intent is there we will find it. Regardless of the activity, if we aspire to live, not just to believe, but to embody and express our higher qualities then we are in the process of coming into alignment with soul's purpose.

As we take the time through prayer, meditation, solitude and silence, to build that bridge with our soul and the Creator we will start to understand the greater purpose for this life. As we cleanse and purify our physical, mental and emotional bodies and bring them into alignment, the soul increasingly has a responsive instrument to use in furthering its purpose.

CHAPTER 21

SOULFUL LIVING

Throughout this program, we have focused on the physical, emotional and mental conditions necessary to build optimal health. As we walk the path and move up the wellness continuum we consciously choose to develop the physical body and the energy fields. As this process continues the physical body and energy fields become stronger, more refined, purified, and synchronized. This is the process of coordinating, aligning and integrating the different energies into one functioning unit. This process is called "personality integration." It is an important part of our spiritual journey.

On several occasions the word "soul" has been used to indicate that which is not physical, emotional or mental, but is the power that animates and enlivens them all. Depending on one's religious tradition or background this word may have different meanings attached to it. It is interesting to note that the study of the soul is entering the realm of psychology. Again, we are seeing a scientific investigation of a truth described by the world's great religions. Figure 13, developed by psychiatrist Roberto Assagioli MD illustrates the psychological constitution of man and the different levels of awareness that are part of our experience.

The point in the center, number 5, is the conscious self, the ego, one's lower self, or what I have referred to as "the personality." For the most part this is our conscious awareness of who we are. It is the part we identify with when we use the word "I", and relates to our physical, emotional and mental experience of life.

The circle around the "I," number 4, is our field of consciousness. This is everything of which we are consciously aware through our five senses and any other means of perception we may have developed. It is the result of all we have learned and experienced throughout our life.

The lower part of the oval, number 1, is the lower unconscious or subconscious mind. It holds information and experiences we have gathered throughout our life. Even though this information and our experiences are below our threshold of awareness or sub-conscious, they affect our perception, decisions and quality of life. This is where painful experiences are repressed so the conscious mind can continue to function. Even though these experiences are not part of our conscious awareness they do continue to have an effect on us biologically and psychologically until they are healed and resolved.

Figure 13

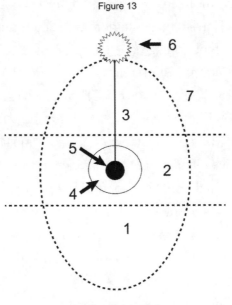

Assigoli Model

Reprinted from An Act of Will with the publishers permission

The middle of the oval, number 2, is the middle unconscious. It contains that information which can be recalled from our memory. We are not conscious of this information, but we have the ability to bring it into our field of awareness when needed.

The top of the oval, number 3, is the superconscious mind and that which relates us to higher consciousness, soul awareness, and the higher dimensions of reality that are beyond sensory perception, emotion analysis, logic and cognition.

The starburst at the top, number 6, is the higher self, the soul or the transpersonal self. The soul is the life energy that animates the physical body. When the link between the soul and the form is severed the form dies. In some traditions the link between the two has been called the "silver cord." The consciousness aspect is anchored in the brain, and the life aspect is anchored in the heart. If the consciousness connection is broken the form is alive but there is no awareness. Nobody is home. Whereas the personality is in the domain of temporal reality, the soul is in the domain of permanent, causal reality. It is untouched by the experiences in the lower arenas of expression.

The field of consciousness outside the oval, number 7, is the collective unconscious of which Carl Jung spoke. This is considered to be the collective gathering of all the thoughts, ideas, emotions and experiences of the human family throughout the ages. As you consider the significance of the collective unconscious of the human family keep in mind that thought-forms are made of mental and emotional matter.

Dr. Assagioli's work provides us with a model that adds to our understanding of man as a multidimensional being with expression on the physical level. As we have seen, man is much more than that. Our perception of man will no doubt be refined and expanded as our understanding grows through the study of psychology, quantum physics, and different spiritual approaches. One of our goals as we progress along the path is to bring the presence of soul into the personality, to make the lower self a vehicle of expression for the Higher Self.

The soul is the essence that underlies the form and substance in the physical, emotional and mental arenas of expression that constitute the personality. It is of a higher vibration and is the consciousness that works through the form. When the energy fields are developed and integrated the personality is ready for the next step. This entails the infusion of soul energy into the substance of the personality.

Refining the Emotional Field

On the path of personal and spiritual growth what can we do to enhance this process of refinement and integration? As you will recall from figure 6, there are different grades of matter in each plane (physical, emotional, mental) which make up our energetic constitution. On the emotional or astral plane matter that is vibrating at a lower, slower rate will be coarser in nature. A person with an astral body or a field made up of coarser matter will experience lower emotions such as anger, envy, lust, resentment and other heavy, oppressive feelings. Because their emotional field is vibrating at a certain level it will attract other people and experiences of a like vibration. Angry and mean people seem to attract other angry, mean people, and those experiences associated with them. Because of the density of matter and the inharmonious, slow rate of vibration at this level it is difficult for the higher vibration of the soul to move into an emotional body composed of this substance.

A person whose emotional field is comprised of a more refined grade of matter and is vibrating at a higher level will experience and express the higher emotions of love, compassion, appreciation, gratitude, and joy. A person whose astral field is comprised of this grade of matter will tend to attract people and experiences of like nature. Many of us have met those people who have a presence of peace, compassion and quiet strength. That is indicative of the quality of matter that makes up their energetic constitution. When confronted with adversity they respond quite differently than people whose emotional field is made of a lower grade of matter.

I recall an amazing story about a Buddhist monk who had spent 25 years in a Chinese labor camp after the invasion and occupation of Tibet. After he had finally been released and made his way to the west he was being interviewed by a newspaper reporter about his experience. After several hours of relating his story, which included physical and psychological torture, depravation, forced labor in freezing conditions with inadequate clothing, starvation, and watching his fellow monks and countrymen brutally beaten and murdered, the reporter was almost stunned at what he heard and the vivid description of what this man had endured for 25 years. Then the reporter asked the monk, "Considering all the horrible experiences you've been through during those 25 years, can you think of any specific times you were in exceptionally grave danger?" The monk thought for a moment and said, "Yes, I can think of several times I was in truly grave danger." The reporter, sensing more for his story leaned forward and asked, "What happened? What were they?" The monk, after reflecting for a moment replied, "There were several times that I *almost* lost my compassion for the Chinese."

I suspect this man's emotional body was comprised of very refined matter made up of the vibration of love and compassion. This certainly would be accompanied by a relatively high degree of soul infusion. The soul, whose nature and essence is divine love, would express this kind of goodness regardless of the external circumstances. To one whose emotional field was vibrating at a more coarse level this kind of a response would be crazy and unimaginable. However, we should remember that the greatest expression of divinity that has ever walked the earth taught those who aspire to follow Him to love their enemies, turn the other cheek, walk the extra mile, and do good to those who despitefully use them. He then set the example as He was dying a painful death, by asking his Heavenly Father to forgive those who were killing Him for they knew not what they were doing.

To return good for evil, to stand as light in the midst of darkness is the mark of a soul-infusing personality. These rare people are found in every religious tradition. Although perhaps not at the level of Christ, they are living what He and other great spiritual teachers taught. Energy follows thought and as we aspire to live the goodness of our faith the vibrational rate and matter that make up the emotional and mental fields are purified, refined and transformed. As we consciously choose to practice more emotions of a higher quality, such as appreciation, love and compassion, we gradually transform who and what we are.

The Infusing of Soul Energy

This process of purification and refinement is often times quite challenging. Often, discomfort is the result when soul energy begins to infuse or flow into the personality. This can cause a cleansing or purging which results in an emotional, mental and spiritual crisis. As the higher, more refined and intense vibration of the soul moves into the lower, denser substance of the personality the coarser matter of the lower sub-planes is stimulated.

As the light and power of the soul pour in, this begins the cleansing process of removing or repulsing that which is not of a like vibration. Old habits, old beliefs, old energy patterns that are no longer compatible with the new rhythm and higher vibration being imposed by soul, are identified, broken down, and swept away. Often, our friends and associates change, living circumstances change, attitudes and beliefs change and perhaps our profession changes. The old vibrational rates are no longer compatible with the new. The new frequency attracts like substances and circumstances that are more in resonance with the increased vibrational rate.

The more we try to hold on to that which is no longer needed in our lives the more painful the experience will be. However, if we understand that this breaking down, cleansing and clearing is a necessary part of the process, then we can work with it rather than treating it as a pathology that needs to be cured.

As the light of soul energy pours in, it illumines the shadows within us, and we begin to see the parts of ourselves that are not so pleasant. As we become aware of these dark, negative, sometimes repulsive parts of ourselves it leads to a crisis. It often feels like we are getting worse. Sometimes, this results in feelings of depression or anxiety. The good news is that the added light is illuminating the areas of ourselves where we need to do the clearing work. We start seeing the limiting belief systems, the self-sabotaging actions, and destructive patterns that have always been there but of which we have been previously unaware. By applying some of the tools and techniques described in this book you will be able to assist the clearing process, thus allowing a greater amount of light to shine in. This will light up more of the shadows that need to be cleared or transformed. Understanding this process is quite helpful because these experiences can be quite intense.

Spiritual Crisis

As uncomfortable as it may be this process is a necessary step in fulfilling the principles of health. As we saw earlier, the result of physical cleansing necessary to building health can cause much discomfort as the toxins are cleared out. In a healing crisis things sometimes appear to get worse before they get better. Nevertheless, this is part of the process. This is true for a spiritual crisis as well. If you understand what is happening you'll be able to work with it rather than feel like you are going crazy.

As we consciously aspire to improve ourselves, bring in more light, choose to live love, and align our lives with higher values and principles, we lessen the need for life to get our attention through a crisis. However, we may find that the growth process itself precipitates the crisis. A caterpillar goes into a cocoon where it completely breaks down into a liquid in order to transform to a higher level. Then it must struggle to break out. The snake sheds its skin. Difficulties inherent in the process of living are necessary for growth.

If you have gone through or are in the midst of experiencing a life crisis where relationships, career, life's work, health, living conditions, and location are changing, and are seemingly beyond your control, realize that this may all be a part of the clearing process. Do your best to increase your meditation time and the quality of your prayer life. If possible, take time to be alone. You may find that life arranges that for you. Experiencing solitude and silence is a wonderful way to nurture the soul. Realize that it is natural for the personality to hold on to that which is familiar and comfortable, while resisting change. However, the harder we hold on, the greater the stress we will create.

A practical and effective technique to increase our identification with soul and navigate the turbulent waters of life, transition, and crisis, is to cultivate the stance of being an observer. Learn to watch yourself from the vantage point of the starburst, the soul in Dr. Assagioli's model. As you learn to detach and assume this role, you can reach the point where you observe your feelings and how you react emotionally. You can observe yourself as you think the thoughts, and start to see the motive behind them. It can be a very effective process of self-discovery, and a way to maintain your center in the midst of trying times. Practice being the observer.

The Caterpillar's Journey

I found that when I have been in the midst of a major crisis, it has been most helpful to remember the experience of the caterpillar's journey, and its transformation into a butterfly. If you are in the process of transition, are melting down and experiencing an overall life crisis, remember: This may be a positive step in your growth and development. If you are successfully moving forward on the path, there will be change. Change produces movement. Movement produces friction, and friction produces heat. If you're melting down from the heat, take heart, because that may be an indication that you're on the right track.

The realm of soul lies above the three arenas we have explored on the living continuum. It is the goal to which we all aspire. In the realm of the soul, new laws apply, and a deeper understanding of energy is necessary. One of the most difficult parts on the path is when the traveler has reached that point where he knows too much to go back to his old way of living, but does not fully know the path that lies ahead. The rules at this level change and he does not yet have enough understanding and clarity to successfully work with them. The rules he has lived by and worked with no longer seem to work. Even though there are road maps in the form of the world's scriptures, and direction from those who have gone before, for him it is still uncharted territory. He walks by faith, and, at the same time, is propelled forward by an inner drive.

As we follow that inner impulse, we do things that may not make sense to the rational mind of worldly convention but are, nevertheless, part of the path. Often, that means leaving that which is comfortable and certain, for that which is unknown and unfamiliar.

As we travel this path, we progress by embodying and becoming a greater measure of soulful qualities. By living and expressing these qualities in daily living we are gradually transformed. The only way we can become an athlete or musician is by training in the selected field of endeavor. As we train the body, the muscles and nerves develop to the point where the movements are automatic. As the mind thinks the thought it is immediately translated into a physical expression.

The process holds true for living as a soul. As the mind is trained to focus and dwell upon positive, healthy, virtuous thoughts it is strengthened and attracts those qualities to itself. Energy follows thought and by dwelling on the nature of the soul the bridge is built to bring soul energy into the form. Through living the principles of health and service the centers are awakened in a safe and natural way. The result is that there is an improved exchange of energy between the energy fields (figure 10), thereby facilitating the integration process, increasing soul infusion and the overall raising of consciousness.

There is a simple technique using your creative imagination that will enhance the process of soul infusion as well as provide a number of other benefits. You may want to look at the figure of the energy fields before you do this and then create your own version in your imagination. Find a comfortable sitting positing. Take a few minutes to relax by placing your attention on the breath and gently following the rhythm of its rising and falling. When this rhythm has been established shift your attention a few inches outside of your body into the etheric field. Continue to breathe and hold your awareness there for a minute or two. If there are colors or feelings associated with that experience just note them and gently hold your attention. Next, shift your awareness a foot or two outside the body into the astral field for a few minutes to sense its presence. If you don't feel anything, that's fine. Just know it is there, hold your attention and be open to what you might experience. Next, shift your attention two to three feet out from your physical body to your mental body and hold your attention there for a couple of minutes. Just be aware. If thoughts come just let them pass and bring your awareness back to the mental field.

Once you have moved through each body/field, shift your awareness directly above your head about two or three feet and imagine a radiant orb of light and love. Hold your attention on that vision for a few minutes, being aware of what you experience as your consciousness becomes one with the orb of light. After holding this positive point of tension for a few minutes, imagine a tube of light descending down into the crown center of your head. When this connection between the orb of light and the top of the head has been made, imagine the light of the orb pouring down the tube and flooding into your physical body.

As the light steadily moves down, see it washing over all of the tissue and cleansing away the diseased cells and toxic material as the light pushes it down. See and feel the light pour down your neck, chest and abdomen, cleansing as it goes. Then, over the waist and down the legs, push the debris into the bottom of the feet. Hold your attention there in your imagination and then, with a deep breath, exhale out the bottom of the feet, blowing the toxic material down into the earth where it will be broken down and absorbed. Don't worry, Mother Earth can reprocess this material easily.

This process of flooding the field or body with light is then repeated for the etheric field, the emotional body and the mental body. As the light pours into the etheric field, it cleanses as it moves through and replaces the old material with the new. As the light of soul floods the emotional field, it dissolves negative emotional matter and coarse emotional vibration, replacing it with light, love, compassion and the higher, more refined qualities of the astral plane. As that light infuses into the mental field, it dissipates and clears away toxic thoughts, errant, decaying thought forms and inharmonious mental vibrations. The light of the soul has substance. As it pours into each body it pushes the lower vibrating matter down and replaces it with the fullness of itself.

When all three fields have been cleared and infused with light, hold that positive point of tension for a few minutes and let the light bathe and cleanse you. Energy follows thought. As you consistently practice this process by focusing your awareness on the light and love of soul that is what you become. As a man thinketh in his heart, so he is, and so does he become.

There is one additional side note that may be of interest regarding the healing power of love. It has been said, "The energy of love has substance, and this substance can be used to drive out diseased tissue and replace it with clean, healthy tissue made of a purer substance." The path to health is the path to wholeness. The infusion of love, guided by your imagination can be a powerful force to heal on many levels.

WELLNESS INVOCATION / AFFIRMATION

As we review the first two sections of this book you now have an understanding of a key cause of degenerative disease at the cell level and the role that the lymphatic system plays in creating health.

You have a greater knowledge of the mind/body connection through the understanding of the energy fields, the centers, belief systems, thought forms, and the power of the imagination to direct energy through the use of visualization.

The following prayer can be viewed as an invocation or affirmation that is an effective way to practically utilize the information we've learned and apply it in the process of healing, the creation of optimal health and performance enhancement. As you affirm this statement, do it in the present tense as if it were already true. At the same time, consciously direct your thoughts to the point in the body being focused upon, remembering that energy follows thought. You may want to use some of the diagrams to assist you in the visualization process.

This prayer, originally written by Dr. Kevin Hartshorn, is intended to serve as a guide in the healing process. It is a way to work with the innate intelligence, which is the source of all healing. I have found this to be a great addition to a workout as it is something that can be done while walking or rebounding. Adding one of the breathing exercises will also enhance the healing effectiveness. I encourage you to adjust it to meet your own particular needs.

As an invocation, fill in the blank with your understanding of the highest source of intelligence from where life, health and healing come. As an example you can use God, Heavenly Father, Great Spirit, Father/Mother God, etc.

_____, I thank thee for blessing my brain, my right side, my left side and my corpus collosum; for washing the cells, feeding the cells and purifying the cells. I thank thee for increasing my brains capacity to function to 100% and directing this energy through my central and autonomic nervous systems into every gland, organ, skeletal muscle, cell and every part of my body from my head to my feet.

I thank thee for blessing my hypothalamus, pituitary and pineal glands; for washing the cells, feeding the cells and purifying the cells. I thank thee for blessing my mind and memory to have total recall from my conscious and subconscious mind.

I thank thee for blessing my thyroid and parathyroid glands; for washing the cells, feeding the cells and purifying the cells. I thank thee for directing this energy to balance and strengthen my metabolism. I thank thee for directing this energy to my lungs and respiratory system enhancing the intake of oxygen and its exchange with the blood.

I thank thee for blessing my thymus gland; for washing the cells, feeding the cells and purifying the cells. I thank thee for directing this energy to my heart, circulatory system and bones. I thank thee for bringing white blood cells from my bone marrow to my thymus gland making "T cells" destroying bacteria, viruses, poisons, cancer and foreign matter in my body.

I thank thee for blessing my pancreas; for washing the cells, feeding the cells and purifying the cells. I thank thee for directing this energy to control, strengthen and balance my digestive system, blood sugar level and body temperature.

I thank thee for blessing my prostate and testes (male) ovaries and reproductive organs (female); for washing the cells, feeding the cells and purifying the cells. I thank thee for balancing my sexual energy and responses to create optimal health and wellness.

I thank thee for blessing my adrenal glands; for washing the cells, feeding the cells and purifying the cells. I thank thee for directing this energy to my kidneys, skin and up and down my spine from my tailbone to the base of my skull.

Now with each of my centers activated to the ideal level to create optimal health I thank thee for blessing my endocrine system, nervous system and immune system. I thank thee for accurately communicating the necessary information to every cell and organ in my body to maximize physical, emotional and mental health.

I thank you for blessing my right and left eyes that they are renewing their ability to see perfectly. I thank thee for blessing my ears that they are hearing perfectly. I thank thee for blessing my sinuses, my stomach, my liver, my spleen, my small and large intestines, my bladder and gall bladder. I thank thee for blessing all my organs for working with the glands increasing anabolic growth, renewal, regeneration and repair. I thank thee for blessing my scalp and hair for functioning and growing perfectly.

I thank thee for blessing my body's pH that my acid and alkaline levels are maintaining balance. I thank thee for strengthening my body ability to manufacture all the vitamins and essential fatty acids that my body needs. I thank thee for balancing all the minerals in my body with all the enzymes, amino acids, calories, and all other nutrients that my body needs. I thank thee for increasing my body's ability to create and store glycogen. I thank thee for blessing me with all the frequencies of all the substances that will promote maximum tissue growth, regeneration and healing.

I thank you for blessing my physical body, etheric field, emotional field, mental field, personality, soul and spirit. For receiving, magnifying and storing all positive energy from my environment, from any and all sources inside or outside of my body. I thank thee for negating, neutralizing and eliminating all energy incompatibility from any and all sources; whether it be poison, allergen, electromagnetic, chemical, plant, animal or anything inside or outside my body.

_____, I thank thee for sending energy from my brain, down the right side of my neck and right shoulder, down the arm into my fingers; down the left side of my neck and left shoulder, down the arm into my fingers; down my spine; into my left hip and down the left leg to my toes; into my right hip and down the right leg to my toes. I thank thee that this visualized energy is activating my lymphatic system and pulling out all dead cells, poisons and excess water while bringing my cells into the "dry state" thus relieving pain. I thank thee for bringing glucose and oxygen from my blood stream into my cells making the proper amount of ATP and turning on my sodium-potassium pumps, and producing the electrical energy to heal and reproduce at the rate of 300 million cells a minute.

I thank thee for blessing the skeletal muscles in my legs that they are growing and becoming stronger, My quadriceps, hamstrings, calves and anterior tibials and all my leg muscles; I thank thee for blessing the muscles in my back; my latissimusdorsi; trapezius scarospinas, spinal erectors and all my back muscles. I thank thee for blessing the muscles in my chest; my pectorals and all my chest muscles; I thank thee for blessing my shoulder muscles; my biceps and triceps and all the skeletal muscles in my body, for growing and becoming stronger. I thank thee for increasing muscle stimulation during exercise and speeding up my recuperation and growth process during rest. I thank thee for increasing anabolic growth secretions building skeletal muscle size and strength.

I thank thee for filling my etheric, emotional and mental fields with the love, light, charity, virtue, knowledge, temperance, patience, kindness, humility, diligence, peace, joy and harmony of my soul and for radiating this out to my environment. I thank thee that as these qualities of my soul fill my energy fields that they drive out all negative frequencies, toxic emotions and mis-qualified thought forms that are not compatible with the highest and best good in my life.

I thank thee for my health and the healing of my body and soul, and all of my many blessings, in the name of _____.

CONCLUSION

Throughout the first part of this book, we have explored the activities, principles and natural laws that will help you develop higher levels of health and wholeness. By consciously choosing to apply the knowledge acquired, you will steadily progress up the living continuum, lessen the chance of serious disease, and continue to develop a high quality of life. As you do this on an individual level, it has a ripple effect throughout the entire hologram affecting all the other parts in a positive way. The higher you ascend the mountain, the stronger, healthier, more wholesome you become and the greater will be your understanding of natural law and universal principles. The more you make these principles a part of who you are the more effective you will be in helping your fellow men/women. The result of this is a happy, fulfilling life.

You know the time you have spent here in temporal reality has been well used and that you have progressed along the path ready for the next step. Those steps will continue whether you are in a physical form or not because it is the consciousness that continues to evolve. You continue holding the balance between focus on the long-term destination and the next step. If you are in alignment with the Creator and you do your part, you can trust the process, because the final destination is wholeness, unity and holiness.

PART III

CREATING SOCIAL AND ECONOMIC WELLNESS

CHAPTER 22

FROM INDIVIDUAL TO ORGANIZATION

Throughout this book we have explored the conditions necessary for physical health on a cellular level. We have seen what is necessary to enhance health in the mental and emotional fields and we understand how these fields can subconsciously affect our physical health and quality of life. As we understand the principles and conditions of health for the entity of the physical body we can observe how like principles apply to an organization or social system. Keeping in mind what we've learned let's move from the cell to the society and from the person to the planet.

We have seen that our body is made up of trillions of individual cells. When the conditions of health for the cells are met the individual cells are healthy. When the individual cells are healthy and functioning at optimal levels then that health is reflected in the life of the greater organism.

Keeping these principles in mind, let's move to a higher level. As individuals, we are the cells that make up the body of the organizations of which we are a part. We are the cells that make up the life of our families, the schools and churches we attend, and our business or place of employment. You and I are the cells that make up the life of our communities and our nation. And we are the cells that make up the body of our planetary life. When the individuals that make up the life of a family, an organization, a community or a nation are healthy physically, mentally, emotionally and spiritually, then that quality of life will be reflected in the life and actions of the greater social organism.

The reverse is also true. If the people that make up an organization are in a state of dis-ease physically, emotionally, mentally or spiritually, then that affects the health, stability and quality of the greater organism.

As in the life of the cell, individuals too must have a supply of essential emotional, mental and spiritual nutrients, a toxin-free environment and a clear flow of life-giving energy. This is influenced, and to a large degree, controlled by the political, social and economic systems of which we are a part. The structure and values of the organizations in which we live and work also have a great deal of influence on our health and our quality of life.

Think back to the difference between the dry state of health and the swamp / disease state in the body. If we place a healthy cell into the state of disease, it won't be long before the cell will be overwhelmed and adjust to the environment. In a like manner, if we take healthy individuals and place them in an organization controlled by a sick system governed by toxic values, unless they are exceptionally strong internally, they will either have to adapt to survive or leave.

The power of a social structure to influence behavior has been demonstrated by numerous psychological and sociological studies. Dr. Philip Zimbardo at Stanford University conducted one of the best-known studies in this area. This experiment involved the structure of a mock prison in the basement of one of the university buildings. The students who volunteered to take part in the study were tested to make sure they were mentally and emotionally stable with a strong sense of ethical values. The students were then randomly divided into groups of prisoners and guards and were told to assume those roles for two weeks.

In a very short time those who assumed the role of guards became aggressive, abusive and, in some cases, downright brutal and sadistic as they exercised their power and control over the prisoners. The prisoners became passive, anxious, depressed and withdrawn as they complied with the orders of the domineering guards. The results of this experiment were so dramatically destructive that the study was terminated after only six days.[1]

What would cause healthy, well-balanced students with a strong sense of ethical values to resort to such behavior? There are several explanations. We have already seen the power that self-image has to control behavior and performance at a subconscious level. Perhaps as students' self-image changed with the perceived role, so did their behavior. On an energetic level, perhaps as an individual tapped into the collective thought-form of what it meant to be a guard or a prisoner, the force of that pattern overrode the beliefs and values of the person.

We do know social, organizational and economic forces have a tremendous effect on the behavior and health of the individual. Just as the environment surrounding the cell will either support or undermine physical health, so will the environment, economic structure, values and attitudes of a social system strengthen or undermine the mental and emotional health of an individual. Please keep the results of this study in mind as you progress through this section.

In a healthy social structure individuals naturally contribute to the greater organism of which they are a part. At the same time the social organism has an obligation to support the personal growth and welfare of its members. By his thoughts and actions the individual has an effect on the environment, and at the same time environmental forces have an effect on the individual. The values and structure of an organization, a social system or economic system will govern the flow of life-giving energy and how it is distributed to its individual members. This affects health and behavior to a much greater extent than has been realized.

As we look at the process of creating wellness on all levels, it is clear that we must address the financial and economic realities of our lives. To address the underlying cause of health and disease in an effective, holistic way, we must consider the whole. We are physical, mental, emotional and spiritual beings who live in a matrix of other living things. Our thoughts and actions affect other people, the organizations of which we are a part, and our greater environment. At the same time, other people, our work, and the environment have an effect on us. As we grow in our understanding of the social and economic principles of health we can then learn how to align our lives with those principles and disengage from faulty belief systems and the actions they produce.

It is possible to create organizations whose values support and nurture the wellness of an individual. At the same time, it is the responsibility of individuals to make sure they support the greater organisms of which they are a part. When we do this, there is a balanced flow of energy and we will be creating health on all levels, individually and organizationally.

CHAPTER 23

MONEY

We have seen how the vital or etheric body of an individual is responsible for the overall health and vitality of the physical body. It is also the interface between the physical body and the mental and emotional fields. This vital energy field is also one of the characteristics of the planet, in that the earth has its own energy field in which we live, move and have our being and from which we draw sustenance. The etheric field of an individual draws energy and life force from the planet's vital energy field allowing it to circulate through and nourish each person's physical body.

In the physical world of individuals, organizations, communities and nations, the form this life-giving, vital energy takes is the form of *money*. Money is concretized or congealed energy. It is crystallized prana or chi. It is the life force made tangible. Although money is thought of as medium of exchange it is more than that. Money is that tangible, physical substance for which you trade your life's energy. Someone may give you ten dollars, fifty dollars, or one hundred dollars an hour for your service. You take an hour of your life that you will never be able to live again, and trade it for money. You now have a tangible unit of your life force that you can exchange to provide for your needs and wants.

There are and have been many different forms of money. For the most part, we think of money being a thing. Gold, silver, shells, tally sticks, stones, paper, plastic and electrons flowing through computers into accounts all have been used as money. However, money is not necessarily a thing, it is an agreement. As individuals, cultures and countries focus their collective thoughts and agree that something has value, money - a medium of exchange - is created by that agreement. Ultimately money is a thought form made physical but a thought form none-the-less. As we have seen, energy follows thought, and this flow of energy can be constructive or destructive depending on how it is directed.

When there is a fair, equitable exchange of energy or life force between people and organizations, the needs and wants are met, and the material conditions of health are realized. When there is an unjust or inequitable exchange, it can be viewed as the *theft* of someone else's life force. As we use our life force to create products and services that produce value for others, we create true wealth and contribute to the health of the whole system. When the system is structured so there is a free flow of life energy, money, then the individuals are prosperous. When there is a blockage of the flow of energy, there is economic dis-ease in the lives of individuals, organizations and nations.

As we have seen, the flow or congestion of energy within the physical body can either lead to health or disease. In fact, Chinese medicine defines disease as too little energy available or too much energy concentrated in a certain part of the body, upsetting the whole system. This same principle also applies to the flow of energy or money within a society and among nations. Since money is concretized life force, and its circulation is necessary to the health of individuals, organizations and nations, it is very important to understand its role in the creation of health or disease.

A wonderful example of how the nature, design and flow of money affect health and well-being comes from the book *New Money for a New World* by Bernard Lietaer and Stephen Belgin. The middle ages stretched for a period of 1000 years, from the fall of the Roman Empire to the Renaissance in the 16th century. As we review history, our view of the Middle Ages usually considers that time to be a particularly unenlightened and stagnant time in western history. The forward progress of humanity embodied in the art, philosophy and legal systems of the ancient Greek and Roman civilizations not only seemed to come to a stop, but in many ways society seemed to slide backwards. When we think of the word "medieval," we usually picture people living in a dark, primitive, backward state of existence.

However, there was a period of this time during the 10th to 12th century in which society, prosperity and health flourished. Recent scholarship in a variety of different areas pointed out by Lietaer and Belgin has discovered a number of findings revealing how progressive this time actually was in economic prosperity and physical health. One of the ways to identify and measure the overall health of the population is by bone structure and height. The height of a population indicates things like better nutrition and the overall quality of care, especially during infancy.

Excavations of skeletal remains in the area of London, dating from prehistoric times until the present have revealed some surprising facts. During the period from the 10th to 12th centuries the height of women was taller than at any other time, including today.[2] We also know that the commoners were fairly well off. Even people in the lower classes enjoyed four or five courses for dinner and usually ate three or four meals each day. Sunday was a day of rest. Most people had Monday off to attend to personal business. There were at least ninety holidays a year. Some scholars believe it may have been as high as a hundred and eighty day a year. The workday was six hours and when the Dukes of Saxony tried to raise it to eight hours the workers revolted. For the most part, everyone, including the working class, enjoyed a relatively high standard of living.

The overall prosperity of this 10th to 12th century era is reflected in the great Cathedrals that were built during this time. Contrary to popular belief, the cathedrals were not built by the church or the nobility. Members of the community built them with the well-being of the community in mind. The cathedrals not only had a religious function but an economic one as well. One of the ways to bring revenues into a community is to increase the numbers of people who visit the area. So, in addition to religious reasons, the cathedrals were built with the intent of attracting pilgrims to the community. The nicer the cathedral the more pilgrims it would attract. Although their motive may have been different, the pilgrims who visited holy places then also served the role that tourists play today. They brought their money into the community, which increased prosperity for everyone.

Although there were certainly spiritual motives for the construction of these buildings there were economic considerations as well. They were built as a long-term investment with the intent of serving the community for years. The cathedral at Chartes is still drawing tourists today and has served as the main source of economic support for that community for 800 years.

An interesting side note to the cathedrals is that they are built on the ley lines and energy vortexes in the planet. Just as there are meridians and lines of force that run through the etheric field of an individual, so are there lines of force that run through the planet. Where these lines of force cross in an individual, you will have a major or minor center or a chakra. Where these lines of force intersect on the planet, you will have an intensification of energy or a vortex. This is one reason why certain sites are considered sacred, and a temple, a mosque or a church marks their location. Often, the energy in these buildings is quite noticeable.

How do we account for this level of prosperity and exceptional health during this period of time? The main reason for this prosperity and health is that were two money systems or two forms of currency working together at the same time. The first type of money, usually in the form of gold or silver, was similar to the national currency we use today. In addition to being a medium of exchange, it also served as a way to store value. This form of money was useful for long-distance trading where a common form of value and exchange was necessary.

The second form of currency was the local exchanges designed to facilitate local trade within a community. In essence each community had its own form of currency. An interesting characteristic of this form of currency was a feature called a "demurrage charge." Demurrage is a charge that is levied when the currency is held longer than a certain period of time. It's like a parking fee for money, a tax that was imposed for *not* spending money or negative interest. The longer you held money the less value it had. The result of this arrangement is that this form of money was a good medium of exchange, but a poor way to store value. People aren't going to save something that incurs a liability by doing so. The effect this had is that people spent money freely and quickly as they didn't want to have to pay an additional fee for holding the money too long. When money (life force) flows the result is economic health.

Since this form of currency was not an effective way to store value it influenced the way people invested. Rather than saving money they used it to invest in tangible goods and also invested in long-term projects like building cathedrals. This form of money made long-term investing in community assets advantageous. People still had the national currency (gold or silver) which was a good way to store value. However, the fact that the demurrage charge was part of the local currency encouraged people to spend and keep the money flowing. This arrangement benefited everyone and dramatically raised the standard of living for the working class. It was the structure and design of the money system that influenced behavior in that it motivated people to invest in certain ways and kept money flowing within the community. It is important to remember that the structure of the money system influences behavior, which in turn influences health. A money system based on flowing abundance will produce a different set of values and behaviors than one based on scarcity.

This period of prosperity came to an end at the close of the 1200's when the church decided to consolidate power by instituting imperialistic kingships. One of the first actions they took was to dismantle the local currencies while keeping the national one. This had an immediate and dramatic effect on the investment patterns. When the medium that facilitated the flow of life force was eliminated the energy exchange of trade and production dried up. When the energy stopped flowing so did the prosperity and health.

A well-balanced money system is very much like having water flowing through an irrigation system. The flow of water will turn a dry desert into a lush oasis. As long as the water flows there is a flourishing abundance of life, vegetation, fruit and other nourishment. As soon as the flow of water stops, so does the rich expression of life. It's not long before there is nothing but a dry, arid, and dusty wasteland. This is, in effect, what happened in Europe at the beginning of the 1300's. The flow of life force dried up and it wasn't long before economic and financial health had been replaced with disease and despair.

This economic contraction slowed the flow of commerce, trade, and the production of food. The social structure as a whole began to melt down. One of the results of this was famine. This restricted flow of life force caused the first European famine in 1315 and 1316, killing over 10% of the population.[3] In 1316, a report in a London chronicle said, "This year was a great dearth of corn and other victuals. The poor ate for hunger cats, horses and dogs... Some stole children and ate them." The downward spiral continued as the life force was restricted even more and other famines followed. These continued to physically weaken the population and epidemics of disease broke out. This physical, emotional and social breakdown culminated in the scourge of the Plague which first hit in 1347. Over the ensuing years the plague wiped out one-third to one-half of the continent.

Some historians who have debated the causes of this social meltdown have attributed it to over working of the land, others to overpopulation or possibly climate change. We have seen in our study of health that the physical expression of illness is usually the symptom or effect of a deeper cause. This too is the case with social and economic disease. Only recently have we begun to realize that a key, contributing event that put this disastrous chain of effects into motion was a shift in the monetary system.

Why is this relevant today? As we have seen, the greater organism of which we are a part (community, nation, and planet) has an effect on the health and quality of life of the individual and the individual by their choices and actions has an effect on the greater organism. It is therefore valuable to identify some of the forces acting on the greater whole that are the result of our choices. Because the nature and structure of money influences behavior, which in turn affects health on all levels, it is vital to have a deeper understanding of the money system as well as the forces and trends that are going to be affecting us and our children.

Trends and Their Impact

In his book *The Future of Money,* Bernard Lietaer describes what he refers to as four mega trends. These four trends are forces that have already begun to impact our lives. The full force will be felt during the next 20 years. They represent a crisis if ignored and an opportunity if recognized and addressed.

The first mega-trend is the **Age Wave**. In 1848, when Otto von Bismark introduced the idea of retiring at age 65, the average life expectancy was only 48 years. When President Franklin Roosevelt introduced Social Security in the 30's, the average life expectancy was 62 years. Starting Social Security was a good idea that was feasible and sustainable. Today, the average life expectancy for men is 76 years and 80 for women. The math worked well in the beginning because there were a high number of workers supporting a small amount of retired people. Now that people live longer, it doesn't work anymore.

An interesting fact pointed out by Mr. Lietaer is that two-thirds of all the people who have ever lived in the history of the planet to reach the age of 65 are alive today. We take it for granted today, but for most of history very few people lived that long. In 1960, one in eleven people was 65 or older. In 2000 it was one in seven. By the year 2030, one in four people will be over the age of 65.

This trend has some interesting and challenging implications. The greatest one is the fact that there will not be enough reserves to fund the needed pensions. The money simply won't exist. In 2000 the Organization for Economic Cooperative Development countries had accumulated 35 trillion dollars in pension liabilities. This does not include health-care costs, which would double that figure if added. As we look at this trend, it is clear that an aging population will be a major economic and political issue in the coming years. In the

United States ten thousand baby-boomers are retiring a day and yet the working population that provides the tax base is growing smaller.

The obvious question is how will society take care of these people as they age? Part of this trend already is that more and more people are taking care of aging parents while trying to raise their own children at the same time. Caring for elderly parents can be a difficult and sometimes a full time job. It is a situation that will be required more and more as we move deeper in the direction of this trend.

The second mega-trend Mr. Lietaer identifies is the **information revolution.** This trend is resulting in a growing movement towards jobless economic growth. Two hundred years ago, Ben Franklin said that if everyone were productive, five hours a day is all it would take to provide the needs of society. Since the 1960's, economists have been predicting a reduced workweek and retirement by the age of 39. In 1967, the New York Times predicted that by the year 2000 people would work less than eight hours a day and four days a week.

What is the reality? Between 1973 and 1993, American labor productivity has increased 30%. However, the amount of pay that workers receive has decreased by 20% during that same time period. During that same time, the world's top 500 corporations increased their profits by 700% while reducing their work force. The growth of technology is replacing the need for labor and not just in blue-collar jobs. In the 1990's, millions of white-collar workers were laid off to cut costs and keep companies profitable. Those who survived the cuts had to carry greater workloads but they rarely received compensation to match the additional work. That tacit acceptance of additional work was necessary for those who wanted to keep their job. Today, people are working more and receiving less. The trend is that businesses will continue to increase their profits and require fewer and fewer employees to do so.

The argument is always made that as new technology displaces workers it opens up new employment opportunities in other areas. That is only partially true. It's very unlikely that someone who has been a construction worker or lumberjack for 20 years will be retrained as a computer technician; not impossible, but unlikely. As we have seen, people employed in the high-tech industry are just as subject to downsizing and job elimination as people in other industries. The fact is, this trend will insure that as technological advancements continue there will be fewer and fewer jobs available.

The obvious question is what happens to the millions of educated, qualified people for whom no work exists?

The third mega-trend is **climate change and bio-diversity extinction**. In regards to climate change, it's interesting to note that much of this information comes from the insurance industry. According to their observations, the frequency and intensity of natural disasters is now three times greater than it was in the 1960's. Eighty-five percent of all insurance claims now go towards compensating for natural disasters. In 1998, there were more insurance claims paid out for floods, storms, droughts, and fires than in the entire decade of the eighties. At present, four times more people die in natural disasters than in all wars or civil disturbances combined. The frequency, ferocity and intensity of these natural disasters continue to accelerate because of climate change.

The second part of this mega trend is bio-diversity extinction. In 1998, the American Museum of Natural History conducted a survey of professional biologists. They were not ecologists and most of them worked for major corporations. Sixty-nine percent of those surveyed concluded that we are in the middle of what they refer to as "the sixth extinction." The previous extinction was that of the dinosaurs. What this means is that we are in the process of losing between 30 and 70% of the planet's bio-diversity in the next 20 to 30 years.

What are the implications of this? Most people might not be concerned with algae in South America, tree frogs in Africa or insects in Asia going extinct. However, if honeybees or the other insects that pollinate crops become extinct it's not hard to imagine the problems that would follow. If this trend continues unabated, one of the possibilities is that the food chain may collapse. The entire eco-system is interdependent. When one part is damaged or destroyed it affects the entire system.

The question to ask concerning this mega-trend is how can we resolve the conflict between short-term financial interests which is what drives most businesses, and long-term sustainability? If a major corporation was responsible for contributing to these problems, and the CEO had environmental concerns, not wanting his grandchildren to inherit the ecological burden being created, he may be motivated to do something about it. However, if his corporation's profits drop as a result of his decisions it won't be long before he is replaced.

There is a myth that short-term planning is just a natural part of doing business; however, as we saw earlier, the money system in the middle-ages supported long term investing. We shall see how the structure of the present money system actually forces short-term thinking and action.

The fourth mega-trend is **monetary instability**. Every day there are two trillion dollars in financial transactions worldwide. Only two percent of these transactions have anything to do with real goods or services. The rest is speculation and paper trading.

There are three causes of this instability. The first is a structural shift, which began in 1971 when President Richard Nixon disconnected the dollar from the gold standard. A period began in which there was no international standard of value. This began floating exchanges, where the value of currency would be determined by market forces and could change significantly in short periods of time.

251

The second cause of this financial destabilization was the deregulation that occurred under President George Bush and England's Prime Minister, Margaret Thatcher, followed by the "Baker Plan." This plan imposed similar deregulation in 16 developing countries. As a result of this more people could participate in currency trading than ever before.

The third cause of this instability was a technological shift. The computerization of foreign exchange trading produced the first 24/7 worldwide global markets to ever exist. This fact, combined with the other two, has allowed for currency trading to move to a whole new level.

These three changes in the system have produced the present level of instability, which has manifested itself in several recent economic crises. They are the Mexican crisis of 1994, the Asian crisis in 1997, the Russian crisis in 1998, and Argentina's in 2000

According to experts in the field (not doom and gloom prophets) there is a 50/50 chance of a major dollar meltdown in the next 5 to 10 years, which would affect the entire world. We came very close to that in 2008.

The questions are: how can we prepare for a possible monetary crisis and how can we change the direction of this trend?

Each of the above trends, which we will investigate in greater detail later, is influenced by, and in some cases is the result of, the design and structure of our present money system. Most people don't know the basis of our present money system, where it originated, or how it evolved. Some who have studied this topic think it has just naturally unfolded this way. Others have concluded that there has been a definite plan and deliberate intent behind it.

As we investigate how the creation of money is controlled and its flow directed, let's take a brief historical look at how the present-day economic situation has developed. The structure of the money system is a major contributing factor to these four mega trends. It should be evident that they will have a tremendous impact on your well-being, your children's, and the planet as a whole. If you are in any way concerned with health and healing, alleviating poverty and other social problems, the ecological crisis and the suffering caused by international conflict, it is essential that you gain an understanding of the creation of money and its control.

How important is it to understand this topic of money creation and its relation to health and the future of your children? Robert Hemphill, credit manager of the Federal Reserve Bank in Atlanta, made this statement regarding the creation of money, "It (the nature of the modern creation of money) is the most important subject intelligent persons can investigate. It is so important that *our present civilization may collapse unless it is widely understood and the defects remedied soon."* We will come to understand in greater detail why this statement is true and what can be done about it. Only by addressing these problems at the level of cause rather than treating the symptoms will we truly be able to make a positive difference.

As with any exploration of little known facts or potentially controversial topics, it is always helpful to examine them from different angles and viewpoints so that we are better able to discern the thread of truth that runs through that which we are investigating. For starters, let's take a brief look at what various people with different religious and political backgrounds have said about the group of people who control the creation and flow of money. This network of the financial elite has brought about the present economic situation. As we shall see, they have affected the course of history on our planet. The design and structure of money continue to cause many of the world problems today.

As mentioned earlier, some economists and financial experts believe the present system just evolved under various forces throughout history. Others believe that the present money system has been guided, directed and is controlled by an elite group of people with their own plans and agenda. The following information is presented from the viewpoint that throughout history those who have controlled money have shaped the destiny of nations from behind the scenes for their own benefit.

The Money Changers

James Madison referred to this group as "the money changers" when he said, "History records that the money changers have used every form of abuse, intrigue, deceit, and violent means possible to maintain their control over governments by controlling money and its issuance."

Pope Leo the XIII observed the power that this group held and the affects they caused when he said, "On the one side there is the party which holds the power, which holds the wealth, which has in its group all labor and all trade, which manipulates for its own benefit and its own purposes all the sources of supply, and which is powerfully represented in the councils of state itself. On the other side, there are the needy and powerless multitude, sore and suffering."

"Rapacious usury, although more than once condemned by the church... is still practiced by avaricious and grasping men... so that a small number of very rich men have been able to lay upon the masses of the poor a yoke little better then slavery itself."

Dr. Carroll Quigley, professor of history at George Washington University, in his book *Tragedy and Hope* made this statement. "I know of the operation of this network because I have studied it for 20 years and was permitted for two years in the early 1960's to examine its papers and secret records. I have no aversion to it, or to most of its aims, and have for most of my life been close to it and to its many instruments. In general, my chief difference of opinion is that it wishes to remain unknown."

Dr. Quigley writes, "The powers of financial capitalism had another far-reaching aim, nothing less than to create a world system of financial control in private hands able to dominate the political system in each country and the economy of the world as a whole. The system was to be controlled in a feudalist fashion by central banks acting in concert, by secret agreements arrived at in frequent private meetings and conferences."

Pope Pius XI stated, "In our days, not alone is wealth accumulated, but immense power and despotic economic domination is concentrated in the hands of a few. This power becomes particularly irresistible when exercised by those who, because they hold and control money, are able to govern credit and determine its allotment, supplying so to speak the life blood to the entire economic body, and grasping as it were, in their hands, the very soul of the economy so that no one dare breathe against their will."

Horace Greeley had this to say. "While boasting of our noble deeds, we are careful to conceal the ugly fact that by an iniquitous money system we have nationalized a system of oppression which, though more refined, is not less cruel than the old system of chattel slavery."

This thought was presented by New Age author, Alice Bailey. "It must be recognized that the cause of all world unrest, of the world wars which have wrecked humanity, and the widespread misery upon our planet can largely be attributed to a selfish group, with materialistic purposes, who for centuries have exploited the masses and used the labor of mankind for their selfish ends... This group of capitalists has cornered and exploited the world's resources and the staples required for civilized living; they have been able to do this because they have owned and controlled the world's wealth through their interlocking directorates, and have retained it in their hands. They have made possible the vast differences existing between the very rich and the very poor; they love money and the power which money gives; they have stood behind governments and politicians; they have controlled the electorate; they have made possible the narrow, nationalistic aims of selfish politics; they have financed the worlds businesses, and controlled oil, coal, power, light and transportation; they control publicly or sub rosa the world's banking accounts. The responsibility for the widespread misery to be found today in every country in the world lies predominately at the door of certain interrelated groups of businessmen, bankers, executives of international cartels, monopolies, trusts and organizations, and directors of huge corporations who work for corporate or personal gain."

Although these people have very different political and religious orientations they do agree on one thing. From their different perspectives they have concluded that there is an elite group of financiers that exercise a tremendous amount of power and control over the economy of the world. These quotes lay a foundation for the understanding that there has been throughout history and exists at this time, a group of people working together to control the economy of nations and the world for their own selfish gain. If the flow of life force on the physical plane, money, is controlled, then ultimately so are the lives of the individuals and countries that depend on it. One might ask, if this is the case how did this economic situation come about?

Let's take a trip into the past and imagine a scene from several hundred years ago. A merchant is transporting his wares in a caravan of several horses. He arrives at a village located at the foot a mountain range. He knows that living in the mountains are bandits, who rob those who are obviously carrying things of value. Rather than risk the trip with his valuables, he sells them and gives the gold, in this case ten pounds, to a gold broker. The broker gives him a paper receipt for the gold and charges a small fee for his services. The merchant makes the journey over the mountains without a problem because he obviously has nothing of value for the bandits. Upon arriving at the town on the other side of the mountain, he takes his paper receipts to another gold broker and is given ten pounds of gold in return minus a small transaction fee. The receipts are a representation for the value of the gold and they are redeemable for gold upon demand. This is an honest, fair, stable system of banking using paper currency backed by something with tangible value. It is a convenient way to facilitate trade and commerce without the difficulty of barter.

One day, one of the gold merchants is thinking about this system. Over time, he has observed that he always has an average of one hundred pounds of gold in reserve at any given time. Sometimes he had a little more and sometimes a little less, but on the average, there was one hundred pounds. Because he knows it is likely he'll always have enough gold to cover the receipts that anyone brings him, he decides to print up receipts representing one thousand pounds of gold. By doing so, he just multiplied his wealth ten times. He can use these receipts just as gold to buy whatever he wants. And there is always enough gold on hand to redeem the demands of the other receipt holders.

This process worked quite well for the gold merchant who could increase his wealth just by printing more receipts. This arrangement is the basis of what is known as "fractional reserve banking." Although it has become more sophisticated over time, this is basically how money is created today.

Now let's suppose that our gold merchant/banker friend wants to increase his wealth even more. He decides to take some of his money, loan it out to his fellow townsmen and charge them interest for using it. He takes paper notes, supposedly backed by gold, and loans them out with interest. The collateral of the home, farm or business he is financing secures his loans. If the borrower is unable to repay the loan and interest, the banker is able to legally confiscate his property for the repayment of the debt. His wealth continues to increase with no risk.

Whenever individuals, businesses or local governments need capital they come to the gold merchant for a loan. Perhaps a small community wants to finance civic improvements. They go to the gold merchant who they know has plenty of money and ask for a loan. The loan is secured by the city council's promise to levy a tax on the people to repay the merchant with interest. In this way, the gold merchant/banker is able to gradually gain influence over government and a degree of control over the people through taxation.

It becomes clear to the banker that one of the best ways to increase profits is to create debt. The greater the debt, the more the interest adds up and the more control the banker has over the people. Over time, as his wealth continues to amass, he graduates from financing business and local endeavors to financing kings and nations.

Keep in mind that if the primary objective is to gain profit, then the best way to accomplish this is to increase debt. The best way to increase debt when dealing with nations is through war. When the issue is war, leaders rarely ask what it will cost. War is expensive, and when a king wanted to go to war he needed a way to finance it. He confers with the now, very-well-to-do gold merchant turned banker about financing his project. The amount of financing he is able to procure will, to a large degree, determine the success of his undertaking.

What about collateral? How does the gold merchant secure his loan? How will the king repay the loan plus the additional interest? A taxation system and a mechanism to enforce it are part of the arrangement. This will assure that the gold merchant will be compensated for all of his risk. The king receives abundant financing to buy arms and pay men thus greatly improving his chances of victory. This creates an advantage to a degree that the outcome of a war can often be determined by the financing.

But what if he loses? The gold merchant has lost everything. What can he do to insure that he profits no matter what the outcome? This problem was cleverly solved by financing the other side as well. If the other side wins, he has the same taxation arrangement to cover all of his losses, including the money loaned to the losing side. By financing both sides, the banker creates greater debt, maximizes profits, increases his control over the citizenry, consolidates power and has a means to punish nations who don't cooperate.

This explanation may sound like an oversimplification. However, Reginald McKenna, a former Chairman of the Board of the Midlands Bank of England succinctly described this process when he made this statement, "I am afraid the ordinary citizen will not like to be told that *banks can and do create money...* And they who control the credit of the nation, direct the policy of governments and hold in the hollow of their hands the destiny of the people."

It is essential to understand that regardless of the nature or form of government involved, it is those who control the creation and allocation of money who have the control and can dictate policy. When one understands this process and looks behind the scenes, many historical events take on a completely different perspective. In most cases the unseen forces behind the wars, depressions and revolutions have been and are the manipulations and financial maneuvering caused by international bankers.

The Bankers Influence of American History

Throughout the history of the United States the international banking establishment attempted to gain control over the issuance of money through a centralized banking system. In fact, it could be said that the struggle for control over the nation's banking system has been a pivotal point throughout American history. Thomas Jefferson stated, "I sincerely believe that the banking institutions are more dangerous to our liberties than standing armies." He was right.

The influence wielded from behind the scenes by these bankers on policy decisions and historical events puts our understanding of history in a totally different context. Let's take a brief look at a few key events in American history, and see how this struggle for the control of issuing money and the establishment of a central bank has influenced these events.

In pre-Revolutionary War times, the American colonies used a form of money called Colonial Script. It was paper money that was issued by the government in amounts that were sufficient to facilitate commerce but not cause inflation.

It is interesting to note that this period of American history was very prosperous. So prosperous, in fact that it caught the attention of the Bank of England. One of the governors of the Bank of England asked Benjamin Franklin, who was living in London at the time, what he attributed to be the cause of the high level of prosperity enjoyed by the colonies.

Franklin answered, "In the colonies we issue our own money. It is called Colonial Script. We issue it in proper proportion to the demands of trade and industry, to make the products pass easily from the producers to the consumers. In this manner, creating for ourselves our own paper money, we control its purchasing power and we have no interest to pay anyone." This was a great arrangement. Money did the job it was intended to do which was to facilitate commerce and there was no interest.

You can guess how that went over when the bankers realized how much interest income they were losing. The Bank of England pressured Parliament to pass the Currency Act of 1764. This act prohibited the issuance of paper money and required the colonies to pay taxes in gold or silver. The effect of this was devastating. Franklin noted, "Within one year the conditions were so reversed that the era of prosperity ended, and a depression set in to such an extent that the streets of the colonies were filled with the unemployed." With the stroke of a pen the economic conditions went from prosperity to depression. The British used this tactic of requiring taxes to be paid in gold or silver to destabilize local economies and control people around the world.

In his biography Franklin made the statement, "The colonies would have gladly born a little tax on tea and other matters had it not been that England took away from the colonies this money, which created unemployment and dissatisfaction. The inability of the colonists to get the power to issue their own money permanently out of the hands of George III and the international bankers was *the primary cause* of the revolutionary war." Colonial Script, paper money worked fine when it was used with the intent to facilitate commerce instead of the intent to control and dominate.

We may have won the Revolutionary War militarily but the economic war with the Bank of England continued. The strategy changed as they attempted to gain influence in the new nation by working with those in government. The plan was to start a central bank they could control and loan money to the US government. In

1790, Alexander Hamilton pushed for a new private bank, and in 1791, Congress passed the bill giving The First Bank of the United States a twenty-year charter. During the first five years the government borrowed eight million dollars from this private bank and prices in the new republic rose 72%. Although we normally don't think in these terms, for the most part, economic conquest can be as bad as military conquest. The Americans had experienced the economic pain and hardship brought on by this banking system. Although the British warned them not to revoke the bank's charter, it was not renewed. This was one of the contributing factors to the war of 1812.

There is nothing like war to increase debt. To the banker's advantage this war increased the national debt from $45 million to $127 million. The fledging nation was in a difficult situation as it struggled to repay the debt. Finally, under pressure to repay the debt, it chartered the Second Bank of the United States with another 20-year charter. This private bank immediately loaned the government sixty million dollars to repay the debts caused by the war.

Over the next few years, the bank inflated (increased the amount of money in circulation) and contracted the money supply (decreased the amount in circulation) causing economic hardship for the people. The renewal of the bank's charter was due to come up in 1836 during Andrew Jackson's second term. The bankers knew Jackson was a staunch adversary of the bank so Nicholas Biddle, the president of the bank, asked Congress to renew its charter four years earlier with the intent of making it an election issue in 1832. Congress granted the renewal, but Jackson understood the danger of the people's money supply in private hands and vetoed it. Jackson once said, "I do not believe that a national bank is a national blessing, but rather a curse to a republic, inasmuch as it is calculated to raise around the administration a moneyed aristocracy dangerous to the liberties of the country."

When he ran for president in 1832 Jackson decided to let the American people decide whether or not they wanted a bank. He ran under the platform of "Bank and no Jackson or Jackson and no bank." When he was re-elected, the people had made their decision. In an attempt to force the people to demand a re-charter, Mr. Biddle ordered a contraction or decrease of the money supply for five months. He then reversed his action and dramatically inflated the money supply. These actions had a devastating effect on the economy causing businesses to fail and mass unemployment. The bank then blamed the financial turmoil they caused on Jackson in an attempt to blackmail the government. In spite of this manipulation and political maneuvering the bankers were defeated and the charter was not renewed. In addition to killing the bank which he said was his most important accomplishment as president, Jackson also completely eliminated the national debt.

Let's consider how these international bankers influenced another key pivotal point in American history, the Civil War. According to Otto Von Bismarck, the chancellor of Germany at the time, there were other forces influencing the Civil War besides the ones with which we are all familiar. As Bismarck put it, "The division of the United States into two federations of equal force was decided long before the Civil War by the high financial powers of Europe. These bankers were afraid that the United States, if it remained one block and one nation, would allow economic and financial independence which would upset their financial domination over the world."

True to form the European bankers attempted to finance both sides of the Civil War from behind the scenes. However, instead of borrowing the needed funds Lincoln circumvented the bankers and had 400 million greenbacks printed in 1862 and 1863 to finance the war. This was done at no interest to the government and created no debt for the people. Lincoln's assessment of the creation and use of money was succinctly expressed when he said, "The government should create, issue and circulate all the currency and credit needed to satisfy the spending power of the government and the buying power of consumers. The privilege of creating and issuing money is not only the supreme prerogative of government but it is the government's greatest creative opportunity... By the adoption of these principles the taxpayers will be saved immense sums of interest. Money will cease to be the master and become the servant of humanity."

Unfortunately, Congress was persuaded by the Secretary of the Treasury, Solomon Chase (after whom the Chase Manhattan bank is named) to create a new national bank which would use a debt-based currency. This resulted in the passing of the National Bank Act in 1863. These new national banks had tax-free status and an exclusive monopoly power to create the new money in the form of bank notes. This act took the power of creating money from the government and again placed it in the hands of private bankers. Chase later regretted his involvement in this decision when he said, "My agency in promoting the National Bank Act was the greatest financial mistake of my life. It has built up a monopoly which affects every interest of this country." Had Lincoln lived, he surely would have killed the bank just as Andrew Jackson had done years before.

There is a convincing body of evidence that international bankers orchestrated Lincoln's assassination. Again, from his vantage point in Europe, Bismarck remarked, "The death of Lincoln was a disaster for Christendom. There was no man in the United States big enough to fill his boots. I fear that the foreign bankers with their craftiness and tortuous tricks will entirely control the exuberant riches of America, and use it systematically to corrupt modern civilization. They will not hesitate to plunge the whole of Christendom into wars and chaos, in order that the earth should become their inheritance."

From the beginning of our country there have been numerous attempts by international bankers to implement a central banking system. They were successful on a temporary basis several times throughout our nation's history but were eventually defeated. Each time they wreaked havoc on the economic lives of common people as a result of their quest for control.

One of the ways bankers have influenced the economy has been by inflating the money supply, which is adding more money or by deflating it, which is withdrawing money from the money supply. Again, Jefferson warned us of this when he said, "If the American people ever allow the private banks to control the issuance of their currency, first by inflation and then by deflation, the banks and corporations that grow up around them will deprive the people of all their property until their children wake up homeless on the continent their fathers conquered."

We can see the truth of this prophetic statement in another contraction that happened after the civil war. In 1866, under pressure from the banking establishment then controlling the National Bank of the United States, Congress issued "The Contraction Act" and began to retire the greenbacks in circulation. The effect this had was devastating.

- In 1866, there were 1.8 billion dollars in circulation. This amount equated to $50.46 per capita.
- In 1867, it had been reduced to 1.3 billion in circulation or $44.00 per capita. As the money supply was reduced there was a loss in purchasing power. People had to work more and received less.
- By 1876, there was only .6 billion in circulation or $14.60 per capita.

- By 1886, that amount was further reduced to $.4 billion in circulation which was only $6.67 per capita.

This was a 760% loss in buying power in nineteen years and this hardship was caused solely by the bankers calling in two-thirds of America's money. They wanted centralized banking under their control. Their strategy was to intentionally cause these recessions to bring people to submission. It's rather difficult to become involved in the political process of self-governance when you're struggling to survive.

Another example of this ability to control the flow of life force necessary for living is this statement issued in 1891 by the American Bankers Association:

"On September 1, 1894, we will not renew our loans under any consideration. We will demand our money on September 1st. We will foreclose and become mortgagees in possession. We can take two-thirds of the farms west of the Mississippi and thousands of them east of the Mississippi as well, at our own price.... Then the farmers will become tenants as in England."

The motive behind this plan was to create a panic so that the people would demand a central bank to control the economy. People were led to believe that by centralizing control it would be possible to prevent fluctuations in the economy. However, in this case the bankers were actually the ones constricting the availability of money, causing economic hardship and driving people out of business. The plan worked and helped to set the stage for public acceptance of a central bank.

Through some political maneuvering, the international bankers were finally successful in 1913 with the enactment of the Federal Reserve Act. This legislation brought into being a privately owned central bank known as the Federal Reserve. This organization is not a government-owned or controlled institution, as most people believe. In fact, during its history, it has never been audited and it is outside the control of Congress. It is a privately held, for-profit corporation that literally manufactures money out of paper, makes loans to the government, and charges interest.

Senator Louis McFaddan of Pennsylvania put it this way: "Most Americans have no real understanding of the operation of the international money lenders. *The accounts of the Federal Reserve System have never been audited. It operates outside the control of Congress... and manipulates the credit of the United States.*"

Should you question this fact, try to look up Federal Reserve in the government pages of your telephone book. If you don't find it there, and you won't, try the business section where you'll find it very close to Federal Express.

This financial arrangement is the source of our national debt and is the dominant, behind the scenes force influencing national and international political decisions for financial gain. The purposes and designs of this organization have been identified and exposed by many prominent and credible people throughout history. Senator Charles Lindbergh Sr., father of Charles Lindbergh, warned the American people when he said, "The passage of the Federal Reserve Act... established the most gigantic trust on earth. When the president signs this act, the invisible government by the money powers... will be legitimized. This new law will create inflation whenever the trust wants inflation. From now on, depressions will be scientifically created."

On another occasion, Mr. Lindbergh said, "The financial system... has been turned over to the Federal Reserve Board. That board administers the finance system by authority of a purely profiteering group. This system is private, conducted for the sole purpose of obtaining the greatest possible profits from the use of other people's money."

It is clear this group has no moral issue about creating economic hardship in the lives of individuals and families. They have no concern about instigating war as a means of controlling nations by debt creation to further their financial gain and consolidate power.

A few years after he signed the Federal Reserve Act, Woodrow Wilson realized what he had really done and he wrote, "I am a most unhappy man. I have unwittingly ruined my country. A great industrial nation is controlled by its system of credit. Our system of credit is concentrated. The growth of the nation, therefore, and all our activities are in the hands of a few men. We have come to be one of the worst ruled, one of the most completely controlled and dominated governments in the civilized world. No longer a government by free opinion, no longer a government by conviction and the vote of the majority, but a government by the opinion and duress of a small group of dominant men."

Just so we are clear on the long range goals and intent of this group, let's repeat a statement we quoted earlier made by Dr. Carroll Quigley. *"The powers of financial capitalism had another far-reaching aim, nothing less than to create a world system of financial control in private hands able to dominate the political system in each country and the economy of the world as a whole. The system was to be controlled in a feudalist fashion by central banks acting in concert."*

As mentioned earlier, some people who have investigated the powers and motives behind these acts are of the belief that there is a gigantic conspiracy driving all of this. Other investigators just view it as greedy, selfish people being driven and guided by bottom-line values. Whatever the case, the damage is the same. The effects of these acts have been articulated by the well-known economist, John Maynard Keynes. In 1919, Mr. Keynes said, *"There is no subtler, no surer means of overturning the existing basis of society than to debauch the currency. The process engages all the hidden forces of economic laws on the side of destruction, and does it in a manner which not one in a million is able to diagnose."*

As we grow in our understanding that money is life force, we begin to see that the restriction and manipulation of life force causes dis-ease. Just as it is impossible for a cell to remain healthy in a toxic environment, so is it difficult for an individual to thrive and grow in a corrupt system. The present world economic system under the control of a private banking system appears to be guided by the intent to control the life force of humanity. If this is the guiding intent (and many believe it is) and not just a flaw in the system, it could very well be considered to be the greatest threat to health and well-being on the planet today.

This corrupt intent and the disease it causes were clearly articulated by Sir Josiah Stamp who was himself a director of the Bank of England in the 1920s and the second wealthiest man in Britain. Mr. Stamp told us, *"Banking is conceived in iniquity and born in sin. Bankers own the earth. Take it away from them, but leave them the power to create money and control credit, and with a flick of a pen they will create enough money to buy it back again. Take this power from them and all great fortunes like mine will disappear, and they ought to disappear, for this would be a better and happier world to live in. But if you want to continue as the slaves of bankers and pay the cost of your own slavery, then let them continue to create money and control credit."*

The information presented above is but a fragment of the greater picture. It is my hope that it will serve as the impetus for you to learn more and, most important, take action. Possibilities for effective action will be suggested later on. If we are ever going to address and heal the social and political problems that face humanity, an understanding and resolution of this money creation and control process is absolutely essential. To gain a more in-depth understanding of this process and its history read *Secrets of the Federal Reserve,* by Eustace Mullins. It is one of the best books on this topic and the years of research done by Mr. Mullins is the source from which many other authors draw. The video *The Money Masters* by Bill Still is also an excellent resource and can be found at www.themoneymasters.com.

CHAPTER 24

INTEREST AND USURY

To understand how this process of creating debt affects our country and the world, let's briefly examine the role and power of compounding interest. Albert Einstein once said, *"The most powerful force in the world is the power of compounding interest."* As an example:

1. If we take one dollar and compound it at 10% annually, at the end of the first year we would have $1.10.
2. At the end of the second year the interest compounding on itself would have caused the amount to grow to $1.21.
3. By the tenth year $2.59
4. By the thirtieth year $17.44
5. By the by the 50th year, $117.39
6. By the 80th year, $2048.40.
7. By the 100th year, $13,780.65.
8. By the 150th year, the one-dollar has grown to $1,617,724 as a result of the interest compounding on itself.

Figure 13a is a graph taken from the book *Money and Debt: A Solution to the Global Crisis,* by Thomas Greco Jr., that illustrates the exponential growth of compounding interest.[4] The second graph comes from the book The End of Money and the Future of Civilization, also by Mr. Greco and shows the progression of the public and private debt our country has accumulated with this system.

This arrangement is great if you are the one loaning the money and earning the interest. However, if you are the borrower, as time goes on, it becomes more and more difficult to repay the loan and interest. In some cases it becomes impossible to repay. This is especially true when one is already in debt and the money supply is contracted. The interest continues to compound, and there is less money available to use.

It is worth noting that throughout history, many religions have forbidden usury or the charging of interest on money loaned. Deuteronomy 23:20 says, "Unto thy brother thou shalt not lend upon usury, that the Lord thy God may bless thee in all that thou settest thine hands to." In the Koran, Sutra 30:38 the admonition is even stronger: "What ye put out as usury to increase it with the substance of others, (life force) shall have no increase from God.

As we grow in our understanding of the energetic nature of money and the parasitic, energy sucking effect created by compounding interest, we can see that this arrangement is literally a siphoning off of one's life force into the control of others. When viewed in this manner, most of us would agree this violates the spiritual principles we aspire to live by.

GROWTH OF ONE DOLLAR
AT COMPOUND INTEREST
Figure 14A

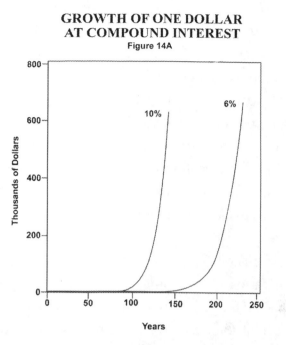

Compound interest

ACTUAL GROWTH OF DEBT
IN THE UNITED STATES
Figure 14B

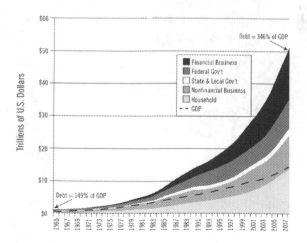

Growth of Debt in US

273

The Federal Reserve, a private banking cartel, loans money to the US Treasury with interest. The Treasury further loans money to commercial banks, which, in turn, loan it to their customers. Keeping in mind the principle of fractional banking, certain banks are allowed to loan out ten times the amount they actually have in reserve or on deposit and charge interest on it. If a bank has $10 million on deposit they can loan out $100 million. From a purely economic and control standpoint, we can clearly see that this is a pretty good arrangement for the private bank of the Federal Reserve and its affiliated banks - create money out of paper and loan it out at interest.

The bank customers use the money to finance businesses, to purchase farms, cars, homes, and consumer goods. These customers pay off the loan plus interest. If they are unable to pay off the loan, the bank forecloses on the farm and house or repossesses the car and sells it to recover the amount loaned. When this occurs, the borrower receives no compensation for the equity he already had built up by paying off part of the debt. He loses everything. Often, this is because he has been unable to keep up with the cost of interest because of the interest compounding on itself.

This same process works with our government. The Federal Reserve creates money out of paper and loans it to the government, with interest. Our government finances its projects with this money. The mechanism for collateralizing these loans and making sure they will be repaid is through taxation. The collection agency for this process in the United States is the Internal Revenue Service.

Although it is incumbent for each of us to contribute to the good of the greater whole of which we are a part, and certain forms of taxation do have a legitimate role, the present tax system is not about helping us or serving society. It is about control.

Some interesting insights about the true nature of the income tax system were presented in a government-sponsored report. In the early 1980's President Reagan appointed Peter Grace to find ways to reduce government spending. By knowing exactly where the money had come from, where and how it had been spent, it was hoped that "pork" could be cut, so to speak, and that the funding situation could be brought under control.

When the Grace Commission released its report on January 15, 1984, one point was extremely interesting, but it did not receive much publicity. Grace said, concerning the income tax, that "100 percent of what is collected is absorbed solely by <u>interest</u> on the Federal Debt. All individual income tax revenues are gone before one single nickel is spent on services which taxpayers expect from their government." Read that again and let it soak in. The next question most of us ask is "What pays government expenses"? The answer: credit the government borrows from the Federal Reserve.

What are the results of this arrangement? The more the government goes into debt, the greater the profits that go to the bankers, the more control they have over the nation and the more the people lose their freedom. Do you think it matters who is in office, and what their policies are (conservative, liberal, pro-this, anti-that) if the privately owned central bank of the U.S. contracts or expands the money supply? Because the Federal Reserve can determine the interest rate, they can control your house payments, car payments, whether or not you have a job, and your overall standard of living. As more and more money goes to pay off interest there is less and less to purchase the necessities of life.

Consequently, it takes both parents working full-time to support a family whereas a generation ago a single parent was able to provide for everyone. When a house is purchased a family will often pay more in interest than the original cost of the house. How many families do you know who have one parent working just to make their mortgage payments? They are struggling to pay interest on money created out of nothing.

When we look at socially destructive behaviors such as drug abuse, violence, teen pregnancy, and gang activity, we find that a root cause of these problems can be traced back to a break-up of the family. Over and over, we hear from educators and psychologists that there is not enough parental involvement. Not enough time is being spent with our children to impart the emotional nutrients required for healthy development because of ever-increasing financial pressures. Although there are numerous causes of these problems finances are at the top. According to many experts financial pressures have been found to be the leading cause of marital break ups.

Let's look at this interest arrangement from a little different angle. Most of us have had the experience of playing musical chairs. In this game, providing enough chairs for everyone except one person creates a "shortage of resources." People walk around the chairs as long as the music plays. As soon as the tune master turns off the music, everyone scrambles for a seat. The person left standing is out, and another chair is removed for the next round. This arrangement dictates that there must be one loser each round. It can be a fun party game, but let's add a couple of different variables.

In this game, the players are all people who are out of work and they have families to support. We will start with 20 people who are going to invest in buying space on a chair for $200. Every time a person wins a seat he is given $100 by the music master. At the end of 20 rounds, the one left has made $2000 from their original $200 investment. This is not a bad return. However, at the end of each round the person left standing after the music stops forfeits all the money he has to the music master. At each round the intensity of competition increases as people vie for limited resources. At the end of each round someone loses all they have accumulated as well as their original investment.

The emotional tension rises and so does the physical conflict as people fight for a chair. As people are eliminated there is a growing group of losers with all the emotional and financial pain that loss entails. An ever-smaller group of winners struggles to be number one. The higher the stakes the greater the conflict. Eventually there is one winner at the expense of nineteen losers. Let's not forget the music master who kept the other $2000 as compensation for setting up the game and managing the accounts.

Artificial Scarcity

The structure of the system in this example created "artificial scarcity" which necessitates some must lose in order for others to win. Did the design of "the system" influence behavior? Did it cause some people to be more aggressive than they normally would be and in some cases lead to outright violence? Is it likely that the losers in this activity might have experienced anger, depression, sorrow, fear, and a general sense of failure and worthlessness?

Some would say that's just the way the world is. The reality is: that is the way we have made the world. By its very nature our money system not only influences behavior, it affects emotional health as well. It creates artificial scarcity in a world of abundance.

In current economic practice what does this artificially created scarcity caused by the money system look like? We now understand that money is created by bank debt. When you borrow $100,000 to purchase your home, that act of borrowing puts $100,000 into circulation. The money you borrowed has been created by the bank, and that is the principle you owe. However, through your loan arrangement, you agree to repay the principal plus another $100,000 in interest. Where does that second $100,000 come from?

The answer to that question is the cause of the artificial scarcity. The money to repay the loan was never created. It does not exist, and yet it must be paid back.

Let's take it a step farther. A million other home owners have made the same arrangement and have the same terms. There has been enough money in circulation to pay for the houses, but there is not enough to pay all of the interest. The result is that people must compete for limited resources. Some will lose everything, especially if there is a contraction in the money supply.

Taking this to an international level, let's take a look at a Third World country trying to develop its resources and uplift its people. It needs extra capital for improvements. The country borrows one billion dollars from the International Monetary Fund or the World Bank at 10% interest. It has the billion dollars to invest in the development. However; at 10% interest it will not only have to pay back the billion but also an additional 100 million in interest. Here's the catch: if there is only one billion dollars in circulation, where does the other 100 million come from? Yes, the country may develop its resources and the skills of its citizenry, but there is only a billion dollars in circulation. That amount must be paid back, plus an additional 100 million. Where does the money for the interest come from and what do they do after they have paid back the original loan.

This is the musical chairs scenario - the losers not only lose their earnings but their original investment as well. The tune master is calling the shots. The country must develop its resources to the point where it can repay the original loan plus interest. If it is unable to do so it will need to borrow again to keep going. By using a debt-based currency with interest attached it must continue to borrow.

Let's expand this model. There are 100 developing countries in the same situation. Each borrows a billion and must repay the original loan of a billion plus an extra one hundred million dollars in interest. They each must pay back more interest than money in circulation. Each develops its resources, and sells them to each other, or possibly to other developed countries. Some of the countries will be successful in raising themselves enough to compete and earn enough to pay back the loan, plus the interest, and hopefully have some left over. Many of the countries won't even be able to pay back the original loan let alone the interest. Often, they must borrow more money just to make the payment on the interest, thus putting them further in debt. The way the system currently works for every dollar borrowed from wealthy nations, Third World countries pay back 13 dollars in interest.

This arrangement results in unhealthy, destructive competition and automatically creates a situation where many must lose in order for a small minority to win. It becomes very clear how this arrangement creates poverty, tension between people and nations, animosity between the haves and have-nots and the destructive behavior that results from these situations.

A study was conducted in 1982 to determine the degree to which wealth extraction via interest occurred in Germany. The population had been divided into 10 groups of 2.5 million households per group. The following graph depicts the amount of Deutsch Marks and from whom they were transferred.[5]

Figure 15

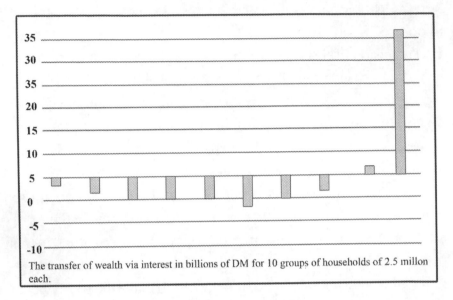

35	
30	
35	
20	
15	
10	
5	
0	
-5	
-10	

The transfer of wealth via interest in billions of DM for 10 groups of households of 2.5 millon each.

German Interest Study

As we can see, the first eight groups lost money as a result of this process. The ninth group held their own and the tenth group increased their income dramatically. Their gain was a result of extracting wealth from the other eight groups. Our money system is designed to redistribute wealth from the large majority to the small minority. When we view money in terms of life force, it is clear how this arrangement is literally a siphoning off of one's life force into the control of others. No wonder the scriptures forbade usury!

What does this mean if you are in the field of education helping youth, or you are a service professional trying to empower people to lift themselves out of poverty? First, it means that the economic system of which we are all a part of is one of the key causes of the poverty. Everyone - individuals, families, and the nation as a whole - is busy working hard to pay interest that doesn't exist, on money created out of nothing. There is an imbalance in the flow of the life force needed to provide the basics of living. There is an ongoing theft of the congealed energy, money, needed to sustain a viable life. There is a systemic flaw in that in order for some to win, others must lose.

Given this arrangement there is too little money to meet the needs in education and the growing challenges faced there. This includes everything from the teacher/student ratio to the poor level of teacher's salaries, from technology and the numerous special programs needed by children today to drug and violence prevention programs. A good deal of the drug and violence issues can also be traced to a constricted life force and feelings of frustration and hopelessness. The needs continue to grow and the resources to meet the needs aren't there.

Looking at the health care issue, we have seen how stress is a major contributing factor to physical disease. How much heart disease, cancer and other diseases are caused by stress resulting from financial difficulty which in turned are caused by the structure of the money system? These are just a few of the problems faced by our country which are caused by this drain of financial energy.

If this can affect a wealthy country so adversely how does this arrangement affect the developing world? Although the above study involved households within Germany we can easily extrapolate this scenario to see how this arrangement on a worldwide basis would extract wealth, resources, and life force from developing countries, and concentrate them in the developed countries who lend the money. This process of establishing a central bank, controlled by a private banking cartel, has continued country-by-country around the world. The lending practices of international bankers through the International Monetary Fund and the World Bank continue to shape governmental policies and economies of the world. Once the tentacles of the bankers establish their hold the grip is gradually tightened. This arrangement is the primary cause of poverty and the ecological crisis not to mention wars and revolutions.

When the IMF loans money to developing countries it makes them dependent on a global economy. Rather than produce the necessities of life for their people, the governments are forced to produce and export cash-based products so that they can repay the loans. Rather than growing beans and rice that they need to eat and feed their families, the peasants work on plantations, or, as sharecroppers, growing coffee, coca or other goods for export that have cash value.

The positive side of this is that it does facilitate trade and allows for the importation of goods produced in other parts of the world. The downside is that the country becomes dependent on a cash economy over which it has no control. It must continue to produce products it can sell for cash to repay its loan. As the economic noose tightens from the original loan by the power of compounding interest the more destructive the governments become to their resources and people.

This financial arrangement is also a driving force behind the ecological crisis. When countries go into debt they must mine, log and exploit nature in the most short-sighted, profit-oriented way to make their loan payments. This can take the form of deforestation to sell lumber and clear land to raise cattle or can lead to environmentally destructive mining practices. Governments are forced to exploit their raw capital which means they have little regard for long-term consequences. They log the rain forests at the rate of one acre a second, and have little or no regulation on mining and manufacturing operations. Consequently, the resources are exploited as are the people. Driven by these destructive financial policies the rape of the planet accelerates. One of the results of this is the third mega-trend we touched on earlier, that of climate change and bio-diversity extinction.

Frequently, what appears to be economic development turns into cultural destruction and the break-up of traditional values that have stabilized the family and society. This results in economic dependency, which in reality is a form of enslavement. This economic arrangement is one of the causes of the ever-widening gap between the haves and the have-nots and is a driving force behind the environmental crisis.

If nations are unable to repay their debts in a timely manner, the interest grows to an unmanageable level. As we have seen, governments must then borrow more money to make the payments on the interest. They are at the mercy of the bankers. If they decide not to pay or default on their loans, there are mechanisms such as instigating revolutions, military coups, or economic strangulation that can be used to induce governments to cooperate. As usual, it is the innocent people who suffer.

In his book *Confessions of an Economic Hit Man* John Perkins tells the story from the view point of an insider who help to engineer these situations. Working as an economic advisor for a private company his job was to induce the governments of developing countries to borrow money to modernize their country. He would "adjust" the numbers so they could qualify for loans from the World Bank or other financial institutions in the business of financing countries. When the developing country would borrow the money it was transferred to his company who built the dams, the electrical grid and other necessary infrastructure the economic advisor suggested was needed to modernize and help the people out of poverty. The money never went to the country, just the debt.

Since the return on the investment was inflated (by the economic advisor) it was very unlikely the country would be able to pay off the debt let alone the interest. If the country was unable to pay off the debt they would renegotiate allowing the "lender" to satisfy the debt by acquiring the countries natural resources, oil, timber, minerals, etc. at rock bottom prices. In cases where the governments understood what was happening and refused to go along Mr. Perkins describes from first-hand knowledge how they were assassinated or over thrown. He pointed out, if fifty percent of the country was in poverty to begin with, seventy five percent was in poverty after we were finished.

Mahatma Gandhi once said, "The worst form of violence is poverty." According to information reported in the Money Masters video program, a prominent Brazilian politician summed up the damage being done by these banking policies. *"The third world war has already started. It is a silent war. Not for that reason any less sinister. The war is tearing down Brazil, Latin America and practically all the third world. Instead of soldiers dying, there are children. It is a war over third world debt. One which has as its main weapon, interest. A weapon more deadly than an atom bomb, more shattering than a laser beam."*

With this understanding of how usury works and its effects, it is no wonder why the scriptures condemn its use. Thomas Edison had this to say about interest. "It is a terrible situation when the government, to insure the national wealth, must go in debt and submit to ruinous interest charges at the hands of men who control the fictitious value of gold. Interest is the invention of Satan." Such is the nature of the collective thought form we have all agreed to.

Mormon scholar Hugh Nibley points out that the Hebrew word for any kind of financial activity is "mamonut," and that the financier is a "mamonai." Nibley says, "Financing in its present form is, in honest language, the business of mammon." He goes on to say, "The Kingdom of God and Babylon both have their appeal but you can't have them both." As we understand the true nature of usury it becomes evident why this is true.

If this is your first exposure to this kind of information you may find it a little overwhelming or depressing. However, there is much that individuals and groups of people can do to remedy the situation if they choose to act. It is certainly worth remembering a historical truth beautifully articulated by renowned anthropologist Margaret Mead. "Never doubt that a small group of thoughtful, committed citizens can change the world. Indeed, it is the only thing that ever has."

The purpose of this brief introduction is to stimulate you to explore this topic further and gather a deeper understanding of the facts, so you will be in a position to act and direct your efforts in an intelligent way. You will be able to address the causes rather than just treating symptoms. As you investigate this topic deeper, you will see that the information shared here is just the tip of the iceberg. It is actually an understatement of what is truly taking place. As you are inspired to help solve these problems, keep in mind the two approaches we discussed earlier. One can either attack the disease or focus on the processes necessary to create health.

Proven Solutions

What is the solution? Have there ever been economic systems or monetary arrangements that have facilitated the flow of economic energy to benefit everyone?

Fortunately, the answer is yes. As we have seen, the early American colonies used Colonial Script, paper money that had been issued by the government in amounts that had been sufficient to facilitate commerce but not cause inflation. There had been a balanced flow of life force. The result was economic and social health.

After the Revolutionary War, a surplus of paper money had been issued to pay for the war causing massive inflation. It wasn't that the use of paper money had caused the problem. It was too much diluted energy, a false representation of life force creating an imbalance. Inflation is *always* caused by a surplus of money in circulation.

Lincoln's creating and issuing greenbacks without any interest attached is another excellent example of successfully directing energy to meet the needs of the times. His statement about the responsibility of government issuing currency bears repeating. *"The government should create, issue and circulate all the currency and credit needed to satisfy the spending power of the government and the buying power of consumers. The privilege of creating and issuing money is not only the supreme prerogative of government but it is the government's greatest creative opportunity. By the adoption of these principles, the taxpayers will be saved immense sums of interest. Money will cease to be the master and become the servant of humanity."*

Isn't that what we all want? The thought-form of money being the servant of humanity rather than its master is a good one to start building through the imagination process. It is also helpful to remember that money is not a thing. Money is a mutual agreement to use something as a medium of exchange. Money is a thought form.

Another example of a community taking control of its financial destiny is that of the town of Worgl in Austria. During the depression that devastated Germany and her allies after the First World War, the town of Worgl had experienced high unemployment and lack of financial resources needed to provide basic needs and municipal services. The city created its own currency much like Colonial Script, only it included an additional feature called demurrage charge. That meant that if citizens held on to money past a certain period of time they had to pay an extra fee for doing so. This motivated people to spend the money quickly. This increased the flow and made sure people wouldn't hoard it. The city government issued just enough to facilitate commerce. It wasn't long before needed roads were being built, infrastructure was being repaired, businesses were opening and most people had employment. In the midst of a terrible depression the town of Worgl became a small, prosperous oasis offering hope and life.

As Worgl's success grew, the idea began to spread to the neighboring communities. By issuing their own local currency, they were able to stimulate the flow of life force and begin to create prosperity in the midst of depression. The miracle of Worgl grew and blossomed for 13 months as a result of the community using its own currency. However, it was so successful that when the central bank of Austria learned about the situation it had the government intervene. Parliament passed laws making anything but the national currency illegal.

The results were similar to those caused by the Bank of England when it prevented the American colonies from using Colonial Script. The flow of life force stopped. It didn't take long before this prosperous, thriving community returned to a hopeless state of economic depression that was plaguing the rest of the continent. This state of despair set the stage for anyone promising economic salvation. A few years later, Austrians welcomed Adolph Hitler with open arms.

Today in Japan, where twenty percent of the population is over the age of 65, complementary currency is being used to offset the impact of the age wave. The medium of exchange is called Fureai

Kippu, which translates into *caring relationship tickets*. It is being used by some 800,000 people.

More than 100 non-profit, health-oriented organizations use a system of credits that allows individuals to exchange time and energy for *caring-relationship tickets*. Here is how it works. The unit of account is for an hour of service. If someone does volunteer work for seven hours they receive a credit for seven *caring-relationship tickets*. Recognizing that there are different values for different skills and jobs performed there are different valuations depending on the type of service rendered.

As an example, an elderly person has difficulty getting around to shop and take care of their basic needs. All they need is some help in doing household chores and going shopping. A college student in his neighborhood helps him for an hour a day doing laundry, shopping, cleaning and preparing food. For each hour, the student receives credit in the form of a ticket for the work he performed. If it was a simple job of shopping or preparing food, that credit had a certain amount of value. If the work were more about personal care there would be a greater amount of value attached to the credit.

These credits can then be spent on the services of any of the hundred organizations, which had agreed to participate in the project. The student can use the credits to help pay for his schooling, save the credits for a time when he might need them in retirement, or he could transfer them to his aging parents who live in another part of the country and need some additional help.

Not only have these caring-relationship tickets helped to ease the impact of the age wave and other socially oriented health challenges, there have also been some interesting positive side effects. One of these side effects is that this energy exchange is building relationships and a sense of community among those participating. The elderly people report a higher quality of care from the volunteers being compensated with *caring-relationship tickets* than those being compensated with the national currency of yen.

From an energetic view point, a neighbor who has time and cares about people in his community will bring a higher quality of service to the work he performs. There is a medium of exchange for the work, but the motive behind the action is different than someone just working for money. Those participating report that they are receiving not only a higher quality of care, but that this arrangement is building a sense of community, cooperation and mutual support.

Another form of exchange that has been successfully used in the U.S. for a number of years is called Time Dollars. This mutual credit system was started by Edgar Cahn in Washington D. C. It is an effective way to connect people who have unmet needs with others who have unused resources. An hour of service is credited with one time dollar. As people accumulate these credits they are able to spend them for other goods and services within the exchange they need.

As with the Fureai Kippu in Japan, one of the greatest benefits is the sense of community this type of exchange is building. People who have never interacted with each other on a personal level are doing so, and meaningful relationships based on service are being formed. A study has been made of retirement homes that used time dollars and those who did not. It was found that those who participated in this type of energy exchange reported a greater sense of community and well-being among their members.

The structure of money does influence behavior. In the case of time dollars, the results have been stronger relationships and a wider variety of friends than one would normally meet. Many people report that they have had a great number of positive experiences with people of other races or ethnic groups with whom they had rarely interacted in the past. The exchange of life force this medium has been providing is proving to be quite effective.

The use of this is becoming more widely accepted and used. Elderplan, a New York City-based insurance company, now takes 25% of its premiums in the form of time dollars. They are better able to use the services of neighbors supporting their elderly clients and provide for their needs in a way that builds healthy relationships. This system is expanding in a number of different places with very positive results. One other positive benefit is that there have been three IRS rulings that make this form of exchange tax-free in the United States. For more information about time banking or to start one go to timebanks.org.

Another recent example of creative currency being used to free the restricted flow of life force is taking place in Brazil. The city of Curitiba has a population 2.3 million. A third of the city lived in slums called favalas where their homes are made of corrugated metal and cardboard. For the people who live here poverty is a way of life.

One of the biggest problems facing the community had been garbage collection. Because the streets are very narrow, the city's garbage trucks couldn't get into the favalas to pick up the garbage. As a result the garbage attracted a large number of rodents and disease began to break out.

The mayor of the city introduced a creative solution. He placed trash bins on the outskirts of these communities. The bins were labeled glass, cans, paper, etc so the trash could be presorted and recycled. Because many of the people living here couldn't read they were also color coded according to the type of trash. In exchange for a bag of presorted trash, the city would give the person a bus ticket so they could go into the city to look for work. The city buses were only half full. Part of the reason for the poverty was that people didn't have a way to get into the city to look for work. This arrangement cost the city very little as the buses were already running and the trash was collected for the cost of printing a bus ticket. A school program was also instituted to help poor children acquire pencils and notebooks, which were given in exchange for trash.

The results of this program were dramatic. Approximately seventy percent of all Curitiba families participated. As a result of their efforts 11,000 tons of garbage was traded for more than one million bus tokens and over 1,200 tons of food. More than 100 schools exchanged over 100 tons of trash for almost 2 million notebooks. The paper-recycling component alone saves 1,200 trees a day.

From this garbage currency a number of other successful, innovative, complementary currencies evolved solving many more problems. Today, Curitiba is the only city in Brazil to have lower pollution levels than they did in the 1950's. The crime rate is lower and the educational level higher than other comparable cities in Brazil. Curitiba is the only city in Brazil that has turned down grants from the federal government because their own solutions are more effective and have less red tape than government-sponsored programs.

The great depression of the 1930's was a terrible time for people in our country but for those in Europe it was even worse. In 1934 a group of business men in Switzerland had all received notices from their banks that their credit lines were going to be greatly reduced or eliminated. This was happening to their customers and suppliers as well. As they pondered what to do they realized they didn't need a bank to issue money. They could do it themselves.

They created a cooperative of businesses and began using a mutual credit exchange system. The credits were linked to the national currency and whenever there was an exchange the company that made the purchase had their account debited and whoever provided the goods or service had their account credited. Their credits were backed by their inventory, real estate or other assets which provided the value backing the currency.

Within 3 months there were 1700 businesses participating and in a year over 3000. This system became known as the WIR Bank and it is still in operation. Today, eighty years later this complementary currency accounts for twenty-five percent of the Swiss economy and is main the reason for the economic stability in that country.

In 2011 the governor of Utah signed a bill into law called the Legal Tender Act making gold and silver legal tender. The Utah Precious Metals Association was set up on a model similar to the WIR as an association of businesses that agree to use gold and silver. This system is practical and using this currency is as easy as swiping a debit card. Just like transferring money from your bank account to a merchant, this will debit a portion of your gold savings and transfer it to the participating business. The association has also created ways to interact with people and businesses that are not part of the association.

This bill gives legal protection to the use of this alternative currency and could be the start of a parallel economic system that is more stable than a fiat currency that can be manipulated. It also gives protection to other forms of complementary currency that may be able to fit under this umbrella. For more information on how this system works or to join, go to upma.org.

These are just a few examples of people taking charge of their own lives and how different mediums of exchange have been used to facilitate the flow of energy between people to enhance the circulation of life force. From these examples, we can again see that money is not necessarily a thing. It is an *agreement* to use something as a medium of exchange. The people in Curitiba didn't just hang around complaining that they didn't have any real money (real money in some circles is defined as gold or silver). They all agreed that garbage and bus tickets would be the medium of exchange. By that agreement, they dramatically improved the quality of their lives and community.

Money is a collective thought form. It may have been created and promoted by bankers but we have agreed to use it. When people understand that money is a thought form created by an agreement, they begin to have control over it and can develop new ways of exchanging life force.

In his book, *New Money for Healthy Communities,* Thomas Greco cites a number of other cases where local communities have gained a degree of autonomy and control over their economic destiny by creating and using their own medium of exchange. This book is highly recommended, as it provides a blueprint and suggestions for arranging your affairs in a way that will free your life force to contribute to the good of your community.

There are two other suggested resources for learning how complementary currencies can be effective solutions to stem the rising tide of social problems we face, and have an effect on lessening the destructive effect of the four mega-trends. The first is the book *New Money for A New World* by Bernard Lietaer and Stephen Belgin and the second is *Rethinking Money: How New Currencies Turn Scarcity into Prosperity* by Bernard Lietaer and Jacqui Dunne. They are both excellent reading and will give you a much deeper understanding of the inherent flaws in the present system as well as practical solutions. Much of the information in this section about complementary currency comes from their work.

For those with a commitment to health, healing, and social justice, it is essential that we find alternatives to the present life-sucking system and work toward the needed change. Until we do, we are literally directing our life force to support those who are actually causing the poverty, armed conflict, educational, environmental, and social problems, so they can line their pockets and strengthen their control.

Beginning to reform the banking system is essential to solving the problems we face on a global level. I suggest that you obtain a copy of the video program "The Money Masters" to gain a deeper understanding of how the problem has evolved and what can be done to help remedy the situation. Their website is www.themoneymasters.com. Until these issues are faced and resolved, we will never be able to truly create wellness on all levels. The problems we work to solve, and the pain we so ardently desire to see healed, will continue to grow and most people will continue to treat symptoms rather than addressing the real cause.

CHAPTER 25

BALANCING THE FLOW

As we have seen, when there is a fair, equitable exchange of life force between people and organizations the material conditions of health are realized. When there is an inequitable or unjust exchange, it is literally the theft of someone else's life force. By using our life force to create products and services that produce value for others, we create true wealth and contribute to the well-being of the whole system.

We are growing in our understanding of the energetic dynamics of imagination, visualization and thought. When we use this knowledge for service and align our actions with the power of purpose we can begin to create alternatives to the present system and learn to redirect our energy. What are some of the other actions we can take that will move us in a positive direction?

Over time you will find that as you grow in the understanding that money is a representation of your life force you will make much more conscious choices about how you handle money, how you earn it and where you invest and spend it. When you write a check to your church or a charity, you, as a cell in that organism, are supporting the goodness that the organization is carrying out. You are giving your life force to the goodness of that work. When you purchase products from socially responsible companies your energy is going to support organizations that give back to the community and planet. Your life force is part of the healing process.

When we purchase from or invest in companies whose products are environmentally or socially destructive we become a part of that destructive process by directing our life energy into those organizations. When we choose to buy products from a country that represses its people, violates human rights, and uses slave labor, even though that country might be on the other side of the world, we, as cells in the body of humanity, are directing our life force to contribute to those actions and values. We have become a cell participating in the autoimmune disease that is attacking the health of the planet. When we purchase products from companies that use sweatshop labor, our life force becomes a part of the exploitation and economic enslavement that contributes to the misery of humanity.

As an example, let's say you're shopping for a jacket. You find one you really love for less cost than the other ones. You note the country where it was manufactured, and you are very certain that some of the activities in which that country engages are not in alignment with the values you believe in. Do you buy the jacket?

Many of us feel frustrated and powerless as we look at conditions in the world. To start taking back your power become aware of where you are choosing to direct your money. Choose to support your values by voting with your dollars. Consciously choose to put your life force into activities and organizations that are in alignment with the principles of health. There are hundreds of socially responsible companies who are using their business as a vehicle for positive social transformation and planetary healing.

In fact, many top business leaders have made the point that business is and can be very much a part of solving the economic problems faced by the planet. Dr. W. Edwards Deming, one of the people responsible for turning a devastated post-war Japan into an economic powerhouse, held and taught the viewpoint that *the purpose of business is to serve society.* It performs that service best by providing jobs. The best way of assuring jobs is to build a stable, productive and profitable company. The best way to make sure the company stays in business is to focus on quality products and service. The focus of the business is on continuous, quality improvement and the understanding is that quality doesn't cost, it pays.

In Deming's teaching, the well-being of the employees came before the profits of the stockholders. Certainly, investors need to be compensated for their capital but not at the expense of the people whose life force is driving the business. Deming's guiding value in his approach to business was service to society. It's worth noting that the highest award a business can receive in Japan is the Deming Award.

Anita Roddick, the founder and president of the Body Shop, a natural cosmetic and skin care business, has made the point that the needed changes in society must be brought about by businesses. Government is too slow and academia is too ineffective. Only business has the power, money and resources to effect positive, lasting change for the better.

Her company redirects a good percentage of its profits into socially responsible activities that contribute to the well-being of the communities of which they are a part. This includes everything from paying employees to work in poverty-stricken areas to building schools and teaching the South American Indians who collect the raw materials for their cosmetics how to read and write. There is an understanding that business is not only about profit, it's about building healthy relationships. The whole company is guided and driven by the values of using the business to create positive social, political and environmental health. Exchange based on healthy relationships with the intent of creating value for all is not only good business but it enhances social and economic health and promotes goodwill. Relationship and fair energy exchange is also the basis of new alternative currencies that are coming into being.

When the mission and intent of a business is to serve society, it can be a powerful force for good. Most of us are aware of how giant multinational corporations use their financial clout to control government and exploit people for their own selfish ends. That's nothing new. However, some companies use their economic influence to stand up for the rights of oppressed people and pressure government for healthy, just policies. Structuring a business to add value and enhance the quality of life for all concerned, rather than sucking off the energy of employees and society at large is simply a matter of intent. It is the result of higher values and a commitment to play at a higher level.

As we begin to view health and finances from an energetic perspective we are able to understand the need for correct regulation of balance and flow. Oriental medicine has approached healing from this viewpoint for a long time. As we noted earlier, Chinese medicine defines disease as a blockage or imbalance of energy. When this happens there is too much energy concentrated in or too little energy available at a given location in the body. When this occurs, the disease eventually affects the whole system. This principle holds true for not only the body of an individual, but also for the body of an organization, a nation and our planet as well.

If we look at our planet as one system, which it is, and we look at the nature of disease that affects different countries, we see the diseases that affect the developed countries are diseases of excess. Heart disease, cancer, diabetes and addictive problems such as eating disorders, or drug and alcohol abuse, are the result of too much energy. There is a consumption of too much food, too much drink, and too much emotional stimulation. When we look at the diseases of underdeveloped countries, we have diseases of too little energy. Malnutrition, starvation, rickets, beriberi, poverty and illiteracy are all forms of dis-ease caused by a deficiency of energy.

The United States is the wealthiest, most affluent country on the face of the earth. Given that fact, it's interesting to note that we are also the leader in violent crime and addictive disorders. Have you ever wondered why, in the midst of so much affluence, depression has reached epidemic proportions? Have you ever thought about the fact that we spend more money on health care and yet are towards the bottom of the industrial world as far as overall health is concerned? Have you noticed that we spend inordinate amounts of money to prolong death, and yet don't have enough to provide the basics of health for many of our children? These are the results of misdirected or misappropriated energy.

Considering that money is life force what happens when we go into debt? When an individual or nation consumes more than they produce and take more than they give it creates an imbalance in the exchange of energy. This drain of energy in one area, and excess in another, leads to a state of dis-ease for the individual as well as the whole system. The diseases of excess we are experiencing in the United States are a reflection of this imbalance.

As the individual cells that make up this nation, collectively speaking, we are presently several trillion dollars in debt. Although we may be using money created out of nothing to pay for it, the fact is that this debt is the inequitable amount of life force we have collectively extracted from the greater whole of which we are a part. As much as we don't like to think about it the surplus we enjoy is often provided at the expense of others. The innate intelligence which governs any living system, whether biological, social, or economic, automatically seeks homeostasis and will eventually balance itself.

Another way to look at energetic debt and the imbalance of energy exchange is the relationship between fossil fuels and food

MICHAEL BROOK

production. Very few people consider this relationship. However, it has profound effect on the way we live, on our society and the planet as a whole. According to research presented by David Pimentel and Mario Giamietro the present food system in the United States consumes ten times more fossil-fuel energy than it produces in food energy. It presently takes ten calories of fossil-fuel energy to produce one calorie of food energy. The use of fossil fuel in food production comes in the form of petrochemical-based fertilizers, pesticides, irrigation, transportation, operation of field machinery, raising livestock, cooking and refrigeration. The next meal you enjoy pause to consider that the food you are enjoying is the result of petroleum products.

Between 1945 and 1994, the amount of energy used by agriculture had a four-fold increase, while the increase of food production increased only three-fold. The amount of energy used to raise food has continued to increase but food production hasn't. Given the damage done to the soil, the amount of pesticides used, and the intensive nature of modern agriculture, it will require more and more energy to maintain our current food production levels as time goes on.

Earlier in this book we examined the relationship between the energy provided by food to nourish the body and the amount of energy it took to digest the food. When we ingest dead, denatured food with no nutritional value it takes more energy to break it down and get rid of it than the body actually receives in exchange. This deficit energy exchange will eventually cause the system to break down because the disproportionate exchange of energy is unsustainable.

This relationship also holds true for the amount of food consumed in the United States and the amount of energy and water it takes to produce it. To feed each American at the present level of consumption requires 400 gallons of oil expended annually per person. To produce an acre of corn requires 500,000 gallons of water per growing season. The amount of energy derived from oil in the form of fertilizers, partial irrigation and pesticides enables the agriculture industry to produce approximately 130 bushels of corn per acre. Without the oil-based energy that production would drop to 30 bushels per acre. Oil and aquifer-stored water are like energy deposits made in the earth that we may use however we wish. However, often overlooked is the fact that these resources are finite.

Just as the physical body must maintain a balance between the energy taken in from food, and the amount of energy expended in daily living, so must the relationship between food production and consumption be kept in balance. For individual and collective health to thrive there must be a balance in the flow of energy that is received and that is given. Too much consumption leads to debt. Whether this debt is in the form of money, fossil fuel energy, life force or nutrients, the debt must eventually be balanced or the organism will reach a point where it can no longer continue.

Here is a rather sobering case in point. Historian Arnold Toynbee studied the 21 major civilizations in the recorded history of our planet to find the causes of their collapse. He found that in every case there were only two causes. The first was an extreme concentration of wealth. The second was the inability to adapt to changing conditions. Given the wealth extraction, wealth concentration nature of usury, the incoming impact of the four mega-trends and the finite limits of our fossil-based energy, we would do well to reconsider our values and choices.

Perhaps, rather than accelerating our quest to acquire more, we might be wise to discover what we can do to voluntarily share our abundance and help balance the world's energy. Sharing is easy, healthy, and gratifying. And, as difficult and sometimes uncomfortable as it might be we would be wise to examine the underlying causes that drive us to consume to the point of self-destruction. We may ask, "What are the emotional principles of health we need to address to balance this flow of energy"?

As we observed earlier, certain emotional nutrients are necessary for our healthy development and growth. When these growth needs are not met the emotional field in a child lacks the substance necessary for healthy development. The child is starved for nutrients. As a result, the child experiences feelings of emotional hunger, emptiness, inadequacy, worthlessness and abandonment. These negative feelings result in "the hole in the soul," an inner void that continually drives a person and demands to be filled. The problem is that it makes no difference how much external stimulus one pours in, it always leaks out.

People in the advertising industry are very aware of this. One of the sources psychologically driving people to over-consume comes from manipulative advertising. In many cases, advertising has gone far beyond informing people about a product. The focus now is to reprogram the thought process and manipulate inner values of the public, especially children, to increase sales. This sophisticated, psychological approach to advertising is literally an over-stimulation of the emotional field. This over-stimulation of the emotional body is the cause of many emotional and social problems that manifest themselves in self-destructive compulsive, addictive behavior. There is a deliberate intent to create psychological needs based on feelings of inadequacy and the belief that a physical object or a product will fill the hole in the soul. People with a poor self-image or low self-esteem are often the targets. Once that belief system is in place it drives the behavior in a way that the person is not even aware of the programming that is running them.

We are finding that children are increasingly the targets of manipulative advertising. Children see approximately 40,000 commercials a year on television. At that young age they really don't have the ability to understand what is going on. Many of these commercials are for foods that are high in fat, sugar, salt and empty calories. In 2002, sales in the children's food and beverage market exceeded $27 billion. A marketing research company, Packaged Facts, found that children between the ages of five and 14 influence approximately 78% of a family's grocery purchases.

There is an increasing use of what marketing professionals refer to as "The nag factor," and "pester power" to use children to influence their parents. Yes, those supermarket squabbles have been engineered and your children have been trained by professionals. Recent marketing studies have found that a child's brand loyalty may begin as early as age two. Their recognition of logos and mascots may be earlier than that. By age three, one in five American children are already making specific requests for name-brand products. The approach of cultivating cradle-to-grave customers is very profitable.

It is quite a commentary on the values driving the economic system (or perhaps it's the design of the economic system that is driving our values) when children are just another target market to be exploited. We say children are our future and we worry about drug abuse, violence, and the difficulty of providing adequate health care. Then we sell them video games that literally desensitize them emotionally, plant images of violence in their minds, poison them with dead food, and then pump them up with Ritalin to control their behavior. Children are being trained by psychologists and marketing professional to nag their parents into buying dead food. At the same time, obesity is up 54% in children, raising the likelihood of heart disease, cancer and diabetes in later years.

There is a difference between fulfilling legitimate needs and creating emotional instability that results in unhealthy wants in order to sell products. These actions are parasitic in nature, sucking off the life force of individuals, especially children, and damaging the well-being of the entire organism, which in this case, is society as a whole. It's amazing how businesses such as the tobacco industry and other poison pushers promote disease and then tout freedom of speech as giving them the right to do it. Abraham Lincoln summed it up well when he said, "You don't have the right to do what is wrong." It needs to be re-emphasized that there can be no freedom without responsibility. The more we relinquish our responsibility, the more we will lose our freedom.

This obsessive condition was beautifully articulated by Chief Sitting Bull at the Powder River Council in 1877 when he said, "The love of possession is a disease with them." That was a very accurate and prophetic statement, one that is certainly descriptive of our present-day society. He went on to say, "These people have made many rules that the rich may break but the poor may not. They take their tithes from the poor and weak to support the rich and those who rule." They not only do this through the law and structure of the economic system but through psychological manipulation.

We saw earlier that in many cases the underlying cause of addiction is the absence of emotional nutrients such as love, care, affection, and attention at an early age. Are not these emotional nutrients the giving of one's life force to another? Because of our values, and because of the nature of the economic system of which we are a part, we have created a society in which it is very difficult to fulfill the emotional conditions of health in many young children. Our country is experiencing the destructive ripple effect that this lack is having in the increase of physical and emotional problems which are reflected in society as a whole. How disconnected, self-destructive, and unbalanced as a social organism have we become?

The following statistics from the Children's Defense Fund 2012 indicate the destructive effect of this misdirected energy as it plays out in the lives of our children. Consider this. In our country every single day:

1. Five children are killed by abuse or neglect.
2. Nine children are murdered.
3. Five children under age 20 commit suicide.
4. 27 die from poverty.
5. 368 children are arrested for drug offenses.
6. 1,115 teenagers have abortions.
7. 1,204 teenagers have babies.
8. 2,573 children are born into poverty.
9. 2058 children are abused or neglected.
10. Over 100,000 children are homeless.

This happens in the wealthiest country in the history of the planet every single day.

How does this over consumption affect the health of the planet of which we are a part? In 1992, the Union of Concerned Scientists issued a statement called, "A Warning to Humanity." This statement was issued and endorsed by over fifteen hundred of the top scientists in the world, over half of them Nobel Prize Laureates. This statement reads:

> *"We the undersigned, senior members of the world's scientific community, hereby warn all humanity of what lies ahead. A great change in our stewardship of the earth, and the life on it, is required, if vast human misery is to be avoided and our global home on this planet is not to be irretrievably mutilated."*

This document outlined the problems that are facing the planet and humanity as a whole. These issues included:

The Atmosphere. Ozone depletion exposes us to increased ultra-violet radiation, which can be damaging or deadly to many forms of life. Air pollution and acid rain are already damaging forests, crops and humans. Increasing levels of gases from human activities may alter the climate on a global level. According to Munich Re, the world's largest re-insurance company insurance claims for 1999 due to natural disasters was greater than for all the claims filed in the decade of the 1980's.

Deforestation. Tropical and dry rain forests are being rapidly destroyed and so is the life they shelter. At currents rates, (10 football fields a second) many of these forests will vanish before the end of the next century. Natural disasters due to deforestation and climate change now account for 86% of all insurance compensation payments worldwide.

Water. The depletion of water resources poses a serious threat to food production and other systems necessary to sustain life. In over eighty countries containing 40% of the world's population, heavy demands on the water have caused serious shortages, and the pollution of lakes, rivers and ground water around the world is reducing the supply of needed water. Some experts have come to view water as a living substance and as it is misused and degraded the life force within it is weakened.

Soil. The depletion of soil has resulted in a loss of productivity. Since 1945, an area greater then India and China combined have been spoiled by destructive practices in agriculture and animal husbandry causing a decrease in per capita food production.

Over fishing. Oceans have been overburdened along many of the coastal regions which produce the world's main supply of fish. Some fisheries have already shown signs of collapse.

Extinction. There has been irreversible loss of living species. What this means is the foundation supporting the food chain is being eroded away. As it continues the interrelationship that supports a balanced eco-cycle is disrupted. Over time it is possible the food chain will collapse. The projection of the third mega-trend is that we will lose between 30 and 70 percent of the bio-diversity on the planet in the next 20 to 30 years. Other scientists say that by the end of 2100, one third of all species on the planet will be lost. With them, go possible medicinal and other benefits.

Overpopulation. The ability of the earth to produce food and absorb wastes is finite. If the destructive environmental practices continue, vital global systems will be damaged beyond repair. At present, one person in five lives is abject poverty, and one in ten is malnourished.

This is a short summary of the challenges we face as stewards of the planet. The consequences of not successfully addressing these issues was summarized by a conference of 2800 economists who unanimously agreed that *"Global climate change is a real and pressing danger, carrying with it significant environmental, economic, social and geopolitical risks.*

A quote attributed to Chief Seattle made in 1854 beautifully sums up what present day science is validating.

"All things are connected.
Whatever befalls the Earth
Befalls the sons and daughters of the Earth.
Man did not weave the web of life; he is merely a strand in it.
Whatever he does to the web, he does to himself."

Perhaps we should take a lesson from the Iroquois confederation of Indian tribes. When making any decision one of the questions that was asked was "how will this affect our children seven generations from now"? If they couldn't answer that question, or the outcome would be detrimental to future generations, they wouldn't take the action even if it were immediately expedient.

That is a little different way of looking at life rather than "How do we get next quarter's profits up?" and "Too bad if we trash the environment, or lay off a thousand people." Interestingly enough, one of Dr. Deming's major criticisms of management is its short-term perspective when it comes to running a company. Producing products that harm people, society and the planet in order to raise the next quarter's profits is a sure sign of a cancerous organization that is destroying the greater whole of which it is a part. It is also the result of the erroneous belief that we are separate from each other. The fact is humanity is one system, one organism.

When considering the mindset of short-term planning, we again must take into account the nature of the money system. As we saw in the 10th to 12th centuries, the design of currency supported investing in long-term projects benefiting future generations. When the nature of the currency changed so did the investing patterns. This produced disastrous effects. We have seen how our present debt based money system creates artificial scarcity as the result of usury. Just like the musical chairs game, this drives competition and the push for short-term gain. Money does influence behavior and values in extremely subtle but powerful ways.

As we look at the problems facing us individually and collectively, what are some of the solutions? The first step is for each of us to take responsibility for fulfilling the conditions of health in the physical, emotional, mental and spiritual arenas of our own lives and our immediate family. Pick several of the health-enhancing points that you've learned and build them into your life one step at a time. Whole live food is as easy to buy as dead refined food. Walking and consciously breathing do not cost anything and the benefits are tremendous. Healthy change must come from within us first. As we change from the inside out, the world around us will change. Ultimately, the only thing that will change the world is a change of consciousness.

The second step is to create healthy organizations that operate according to a higher level of spiritual values and right human relations. This can be our place of employment, a club, church, school or business. Ideally, the values and systems will support the growth and development of its individual members on all levels. If you are a business owner, start viewing your business as a vehicle that enhances the personal growth of your employees. You will find, as many others have, the return is greater than you would have imagined. Business can be a very effective tool for positive social change.

The third step is to understand the true nature of the economic system of which we are a part and to begin creating viable alternatives. The book *New Money for Healthy Communities* offers a number of tested solutions. As we have seen, community-based, complementary currencies can be very effective in facilitating the flow of life force, and participating in their circulation can make a significant difference. Learn to give forth and redirect your economic life force so it is in alignment with those principles which produce health, individually and socially. When you have an opportunity to participate in an alternative or complementary currency system take advantage and do so.

The video program "The Money Masters" proposes monetary and legislative reforms that have a very positive effect and address the problem at the source. Taking advantage of the political process by educating your elected representatives can serve as an impetus towards positive change.

Fourth, learn how to withdraw your life force from individuals and businesses that engage in socially or environmentally destructive practices. Let them know what you are doing and why. When they receive one letter of complaint they know 100 other people are thinking the same thing. No matter how big and powerful the business or multi-national corporation may be they can only survive if people continue to direct their life force to the business by purchasing their products or investing in them. Choose otherwise.

Gandhi used a system of active non-cooperation to free India. Enough people in India just said "We're not going to play your game anymore." When we withdraw or redirect our life force from the money system, destructive companies, or values and beliefs that don't serve the good of the whole their power dissipates and eventually evaporates. Focus on what you choose to create and consciously build those principles of health. Disengage from that which is counterproductive.

Fifth, become involved in some kind of a support group. When we look at the direction in which most economic, mental and emotional energy is being directed it is mostly running contrary to the principles that produce health. When the driving values are "to have" and "to consume," it is challenging to maintain our commitment to live at a higher level. One of the reasons organizations like Weight Watchers or Alcoholics Anonymous are so successful is the support system they provide. Companies that provide corporate wellness programs to support employees in making healthy choices and lifestyle changes not only provide a valuable benefit to employees but realize substantial savings in health care costs. To make the needed changes it's essential to develop a support system of like-minded people who are committed to personal and spiritual growth and the wholesome lifestyle you choose to create.

Along with developing a support system, find a financial advisor who really understands the true nature of the economic system and has a value system compatible with yours. Many socially conscious people are horrified when they find out their investment have been going to support companies whose policies and practices were contributing to the very problems they were fighting. Look for someone who has strategies for working within the present system and the ability to maintain balance. Make sure the money you invest, your life force is directed to companies that support life. You may get a good return off companies who profit from the misery of others like defense contractors, financial institutions and private prisons but your life force is contributing to the cancer killing the planet. There are many socially and environmentally responsible companies that can provide a good return and your money will be contributing to healing and wholeness rather than death and disease. Most financial planners, insurance sales people and others in the financial field have yet to learn of the forces behind the economic scene. Although well-intentioned, in many cases they actually participate in and direct your money towards companies that are causing the problems. As you educate yourself in these areas you will know what to look for and what to avoid.

These are a few things you can do on an ongoing basis that will dramatically improve your overall level of health, sustainable abundance and quality of life. They will help to facilitate the healing of the economic and environmental trauma that has been caused by our present values and money system.

CONTINUING THE ASCENT

Throughout this book we have explored the physical, emotional, mental, spiritual, social and economic conditions of health necessary to create high-level wellness and prevent disease. We have seen the energetic nature of thought and emotion and its role in contributing to health or illness. We understand that the organizations in which we live and work can contribute to our wellness or dis-ease. We have been introduced to the fact that the very nature and structure of the present money system is to a large degree the main cause of much of the world's social and economic dis-ease and dysfunction creating unnecessary suffering and misery. There is much that needs to be done however; we have the necessary tools and knowledge to solve many of the problems facing our world today.

There is a wonderful song that goes "Let there be peace on earth and let it begin with me." This is where it all starts and this is the place where we have the most ability to affect change. As we start to change from the inside out there is a ripple effect on our immediate environment and those around us. We change first and then the world around us changes.

As we have continually emphasized, the focus is on health creation rather than disease treatment. We can either continue to live the way we always have in which case we will continue to produce the same results, or we can choose to move our lives into the high-level wellness zone. It has been said that the definition of insanity is to continue doing the same thing and expect a different result.

My experience has been that when we embrace these challenges as an opportunity to grow, we participate in the uplifting of others and ourselves. As we look at the challenges that we face individually and collectively let us remember that challenges build strength. As we live the principles of health, we become health. As we strive to embody the qualities of wholeness and goodness, we become that wholeness and goodness. This concept of becoming was beautifully stated by Mahatma Gandhi when he said, "*You* must become the change you wish to see in the world."

If we do this, we can make real the shared vision of so many people from various backgrounds, political ideologies and religions, which is to build a world that is sustainable, equitable, just and free from disease, a world based on right human relations and brotherhood in its truest sense. As a cell in the body of humanity, it starts with you here and now.

BIBLIOGRAPHY

1. Dictionary of Word Origins, John Ayto,
    Arcade Publishing, 1990   p. 2
2. New England Journal of Medicine, July 1993.   p. 7
3. Journal of the American Medical Association. April 1998 p. 9
4. Lymphology: The Hidden Science, Laura Hensley RN,   p. 18
    Dakota Publishing, 2001
5. Scientific American, June 1963, the Lymphatic System,
    H.S. Mayerson   p. 21
6. Text Book of Medical Physiology, 5th edition,
    Arthur C. Guyton   p. 22
7. Lymphology, v25, n4, Dec 1992 p. 147.
    Dr. J. W. Shields   p. 26
8. Scientific American, October 1962,
    Electricity in Plants, Bruce L. Scott   p. 29
9. Food is Your Best Medicine, pg 128, Henry Bieler MD   p. 30
10. Science Magazine, February 1956,
    On the Origin of Cancer Cells   p. 31
11. Scientific American, February 1951, White Blood
    Cells Vs Bacteria, W. Barry Wood Jr.   p. 33
12. Text Book of Medical Physiology, 5th edition,
    Arthur C. Guyton   p. 38
13. Diet & Nutrition, Rudolph Ballentine MD.   p. 41

Part II

10. Healthcare Study: The Use of Meridian
    Stress Assessment, ICON   p. 116
    Health & Fitness, Douglas Younker
11. Spiritual Nutrition pg. 19, Gabriel Cousins MD,
    Cassendra Press   p. 120
12. H. Motoyama and R. Brown, Science and
    Evolution of Consciousness,   p. 121
    Brookline, MA: Autumn Press 1978, pp. 99-119
13. Brain / Mind Bulletin, vol. 3 no. 9 (March 20, 1978)
    Electronic Evidence   p. 121
    of Auras, Chakras in UCLA Study
14. Institute of Heart Math   p. 131
15. Biology of Belief, pg. 53 Bruce Lipton, Hay House   p. 138
16. Sybervision: The Neuropsychology of Achievement   p. 150
17. Changing Your Destiny, Mary Orser& Richard Zarro,   p. 160
18. Sybervision: The Neuropsychology of Achievement   p. 164
19. Archives of Pediatrics and Adolescent Medicine   p. 166
20. R. Miller, The Positive Effect of Prayer on
    Plants," Psychic, April 1972   p. 168
21. Boulder Center for Accelerated Learning, Training   p. 183
22. Noetic Science Review , Spring Issue, 1996, No 37   p. 184
23. The Johns Hopkins Medical Journal, vol. 134 (1973)
    Closeness to   p. 199
    Parents and the Family Constellation in a
    Prospective Study of Five
    Disease States: Suicide, Mental Illness, Malignant Tumor,
    Hypertension and Coronary Heart Disease.
    C. Thomas and D. Duszynski.
24. Parade Magazine, Jan 18, 1998   p. 202
25. Taped Lecture by Dr. Petit, 1994   p. 203

Part III

The foolish physician treats the disease. The wise physician fulfills the conditions of health and the disease will leave of its own accord.

The New Dimension explores conditions of health in the physical, emotional, mental, spiritual, social, economic and environmental arenas of our life.

The New Dimension explores how to use natural laws to further the process of personal and spiritual growth leading to high level wellness and optimal health.

The New Dimension explores simple, yet little known, causes of low energy and disease at the cellular level, and what can be done to support true healing.

The New Dimension moves from a Newtonian, mechanistic understanding of reality to an Einsteinian, energy based viewpoint. It applies to attitude, belief systems, self-esteem, self-image and forgiveness and how these can enhance or hinder spiritual growth.

The New Dimension synthesizes science and spirituality and finds the commonality in both approaches to Truth.

The New Dimension explores how systems, particularly the design of an economic system, affects health and behavior. It offers practical solutions to current social and environmental problems.

It's time to step into a **New Dimension**

Michael Brook draws on a wide variety of experience as a professional athlete, an educator, trainer, public speaker, insurance professional, and a life-long student of holistic health and high performance living. As an athlete he was a trampoline champion, a world-class aerial acrobatic freestyle skier and professional high diver. These disciplines gave him first-hand experience of the mind/body connection and the power that thought has in producing physical effects. At the high point of his skiing career, an experience of his higher self working through his physical body, moved him from the sports arena into the area of holistic health and healing.

As Michael investigated various alternative healing modalities it became clear that many of the physical ills that effect us today are preventable. Through the study of various mind / body / spirit teachings, he learned that there were certain principles of health, that, when incorporated into one's life, dramatically lessened the likelihood of disease. At the same time they enhanced one's vitality, performance and the over-all quality of life.

Michael founded the Positive Air Team to take the message of prevention and optimal health creation to young people. Using a dynamic trampoline performance this group of professional athletes presented "High Performance Living Programs" to over a million students, staff, and parents across the western U.S. In addition Michael has presented his High Performance Living and Wellness message to numerous businesses and organizations.

Exploring a holistic approach to health inevitability leads to a spiritual dimension in life. Michael's spiritual path has been wide, inclusive, and eclectic. He embraces a variety of disciplines and teachings, but always aspires to follow the golden thread of truth - the essence of health, healing and wholeness.

For more information on trainings, events and health enhancing products visit newdimensionsinhealth.com